CHARLES E. HIRES
and the Drink that Wowed a Nation

Hires to you Michael!

Bill Dooble

CHARLES E. HIRES

and the Drink that Wowed a Nation

THE LIFE AND TIMES

OF A PHILADELPHIA ENTREPRENEUR

Bill Double

TEMPLE UNIVERSITY PRESS

Philadelphia • Rome • Tokyo

TEMPLE UNIVERSITY PRESS
Philadelphia, Pennsylvania 19122
www.temple.edu/tempress

Published 2018

Library of Congress Cataloging-in-Publication Data

Names: Double, Bill, author.
Title: Charles E. Hires and the drink that wowed a nation : the life and
    times of a Philadelphia entrepreneur / Bill Double.
Description: Philadelphia : Temple University Press, [2018] | Includes
    bibliographical references and index. |
Identifiers: LCCN 2017052256 (print) | LCCN 2018009967 (ebook) |
    ISBN 9781439915929 (E-book) | ISBN 9781439915912 (pbk. : alk.
    paper)
Subjects: LCSH: Hires, Charles E., 1891-1937. | Soft drink
    industry—Pennsylvania—Philadelphia—Biography. |
    Businesspeople—Pennsylvania—Philadelphia—Biography. |
    Pharmacists—Pennsylvania—Philadelphia—Biography. |
    Inventors—Pennsylvania—Philadelphia—Biography. | Soft
    drinks—Pennsylvania—Philadelphia—History.
Classification: LCC HD9349.S632 (ebook) | LCC HD9349.S632 D68
    2018 (print) | DDC 338.7/66362092 [B]—dc23
LC record available at https://lccn.loc.gov/2017052256

♾ The paper used in this publication meets the requirements of the
American National Standard for Information Sciences—Permanence
of Paper for Printed Library Materials, ANSI Z39.48-1992

Printed in the United States of America

9 8 7 6 5 4 3 2 1

To Patricia whose courage and fortitude
are an inspiration.

CONTENTS

Illustrations follow page 104

ACKNOWLEDGMENTS

I WISH TO ACKNOWLEDGE and thank all whose generous assistance informed and enriched my telling of the Charles E. Hires story.

Members of the Hires family were singularly helpful. Karen R. Hires graciously allowed access to the family archive amassed by her late husband, William Hires, a grandson of the founder. Jeff Groff, a great-grandson, provided insightful information on the Hires family and their houses as well as an invaluable collection of family photographs, several of which appear in this book. Charles E. Hires IV, another great-grandson, kindly shared his early recollections of family life.

Dan Flanagan of the J. W. England Library of the University of the Sciences in Philadelphia helped me to navigate the archives at the school where Hires attended night classes when it was the Philadelphia College of Pharmacy. Cynthia Cronin-Kardon at the Lippincott Library of the University of Pennsylvania's Wharton School was similarly helpful in assisting my search of the Charles E. Hires Co. historical financial records.

The Lower Merion Historical Society in Bala Cynwyd, Pennsylvania, proved a rich source of Hires articles, interviews, and images. I am indebted to society members Jerry Francis, Ted Goldsborough, and Max Buten for their assistance.

Bob Francois of the Millville Historical Society in New Jersey and Warren Q. Adams of the Lummis Library of the Cumberland County Historical Society in Greenwich, New Jersey, provided illuminating details on Hires' family and his early years in southern New Jersey. I also thank Mary Beth Tait, former archivist at the Dr. Pepper Museum and Free Enterprise Institute of Waco, Texas, who kindly produced a scan of articles, advertisements, and marketing plans from the museum's Charles E. Hires Co. collection.

I am extremely grateful to the late Nancy B. Schmitt of the Malvern Historical Commission and her daughter Kelly Schmitt. They generously shared Nancy's unpublished article and a collection of newspaper clippings, gleaned from the Chester County Historical Society's archives, detailing Hires' operations in Malvern.

Susanna Morikawa, archival specialist at the Friends Historical Library of Swarthmore College in Pennsylvania, enlightened me about Charles and Emma Waln Hires' connections to the Quaker faith. James Davis, development and archives associate at Friends' Central School in Wynnewood, Pennsylvania, supplied documents detailing the role of Charles and Emma in relocating the school from Philadelphia's Center City in 1925. Doug Costa, clerk of the Merion Friends Meeting in Merion Station, Pennsylvania, shared anecdotal information regarding Hires's efforts to restore the old meeting house and maintain services there.

The staff of the Free Library of Philadelphia exceeded the call of duty in providing access to often obscure works and articles from their collections and those of other libraries. Juanita Vega DeJoseph and her colleagues in the Business Resource and Innovation Center and the Interlibrary Loan Department of the Parkway Central branch were especially helpful. The enthusiastic staff at Temple University's Urban Archives supplied vital information from their collection of Philadelphia Bulletin news clippings.

I am grateful to Linda Gross and Lynsey Sczechowicz at the Hagley Museum and Library in Wilmington, Delaware, for sharing the library's impressive collection of Hires ads and related information with me. I wish to also thank Christine Windheuser at the Smithsonian Institution in Washington, DC, for her assistance in ferreting out Hires holdings at the Archives Center of the National Museum of American History. Her colleague Walter Hursey was also helpful in identifying Hires ads in the Smithsonian's N. W. Ayer and Son Advertising Agency Records.

Finally, I would like to thank my wife and computer guru, Patricia Callahan, for her skillful editing, support, and patience.

Charles E. Hires

and the Drink that Wowed a Nation

INTRODUCTION

I FIRST ENCOUNTERED HIRES Root Beer at Mary's, a cluttered corner store on Pittsburgh's gritty North Side. Neighborhood teenagers hung out there, determined to boost their blood sugar by devouring Clark Bars, Devil Dogs, and other snacks, washed down with ample amounts of soda pop. Mary chilled her soft drinks in a red chest-style cooler emblazoned with the familiar "Coca-Cola" script. Customers were allowed to fish out their favorites. An icy Hires occasionally came to hand among the more numerous bottles of Coke, Pepsi, 7 Up, and Orange Crush.

My boyhood Hires emerged from the cooler in a sturdy returnable bottle unlike today's flimsy throwaway can. It was sweetened with cane sugar, not high fructose corn syrup, and probably contained fewer, if any, artificial ingredients. I seem to recall it as being more intensely carbonated and spicier than its modern successor, though I cannot say this with certainty. Had I dreamt that my fascination with Charles Elmer Hires would one day spawn the research that led to this book, I would have paid closer attention to his signature creation.

Cursory accounts of Hires' humble origins and meteoric business success encouraged me to delve more deeply. Clearly, this inventive druggist who parlayed a humble home-brewed tea into an iconic brand enjoyed by millions deserves a place among the outstanding entrepreneurs of America's Gilded Age. Launched ten years before Coca-Cola, Hires Root Beer blazed the trail for development of the American soft drink industry. And root beer was but one of Hires' successful ventures.

I was surprised to find that the details of his life had not been more fully explored or documented. Despite Hires' accomplishments, he seems to have been oddly underappreciated by succeeding generations. This neglect became more evident as I broadened my search for information that might shed a brighter light on his history. Save for a handful of articles and a few biographical summaries, little of substance had been written about him. Dozens of volumes had been published about the other seminal soft drinks—Coca-Cola, Dr. Pepper, Vernors Ginger Ale, Moxie, and Pepsi-Cola—and their founders. But no biographer had told the story of the man who, in a real sense, started it all. I became convinced that Hires' story deserved a fuller telling.

Creativity, tenacity, and a gift for recognizing opportunities propelled this southern New Jersey farm boy, who left home in 1863 as a twelve-year-old drugstore apprentice, into the ranks of industrial magnates. Nineteenth-century America is fondly recalled as a time of possibility when wits, initiative, and a bit of luck might enable one of modest means and little formal education to ascend to heights of wealth and influence. Like other myths that inhabit our national memory, unfettered opportunity was more an illusion than reality for many. Yet the era certainly did not lack for exemplars of entrepreneurial success.

Several of these self-made men, like Hires, would earn fortunes by introducing products destined to become staples of the nation's diet. For example, Hires' fellow New Jerseyan Joseph Campbell opened a canning factory in Camden in 1869, the precursor of the soup company that bears his name today. Milton S. Hershey, who like Hires apprenticed at an early age, established the Lancaster Caramel Co. in 1886. He would later sell that business to focus his efforts on chocolate bars. Pittsburgh's Henry Heinz began his business career hawking vegetables from his mother's garden. He would later peddle horseradish and other condiments before launching the H. J. Heinz Co., eminent purveyor of ketchup, pickles, and soups.

Indeed, Horatio Alger Jr., who celebrated rags-to-riches flights like theirs in *Ragged Dick*, *Strive and Succeed* and dozens of other novels, was also a contemporary of Hires. Had they met, the young druggist's precocity may well have impressed the novelist. Hires completed his apprenticeship at sixteen. By age twenty-one he had saved enough money to open his own drugstore in Philadelphia. Here the entrepreneurial flair and marketing savvy that would define his career quickly surfaced. Spotting gold where others saw dirt, Hires transformed a mountain of fuller's earth salvaged from a construction site into a profitable branded fabric cleaner.

Three years later he sold the drugstore to found what would become a prosperous business wholesaling drugs and botanical products. The budding capitalist's career path took a fateful turn following a farm vacation with his recent bride, Clara Kate, in 1875. Their hostess served the prim young couple an herb tea brewed from roots, bark, and berries that she had foraged. Smitten with the drink's flavor, Hires returned to Philadelphia with its recipe in his pocket. Reformulated, refined, and renamed, the concoction that emerged from Hires' drugstore was an early convenience food. No longer would housewives be required to gather and process a slew of ingredients to prepare a refreshing beverage for their families. A twenty-five-cent box of Hires' Household Extract, when combined with water, sugar, and yeast, yielded five gallons of delicious "root beer."

Hires' success, however, was not primarily due to his drink's distinctive taste or pure natural ingredients, although many purchased and obviously enjoyed it. Charles Hires was a born innovator and entrepreneur, to be sure. But perhaps his greatest gift was his ability to harness and exploit the nascent power of advertising. His ad campaigns, bold and persistent, catapulted his humble homemade beverage into millions of households and transformed the country's drinking habits. It began with a daily one-column by one-inch ad in Philadelphia's *Public Ledger* that a hesitant Hires felt he could not afford. Despite his anxiety, something in the young man's character inspired confidence. The newspaper's publisher agreed to delay billing Hires for the ads until sales increased enough to cover their cost.

To Hires' good fortune, advertising in America was becoming a potent force for selling products of all kinds. A second industrial revolution was transforming an agrarian society of small producers into an urban society where large industries held sway. Aided by new technology, manufacturers had begun to churn out standardized products ranging from cigarettes to soap in massive quantities. They turned to advertising to create markets for their wares. The medium's surge was fueled by the growth of large-circulation newspapers, the advent of color trade cards, and the emergence of national magazines. Pitches for patent medicines, which had dominated the rural journals of the early nineteenth century, were joined by ads for the products of mass production. Advertising agencies began to shed their traditional roles as mere space brokers to become the catalysts of an advertising age.

Hires exploited these trends with the optimism of youth and the commitment of a convert. Adopting a strategy many regarded as foolhardy, he poured every spare penny of profits from his botanical drug business into promoting his root beer. As sales increased, Hires pressed the *Public Ledger* to abandon newspaper tradition and allow his ads to run across multiple columns. Hires Root Beer ads in color began to adorn the pages of *Ladies' Home Journal* and other national magazines. Trade cards and billboards also were fair game for Hires' blitz. After a modest start, root beer sales achieved astonishing momentum. Hires' unprecedented advertising campaign propelled his once obscure beverage extract into a national brand within ten years. "Doing business without advertising is like winking at a girl in the dark," Hires was fond of saying. "You know you are doing it, but nobody else does."[1]

Despite the heady results of his extraordinary promotional push, Hires' feet remained firmly planted. He understood that advertising might persuade a buyer to try his product, but that its quality was crucial to repeat sales. He insisted on using only the finest natural roots, herbs, and berries obtainable. It was said that he complied with the strictest provisions of the pure food laws years before the enactment of such statutes.

Hires earned his reputation by perfecting his root beer and building it into a national brand, but his commercial interests ranged beyond soft drinks. He invented other products, including patented cough remedies, colognes, and a line of flavorings and extracts that were used by other manufacturers. He also presciently marketed spring water and instant coffee while growing his botanical drug business into one of the largest on the East Coast. One botanical, the vanilla plant, held a particular fascination for Hires. He mounted an expedition through Mexican jungles to view its growth firsthand and became an acknowledged expert on the exotic bean.

In 1900 he incorporated the Hires Condensed Milk Co. Canned milk was a growth industry that fulfilled an important nutritional need in an era lacking home refrigeration. Hires' initial investment grew into a chain of twenty-two condenseries.

While my book chronicles the commercial ventures of this extraordinary entrepreneur, it also seeks to examine Charles Hires, the person. What traits of character, beliefs, and morals defined his personality and motivated the decisions that shaped his life? Information about Hires' personal life is admittedly fragmentary, but the existing pieces offer revealing insights.

From an early age, Hires displayed an independent nature. He declared that he had left home at age twelve determined to make it on his own without assistance from his family. Hires used $400 in personal savings to outfit his first drugstore. He got some help from drug wholesalers who, impressed by the young man's ambition, advanced credit for the store's initial inventory. There is no evidence that he sought or received other aid.

A letter to his brother William reveals an idealistic twenty-three-year-old correspondent clearly focused on making his mark in the world. But his writing resonates as well with the spirituality and moral purpose that would come to characterize his life and work. "Truthfulness, integrity and goodness form the essence of manly character," Charles reminded his brother. "I should always be happy if I followed the directions of my own conscience and leave the consequences to God."[2]

Religious faith was a guiding force in Hires' life. Raised in a staunchly Baptist family, he conscientiously transferred his membership from the rural church of his youth to another in Philadelphia. Here he also forged a life-long friendship with prominent

Baptist clergyman and Temple University founder Russell Conwell. Like Conwell and other religious leaders of the day, Hires would become a vocal temperance advocate. Over the years Hires became increasingly attracted to the Quaker faith. He donated generously in support of Quaker causes, including the restoration of the historic Friends meeting house where William Penn had worshipped. At its dedication, he exhorted Quakers to fulfill their obligation to God to live a pure and correct life.

Hires' business dealings at times fell short of his religious rhetoric. For example, he steadfastly rejected the pleas of Chester County dairy farmers who suffered when his condensery abruptly reduced the price it paid for their raw milk. Hires maintained that industry competition had forced the cut. Later, he sheepishly threw a grand party to assuage his dismayed suppliers. The erstwhile apprentice had by then become a seasoned capitalist with a well-honed survival instinct.

Hires was devoted to Clara Kate, whom he wed at age twenty-four, and their five children. Letters to his wife and family reveal a touchingly compassionate side of his personality. He was devastated when Clara died unexpectedly in 1910. The lonely widower married again at age sixty to a family friend who shared his dedication to Quaker beliefs. Hires would later formally join the Society of Friends.

In a reflective moment Hires attributed his business success to "a great deal of ambition and absolute honesty."[3] Certainly, a strong will to succeed was key to launching and sustaining his several businesses. Evidence also suggests that his integrity, if not always absolute, figured prominently in his business dealings and personal life. The truthfulness of some of his more outlandish advertising claims is open to challenge, especially those extolling the health benefits of Hires Root Beer. Yet his dedication to producing honest products using only pure natural ingredients was exceptional given the standards of his time. Hires adamantly refused to follow the competition by adulterating his root beer with synthetic flavors, caffeine, or other habit-forming chemicals.

Hires has been described as a tycoon with the soul of a chemist. He continued to refer to the factory floor where his root beer and other products were blended as the "laboratory." At times his continuing experiments with flavoring extracts and scents lured him from the demands of routine business. He seemed most contented while fine-tuning the formulas of existing products and concocting new ones. He compiled his favorite "recipes" in a do-it-yourself manual for pharmacists that he marketed for a dollar.

There were other diversions from Hires' workaday world—namely, public speaking, amateur theater, and sports. A bit of a ham, he did not shy from the opportunity to present his thoughts in a public setting. He burnished his oratorical skills with readings and recitations before church and civic groups. The title of one such talk, "Orators, Ancient and Modern," suggests his desire to master that art. He also performed in numerous amateur theater productions. His acting credits, gleaned from playbills and reviews that he saved, indicate a seamless segue from dais to stage.

Hires admired fine horses. Once he could afford to own one, he purchased a sleek pacing mare to pull his private carriage and, in winter, his sleigh. Slower traffic scattered as Hires competed with other gentleman racers in dare-devil contests on the streets of Philadelphia and Camden. In his later years, Hires took up deep-sea fishing with equal enthusiasm. He relished carefree days aboard his modest yacht with family and friends pursuing marlin and other trophy-worthy denizens of Florida waters.

Charles E. Hires and the Drink that Wowed a Nation relates Hires' story in the context of his place and time, America in the late nineteenth and early twentieth centuries. His long life (1851–1937) spanned eventful eras of the nation's history from the Civil War through World War I onward to the Roaring Twenties and ensuing Great Depression. The dynamic economic and social forces that thrust the nation into a new century exerted a gravitational pull on the trajectories of Hires' life and career as well. These included the surge of native ingenuity that paved the way for modern America, the rough-hewn capitalism of the Gilded Age, the evolution of the neighborhood drugstore, the rise of advertising in creating mass markets, and the emerging temperance movement.

Although the milestones of Hires' attainments have been documented, the details are often unrecorded or ambiguous. Apart from a few personal recollections gleaned from articles in newspapers and trade journals, his paper trail is sparse. Hires, of course, must share responsibility for his relative neglect. He was a doer with little time or inclination to chronicle his insights or polish his legacy. He left no accessible memoirs or diaries to illuminate the experiences of a long and productive life and business career.

Moreover, ostensibly factual accounts of Hires' life are frequently dogged by inaccuracies, contradictions, and myths. For example, one major achievement frequently attributed to him is patently false. Charles Hires did not invent root beer! That drink had existed since Colonial times in America and earlier in Europe. Other significant events in his life are difficult to confirm through primary sources.

In recounting Hires' story, I have relied upon published interviews, correspondence, newspaper reports, magazine articles, financial data, and a small family archive. I have endeavored to stick to verifiable information and to highlight historical inconsistencies where they exist. Hopefully, I have managed to avoid most of the mythology and tall tales however beguiling.

1

FARM TO PHARMACY

CHARLES ELMER HIRES was born August 19, 1851, on a farm in the southern New Jersey township of Elsinboro in Salem County. He was the sixth of ten children of John Dare Hires and Mary Williams Hires, who were married in 1839. John was born in 1817 and Mary in 1819. To support his large family, John augmented his farming income by selling cattle and other livestock on commission. He also worked as a blacksmith according to 1850 census records. A loyal Democrat, John held various local offices, including that of township tax collector.[1]

Charles Elmer could trace his paternal lineage back to one Gunrod Hoyer, his great-grandfather, born in Germany in 1744. After migrating to America, Hoyer modified his name to the easier "Conrad Hires" before marrying Christiana Hitchner in Deerfield, Cumberland County, New Jersey, in 1771. Conrad served in a New Jersey unit during the Revolutionary War. Charles's maternal ancestry also bore a Revolutionary connection. His mother, Mary, John Hires' third wife, was said to be a descendant of First Lady Martha Custis Washington from her first marriage to Daniel Custis.[2]

Two events occurred in the year of Charles' birth that presaged what would prove to be significant chapters in the newborn's future: Maine became the first state to prohibit the manufacture and sale of alcoholic beverages, and inventor Gail Borden visited a Shaker community in New Lebanon, New York.

The Maine law signaled an early triumph for the temperance movement and was hailed as a milestone on the road to national prohibition. A firm supporter of the cause, Hires would proudly market his root beer as "a temperance drink for temperance people."[3] To his chagrin, his presumed ally, the Women's Christian Temperance Union (WCTU), would declare root beer to be an intoxicating beverage based on its slight alcoholic content. The group's boycott of his drink would threaten the existence of Hires' thriving company.

Borden observed with fascination the Shakers' use of an airtight pan to produce sugar.[4] The inventive Texan, a native New Yorker, soon patented a similar process for preserving fresh milk without refrigeration, spurring the growth of a new industry. Beginning in 1900, Hires would invest millions in the manufacture of condensed milk in an effort to diversify his soft drink business.

Southwestern New Jersey in the mid-nineteenth century was a patchwork of small farms and rural villages, punctuated by a few larger regional centers. While agriculture was the backbone of the region's economy, manufacturing also contributed. The production of iron from local bog ore had about petered out by Charles' birth. But glass manufacturing, based on the region's ample resources of sand, soda ash, and silica, proved more lasting. Hires showed little interest in pursuing the glass-making trade, although members of his family were involved in that business.

Born ten years before the attack on Fort Sumter, Charles was young enough to avoid personal involvement in the Civil War. Public sentiment about the war was divided in the state. Northern New Jersey residents tended to support the Union cause. The state's southern counties were more sympathetic toward the Confederacy. Nevertheless, New Jersey sent an estimated seventy-seven thousand native sons to serve in the Union army, of whom almost six thousand died.[5]

Charles would later be baptized at the Cohansey Baptist Church, where his father served as a deacon.[6] The youngster revealed an early attraction to the trappings of the pharmacist's trade. At the age of six or seven he would gather up old bottles from around the house and farm. After cleaning them thoroughly, he filled the bottles with colored water made from poke berries, dandelion flowers, elderberries, and other plants. He set up a makeshift store in the family's apple orchard by suspending boards between stakes that he had driven into the ground. He displayed his bright bottles on the crude shelves alongside fruit jars and jelly glasses that he had filled with sand and dirt to represent powders. There it was recalled he played druggist or doctor for hours on end. His seriousness of purpose prompted gibes from other children who called him "the old man."[7]

As he grew older, Charles helped out on the family farm and attended the local public school. By an early age he had experienced enough of farming to decide that it would not be his future. "Although my family was fairly well off," he recalled, "I was not interested in farming. I wanted to make my own way in the world."[8]

APPRENTICED AT AGE TWELVE

Influenced perhaps by their son's fascination with pharmacies and his aversion to agriculture, Charles' parents agreed to place him in an apprenticeship. Fortuitously for the twelve-year-old, his two elder sisters, Cecilia and Rebecca, had married pharmacists. Their respective spouses, John Anthony Wright and Daniel Brooks, operated a drugstore at High and Sassafras Streets in Millville, a small city about twenty-five miles from the Hires' farm. Charles would complete a four-year term as their apprentice. He received a dollar a week plus room and board for his service.[9]

This was young Charles' first experience living away from home. Despite his enthusiasm for his prospective vocation, as spring approached Charles showed symptoms of homesickness. His understanding employers agreed to allow him to return to the farm for a couple of weeks. Once there, Charles coaxed his father into letting him help plow the corn and potato fields. He had never plowed by himself before. Somewhat reluctantly, his father hitched a plow to a pair of elderly nags that he felt the lad would be able to handle. He was certain his son would soon tire of the labor and quit.

The work was a lot harder than the boy had imagined. The sun was hot and the aging horses lethargic. Two other plowmen who were working the field lapped him frequently, taunting the slowpoke to "get out of the way with that snail team," as they passed. By lunch Charles was exhausted. His father suggested he take a rest, but Charles doggedly returned to the field and finished the day's work. He was too tired to eat much dinner before falling into bed. When his homecoming respite ended, Charles was more than ready to resume his apprenticeship.[10]

Back at the drugstore, his usual assignments were less rigorous. In fact, after completing them, Hires would sometimes have time on his hands. Instead of repolishing the glassware or finding other make-work projects, Charles asked whether he might purchase a load of watermelons and peaches and resell them at the curb outside the store. His employers consented, allowing the boy to earn a small profit and gain his first experience as an entrepreneur.[11]

The era was auspicious for an ambitious lad to embark on a career in pharmacy. An apprenticeship offered a path to advancement for those with limited formal education and modest means. Once the apprenticeship was completed, the erstwhile trainee might assume the mantle of "pharmacist" and be generally accepted as a bona fide member of that profession. Formal education or licensing examinations were not yet required. Self-anointed pharmacists and apothecaries were common.[12]

Pharmacies benefited as well by taking on apprentices. Their low-cost labor relieved druggists of routine and laborious tasks such as chopping roots and bark, crushing minerals and organics in large-volume mortars, rolling and cutting out pills, and packaging standard products. "Drug store boys," as they were known, also kept the glassware sparkling, swept floors, stocked shelves, waited on customers, and made deliveries. These mundane labors aside, an apprenticeship under the tutelage of an amenable employer offered an ambitious novice an opportunity to master the rudiments of pharmacy. Big cities also offered the possibility to supplement on-the-job training with night school classes. But this informal route from apprentice to professional was beginning to close.

Throughout the nineteenth century, pharmacy in America was evolving from an unregulated practice, often carried out by physicians or their assistants, to a profession with specialized training and licensing requirements. The medical community first recognized the value of pharmacological training. The College of Philadelphia (later the University of Pennsylvania) began teaching chemistry to its medical students as early as 1769.[13] Physicians and their apprentices prepared or purchased drugs and dispensed them to their patients. Thus the earliest retail pharmacies were established by physicians based on European models. They supplied medicines, frequently acquired from abroad, as well as a variety of patented nostrums and folk remedies.

The early dominance of the physician-apothecary, however, afforded an opening for independent drug outlets. Wholesale drugstores, run by "chemists and druggists," provided the raw materials, imported and domestic, that doctors required in their practices. Some early druggists also manufactured chemicals.[14] Professional pharmacy schools were beginning to emerge. The Philadelphia College of Pharmacy, the nation's first, was founded in 1821. A growing push for professional standards by academics and practitioners led states and cities to begin to establish pharmacy boards with licensing authority.

In 1872 the City of Philadelphia launched a local Pharmaceutical Examining Board and required that persons conducting business as retail apothecaries register with the board. Those in charge of stores where medicines were sold were further required to apply for a certificate of competency and qualification. Graduates in pharmacy were not required to meet these requirements. New Jersey would adopt a pharmacy licensing law in 1877. Pennsylvania enacted a similar statute in 1887 based on the Philadelphia model.[15]

THE BIG CITY BECKONS

Despite these trends, pharmacy had not attained full professional status by the time Hires completed his apprenticeship in 1867. His employers had grown to appreciate his diligence and intelligence. When his four-year term ended, they offered him a clerkship with an increase in salary, but the ambitious sixteen-year-old had other plans.

Demonstrating the restless energy and entrepreneurial zeal that would characterize his business career, Hires decided to pursue his future on a larger stage. On a Sunday afternoon, he traveled to nearby Bridgeton, New Jersey, where he boarded a Cohansey River steamer for the eighty-mile voyage up the Delaware to Philadelphia.[16] He carried a small suitcase containing a second suit of clothes and clean undergarments that his mother had packed. She had at first opposed her son's plan, fearing that the temptations of the city might lead a callow country boy astray. Her parting words of caution lingered in Charles' mind.[17]

Philadelphia, a growing city of some 675,000 residents, had until recently been preoccupied with the Civil War. The city had supported the Union armies with soldiers, armaments, and ships. Its factories delivered logistical support for the war effort ranging from uniforms to rations. Thousands of wounded soldiers and sailors were treated in Philadelphia hospitals. Following the war, the country's productive energy turned to peacetime enterprises. A workforce of returning soldiers and capital investment in new communication and transportation technologies spurred the industrialization of northern cities. Philadelphia's geography and manufacturing diversity positioned it well to prosper in the postwar economy.[18]

Hires joined an influx of immigrants that was rapidly altering the demography of the conservative Quaker city. A stream of Europeans, mainly from Germany and Ireland, debarked from steamships at Philadelphia's Washington Avenue piers. They would be followed later in the century by even greater numbers of Russians, Italians, and Eastern Europeans. The population of Hires' adopted hometown would nearly double to almost 1.3 million over the next thirty years.

Southern migration swelled the ranks of the city's African Americans as well. Between 1860 and 1880 their numbers increased from twenty-two to thirty-two thousand, the most of any northern city. They were not warmly welcomed by many in the majority community. For example, the Fifteenth Amendment, ratified in 1870, granted African American men the franchise. But it failed to dissuade a band of nativist yahoos determined to prevent them from exercising this right. Federal troops patrolled the city's polls in 1870 to protect African American voters. However, at polling places the following year, with no federal enforcement, white rioters killed three black residents and wounded many more. Among the dead was Octavius V. Catto, a thirty-one-year-old leader in the struggle for racial equality in the city.[19]

Boosters labeled nineteenth-century Philadelphia the "Workshop of the World." The city's eclectic mix of factories turned out products ranging from locomotives to clothing. A thriving transportation sector was led by the Pennsylvania Railroad, destined to become the country's largest corporation. Banking, publishing, and retailing firms also flourished; their headquarters occupied stolid Victorian office buildings in the city's compact central business district. A few large factories, including the Baldwin Locomotive Works and saw maker Henry Disston and Sons, were interspersed throughout the outlying neighborhoods. But most firms were of smaller scale. Consolidation of the city with its surrounding county in 1854 had provided room for expansion. Instead of occupying tenements, the city's working-class residents lived in ranks of three-story "row houses," often within walking distance of the places where they were employed.

By the time Hires arrived, the municipal bureaucracy was fast outgrowing its allotted space at Independence Square. Plans were afoot to find more spacious digs. In 1870 voters decided by referendum to move city government to Center Square, the site that William Penn had designated for that purpose in 1683. It would take almost twenty-five years for Philadelphia's grandiose French Second Empire–style city hall—beset by graft and seemingly endless delays—to be completed.[20]

A project finished on a swifter schedule, the 1876 Centennial Exposition, was the venue where Hires would introduce his root beer to the world. A herculean construction effort produced the expo's five massive exhibition halls, fifteen national and twenty-four state pavilions, and numerous ancillary buildings within a mere three years. America's first world's fair with nearly ten million paid admissions proved a defining event for the city. For six months it placed Philadelphia in the national, even international, spotlight and provided a welcome boost to its construction and hospitality industries. Perhaps more importantly, the Centennial buoyed citizen morale: "Over and above the economic benefits Philadelphia had acquired a sense of accomplishment, a conviction that its citizens could achieve results, that the city was no longer just a stop on the way to New York."[21]

The possibilities offered by this dynamic metropolis must have enthralled an ambitious youth eager to launch his business career. Hires stepped onto the city's Arch Street wharf on a Monday morning. He had fifty cents in his pocket. The young man from rural Millville (population six thousand) did not appear daunted by the pace of life in the nation's second largest city. He went directly to the home of a Quaker lady to whom he had a letter of introduction. She offered him a room in the attic of her home on Sixth Street north of Vine. The rent was four dollars a week, due upon his finding employment.

Hires stowed his grip and set out to present his credentials to drugstore proprietors in the area. He soon found a position as clerk for a Dr. Brown, a physician-apothecary who operated a drugstore on Ninth Street. Hires went to work that evening behind the counter. No mention was made of wages. On Saturday Dr. Brown handed him an envelope containing ten dollars and asked the young man if that was enough. Hires had not expected so handsome a salary. Concealing surprise with his employer's apparent largess, he tactfully replied that if the doctor felt his service was worth this amount, he was satisfied.[22]

One responsibility of Hires' first professional job was to cultivate Dr. Brown's trade with captains of ships berthed at the busy municipal port. He offered them a cleverly designed kit for treating common illnesses that might beset their crews while at sea. It consisted of a chest of medicines labeled by number. A numeric index affixed to the chest's inner lid described the disorders for which each medicine was intended. Hires visited the nearby piers almost daily to drum up new business and replenish the medicine chests of returning ships.[23]

As the home of the nation's first pharmacy college, Philadelphia was a leader in advancing professional training in the field.

Both the Philadelphia College of Pharmacy and Jefferson Medical College offered evening classes for drugstore clerks. Hires seized this opportunity to enhance his professional skills by attending sessions at both institutions.[24] Instruction in the medicinal properties of roots, barks, herbs, and other plants would serve him well in future endeavors as a soft drink experimenter and wholesale botanical druggist. He spent other evenings following up on classroom topics at the city's Mercantile Library. This private institution had been established in 1821 for the enlightenment of workers employed in the city's commercial enterprises.

After about a year, Hires left his position with Dr. Brown for one that paid more at a wholesale drug house. He was assigned to a department that manufactured fluid extracts.[25] Not content to continue working for others, Hires resigned this job a short time later to return to Millville. There he became a partner in the drugstore where he had apprenticed. Details surrounding Hires' return to Millville are sketchy. Certainly, the prospect of a partnership in an established business presented a promising opportunity for the nineteen-year-old. Why his brothers-in-law, Wright and Brooks, would seek a third partner in their small-town drugstore is not clear. An undated handwritten note in the Hires Family Papers states he bought "one third interest in the drug store in Millville." No price is noted. Hires' short stay, less than two years, also raises questions about the circumstances surrounding his departure.

Nevertheless, the new junior partner displayed a knack for concocting herbal remedies. "Hires' Dyspepsia Mixture," a blend of dry roots and barks, was claimed to banish that worrisome malady that its label described as "a constant pain or uneasiness in the pit of the stomach."[26] Advertisements for Hires' blend portrayed it as a panacea for an assortment of ailments. When brewed as directed, it was claimed to alleviate "stomach pain, acidity, costiveness [i.e., constipation], lack of appetite, depression, heart palpitations, sleeplessness, vomiting, dizziness, dimness of vision, staggering, memory loss and headaches."[27] Whether Hires attempted to patent his nostrum is unknown. However, his partners were sufficiently impressed with his creation to advertise it in the local newspaper under his name.

A Drugstore of His Own

The Millville partnership proved less attractive than Hires had anticipated.[28] By 1871 the twenty-year-old pharmacist had an itch to return to the big city. This time, instead of seeking work with an established pharmacy, he planned to strike out on his own.

The frequent financial meltdowns that beset the nation's economy in this era of untamed free enterprise might have given pause to an aspiring entrepreneur less confident than Hires. The gold panic of 1869, for example, added the term "Black Friday" to the national lexicon. It was triggered by speculators who pushed the price of the precious metal to astronomical heights, hoping to reap huge profits when the federal government returned to the gold standard. President Ulysses Grant foiled the speculators by ordering that $4 million in federal gold reserves be made available for trading. The price of gold plummeted, creating financial havoc and a wave of bankruptcies.[29] Four years later another panic paralyzed the nation's economy following the collapse of Jay Cooke and Co., a Wall Street banking house. More than ten thousand businesses went under in the ensuing three-year depression.[30]

Fortunately for Hires, his first business venture would not depend on such high-stakes financing. It relied instead on his own resources augmented by sweat and youthful optimism. He had managed to save $400 while working at the Millville drugstore. Using part of this stake, Hires rented a property at 602 Spruce Street, near downtown Philadelphia, and set about to turn the first floor into a retail drugstore. The structure was second from the corner in a block of three-story federal-style brick row houses a half block from Washington Square.

The square, plotted as part of William Penn's 1683 city plan, was an oasis of urban serenity. It had served as the city's potter's field through the Revolutionary War. The moldering remains of paupers, prisoners, and wartime casualties rested beneath the park's grassy expanse. Directly across the street from Hires' store stood the red brick Holy Trinity Roman Catholic Church, a precisely pointed structure erected in 1789.

After paying his rent, Hires had enough money left to cover needed renovations. He hired a carpenter and worked alongside him to outfit the shop with wooden shelves and simple showcases. They painted the walls white while adding a touch of pizazz with a gold border. Hires economized by sleeping in a room over the store.[31]

He managed to arrange a $3,000 credit with suppliers to purchase additional fixtures and his initial stock of drugs and sundries.[32] "The wholesale drug companies knew me from dealing with them while I was a clerk," Hires explained, "and evidently realizing that I was to be trusted, since I was ambitious and eager to get ahead, they gave me the supplies on credit."[33]

The finished store measured eighteen by sixty feet with a twenty-foot rear extension leading to a small backyard. Customers entered through a door on the left. A sales counter on the right side of the store sported a marble top. Over the counter, shelves held tinctures in bottles of various sizes and prominently displayed jars of pharmaceuticals. Shelves along the left wall held an assortment of popular patent medicines. These were good sellers, Hires said. One end of the sales counter was reserved for the store's showpiece. This was, as Hires recalled, "a small octagonal soda fountain in Tennessee marble with a gas light on the top. Of Lippincott make, which at the time I thought was very pretentious but which I would imagine would not find room in a second or third class store today."[34]

The prescription counter extended across the rear of the store. Behind it a working laboratory held tools of the druggist's trade: a pharmacy scale, glass graduates, mortar and pestle, and a wire hook where completed prescription forms were skewered.

Victorian-era druggists did more than interpret physicians' scrawls, counsel ailing customers, and count pills. They were required to actually prepare many of the products they sold. These included tonics, tinctures, tablets, plasters, and other medicines used by doctors and the public. The rise of pharmaceutical manufacturing following the Civil War would begin to relieve pharmacists of such hands-on chores. Neither were drugstores of the day devoted solely to the preparation and sale of medicines.

They were quasi hardware stores as well, stocking everyday necessities such as paint, glass, dyes, putty, and lamp oil. Some retail druggists also manufactured and wholesaled drugs and other chemical products.

Hires issued an "earnest invitation" to the opening of his drugstore in a handbill dated February 26, 1872.[35] He promised prospective customers a choice selection of drugs, chemicals, and spices of every description as well as the popular patent medicines of the day. The handbill reflected what would prove to be Hires' lifelong dedication to selling products "which are fresh and of the very best quality." He pledged to compound physicians' orders with accuracy and dispatch. He further assured the public: "My tinctures and syrups are made only by percolation and baths, from carefully selected drugs and herbs, with no fluid extracts used in their formulation, and therefore can be relied on as being of full strength and purity."[36]

In the manner of modern drug emporia, Hires' fledgling store advertised an array of nondrug items. In addition to spices, these included "perfumery, pomades, cosmetics, tooth, nail and hair brushes, note and letter paper, envelopes and postage stamps."[37]

Hires' invitation concluded with a pledge to his customers: "I shall endeavor by my practical knowledge and personal attention to the business to keep a First Class Establishment, feeling assured that all who may favor me with their patronage will receive entire satisfaction. C.E. Hires, Compounding and Dispensing Druggist."[38]

After getting his business on firm footing, Hires found the humdrum day-to-day duties of a retail druggist something less than fulfilling. "I have always been active and energetic," Hires recalled. "The time spent behind a prescription counter, especially in the dull part of the day, often became irksome. I longed for greater things to do." Thus it is not surprising that the inspiration for his "first conspicuous success," as he would later characterize it, occurred not while presiding over his prescription counter but during a midday walk along Spruce Street.[39]

A pile of a "lead colored clay-like substance" beside a cellar excavation site attracted the stroller's attention. It was smooth and heavy with a consistency like putty. The curious druggist picked up a glob of the stuff and rubbed some between his fingers. After drying a sample and examining it more closely under a microscope back at his store, Hires' suspicions were confirmed. The substance was potter's clay, also known as fuller's earth. The highly absorbent mineral-rich clay was a commodity of some worth. It was widely used in this era before chemical solvents to clean and remove stains from wool and flannel. The word "fuller" referred to a tradesperson engaged in the cleansing and thickening of cloth. Fuller's earth was also used as a filtering agent and as a base for baby powders.

Hires quickly grasped the potential value of his discovery. He returned to the construction site the next day and asked if he might have the excavated clay. Because Hires' drugstore was closer than the contractor's disposal site, he readily agreed to dump the excavation spoils at Hires' cellar door. Eventually, the entire cellar became piled high with fuller's earth, save for a narrow passageway that Hires boarded off. Fine particles from the drying clay filtered through the structure. "My store was a dusty dump," Hires recalled.[40]

Molding Clay into a Profit

Druggists customarily kept fuller's earth, in the form of lumps and powder, in a large container. When requested by a customer, the substance had to be scooped out, weighed, and wrapped to go in five- or ten-cent packages. It was a tedious process at best and one that created a great deal of dust and grime. Hires had a better idea. If the powdery clay could be packaged compactly in a uniform shape, he surmised, it would be much more convenient to handle and use.

Hires had been taking his meals at a boardinghouse operated by a widow near his store. In pondering how he might moisten the clay and mold it into cakes, he recalled the metal ring on which his hostess rested her iron. It was about three inches in diameter and one inch high. Hires asked to borrow one of the rings. Back at his store he filled the ring with a thick slurry of fuller's earth mixed with water. After fashioning several cakes in this manner, he allowed them to dry thoroughly in the sun. The finished product elated the budding entrepreneur. The molded cakes held their shape while retaining the granular texture and cleaning quality of fuller's earth. He reckoned they could be sold at retail for five cents apiece. He also recognized the importance of branding his earthy invention. He ordered a cast-iron stamp to impress the words "Hires' Special Cleaner" on each cake before it fully hardened.[41]

After securing additional ironing rings, Hires worked with his assistant and another hired hand to mold ten gross of the clay cakes, enough to fill a barrel. He wrapped several samples neatly in tissue paper and began making sales calls to drug wholesalers. Hires offered the cakes at $3.50 a gross. This would allow their profitable resale at thirty-five or forty cents per dozen. The first prospect declared Hires' product an "excellent idea." He was especially impressed by its promise to save druggists' time and eliminate the dirty work required to weigh and dispense fuller's earth in the traditional manner. He ordered ten barrels. Almost every drug wholesaler he called on ordered three to five barrels, Hires recalled. The Clayton French wholesale house took twenty-five barrels.[42]

Hires shrewdly opted to take payment for his product in kind rather than cash. "I sold this mostly with the understanding that the amount was to be taken out in drugs or sundries as I should want," he recalled. "In this way . . . it was much easier to sell the quantity I did. From these sales I was able to better stock my store."[43] These transactions also enabled Hires to establish lasting business relationships with the city's major drug wholesalers.

Hires expanded sales by renewing his supply of raw material from other cellar excavations. "I found that nearly all Philadelphia is underlain with a stratum of three or four feet of potter's clay," he explained. After supplying the local market, Hires took his product to New York City, where sales were brisk at first. These sales were also made in exchange for credits. But, as Hires would later learn only too well in his root beer business, success in the marketplace attracts competition. Within two years, Hires noted, larger competitors were selling knockoffs of his product at prices hardly sufficient to cover the cost of his labor. Hires decided it was time to abandon his brief but rewarding fuller's earth enterprise.[44] His total sales for Hires' Special Cleaner were reported to exceed $6,000.[45] "It was my first experience with a side line," Hires recalled. "I have found side lines more or less interesting ever since."[46]

His profits made it possible to hire a full-time clerk for retail sales, allowing Hires to turn his attention to a growing wholesale trade. He also had enough money to improve his Spartan original store. A woodcut of Hires' store from the 1870s shows a converted Philadelphia row house, a full story higher than the adjacent residential structures.[47] The first floor had been transformed into an inviting storefront with high arched display windows and door panels. A bold sign across the top of the façade identifies the building as a "Drug Warehouse." Less prominent banners above the third and second stories announce other wares sold within: "Paints, Oils and Varnishes" and "Quinton Glass Works."[48] Hires' reference to Quinton Glass probably reflected a family connection to this business in Salem County, New Jersey.

In 1872 Hires registered with the city's Pharmaceutical Examining Board and received a "certificate of competency" to practice pharmacy.[49] A report by the board indicated that 50 percent of the pharmacy owners who applied for certification that year were deemed unfit.[50] However, Hires had no intention of remaining strictly a retail pharmacist. He had begun to import botanical products and crude drugs while developing what he described as "a fairly substantial business" concocting and selling flavoring extracts. At about this time he also formally joined the congregation of the Spruce Street Baptist Church, transferring his membership there from the Cohansey Baptist Church of Roadstown, New Jersey.[51]

SOME BROTHERLY ADVICE

A letter Hires wrote that year to his younger brother William offers insights into values and the principles that would guide the twenty-three-year-old druggist's business career. The letter took the form of a pep talk. It was intended to arouse William from what Charles perceived to be a state of ennui and to encourage him to engage the world boldly. Although Charles' formal education had ended at age twelve, his writing is grammatical and articulate. The letter reveals an idealistic author who had seriously considered his own way forward.[52]

"It is foolish to say we have no time, and say 'if . . . if,'" he wrote. "We must make up our minds to sacrifice minor pleasures and look higher, with a determination that we will accomplish something even if we die in the attempt. How glorious it is when one has been baffled in his efforts for many years to come out victorious in the end."[53]

Hires recounted lessons he had gleaned from reading the biographies of prominent men—Peel, Arkwright, Wedgewood, Vanderbilt, and Melbourne—to support his belief in positive thinking and hard work as prerequisites to success.

"We must not allow time to pass without yielding fruits in something for our good, some good principle cultivated or some good habit strengthened," Hires exhorted his brother. "It is not accident then that helps a man in the world, but purpose and persistent industry. These make a man sharp to discern opportunities and turn them to account."[54]

But, as Charles reminded William, merely studying the examples of others was not enough:

> We must ourselves be and do, and not rest satisfied merely with reading and meditating over what other men have written and done. Our best light must be made life, and our best thoughts action. . . . To think meanly of ourselves is to sink in one's own estimation as well as in the estimation of others . . . as the thoughts are so will the acts be. A man cannot live a high life who grovels in the moral sewer of his own thoughts. He cannot aspire if he looks down; if he will rise, he must look up. It is a noble sight to see a poor man hold himself upright amidst all his temptations and refuse to demean himself.[55]

Hires bade his sibling to remember the words of the Spartan father who urged his son to "add a step to it" after the lad complained that his sword was too short. "That is applicable to everything in life," Hires said. "Where there's a will, there is a way."[56]

The letter resonates with a strong sense of moral purpose. "Truthfulness, integrity and goodness form the essence of manly character," he reminded his brother, "for it is when misfortune comes, the character of the upright man shines forth with greatest luster, and when all else fails he stands upon his integrity and courage. I truly believe I should always be happy if I followed the directions of my own conscience and leave the consequences to God."[57]

Hires signed the letter "your affectionate brother, Charlie." William would later serve as treasurer of the Charles E. Hires Co.[58]

With his business firmly established and future prospects encouraging, Hires was prepared to begin a family. He had begun courting Clara Kate Smith of Philadelphia. The comely Clara was twenty-three, a year younger than Charles. She came from a family of prosperous Quaker merchants. Her parents were Rebecca Jane (née Keyser) and Charles Shepard Smith. He was a partner in a firm that sold cement, lime, and other building supplies, while her mother's family operated a dry goods business. Clara attended the Friends Meeting at Fifteenth and Race Streets in Philadelphia. Charles was a Baptist who would not formally affiliate with the Quaker faith until much later. Thus the couple was wed in a simple civil ceremony on January 5, 1875, at which the mayor of Philadelphia officiated.[59] If they had been married by a minister or priest, Clara may have forfeited her right to membership in the Society of Friends, according to their grandson William.[60]

Charles and Clara would enjoy a harmonious and fruitful union that would bear them six children. Their first child, Linda, was born in 1878. Rebecca was born in 1883 but died at the age of six months due to whooping cough and convulsions.[61] Linda was joined by brothers John Edgar in 1885, Harrison in 1887, Charles Elmer Jr. in 1891, and a sister, Clara, in 1897.

Later in 1875 Hires sold his Spruce Street drugstore and opened a wholesale firm dealing in a range of products, including vanilla beans, botanical drugs, and flavoring extracts. A small ad in the *Philadelphia Inquirer* in 1876 also offered "sponges and chamois for sale by Charles E. Hires at 41 N. Front St."[62] Yet none of those items would ultimately wow a nation.

2

A RUSTIC TEA PARTY

N̲O ONE KNOWS FOR SURE why Charles, twenty-four, and his recent bride, Clara Kate, were boarding at a farm near Morristown, New Jersey, in 1875. Some have speculated they were on their honeymoon, but credible evidence is lacking. In recalling the visit, Hires made no reference to such a romantic scenario.[1] Neither is it known what attracted the couple to vacation at this particular farm or what activities occupied their time while there. One ostensibly trivial event that occurred during their stay, however, is well documented. Their hostess, a locally renowned cook and concocter, "plied her young guests with a strange, cool, sparkling beverage—'temperance of course'— brewed from native roots, herbs, barks and berries. It was a very moral thirst quencher for a prim young couple."[2]

Farm wives of the era, whose domestic skills sustained their families in so many ways, commonly created drinks for them in this manner. While farm families often found these beverages pleasantly refreshing, they tended to believe they were good for them too. Many of the roots, herbs, and berries used to flavor the drinks had tonic or medicinal properties. Also, the liquid used in their preparation was boiled, making it safer than tainted drinking water drawn from shallow wells or creeks that ran through cow pastures.[3]

"The farmer's wife was accustomed to gathering teaberry leaves, sassafras bark and berries, and to steep them, making a tea," Hires recalled. "The result, when boiled with sugar and fermented with yeast, was called 'homemade root beer.'"[4] The brief fermentation period yielded a pleasant carbonation but added no more than a trace of alcohol. The beverage intrigued young Hires. "It was highly agreeable to the taste," he recalled, while noting that overindulgence was apt to produce a less pleasant laxative effect. "I thought I saw a chance to put a similar product on the market if that fault could be corrected," he said. He persuaded their hostess to share her recipe with him.[5]

This rustic tea party, though seemingly mundane, would trigger future events beyond the imaginations of those present. A "Eureka!" moment it was not. But the flavor of that unpretentious drink lingered on the palate of the budding entrepreneur. After returning to Philadelphia, Hires set about to refine the humble brew, expunge its purgative proclivity, and transform it into a commercially viable beverage.

Hires' efforts were not unusual among pharmacists of his day. Soda fountains where flavorful drinks were concocted by blending soda water with fruit flavors had become a profitable adjunct to many neighborhood drugstores. Hires and his fellow druggists—not unlike farm wives—experimented by mixing various fruit syrups and other flavors with soda water, hoping to hit upon a tasty new beverage. Hires recalled his experience at the modest soda fountain he had proudly installed in his first drugstore. "I often experimented in getting up new flavors for soft drinks," he said. "Thus I learned a good deal about public taste. What sort of flavors would please patrons from the start and the kind of flavors which would remain in public favor."[6] This knowledge would prove invaluable in his quest to concoct an appealing root drink.

A NEW CONVENIENCE FOOD

While building his recently established trade in botanical drugs and flavoring extracts, Hires experimented off and on for more than a year to create a zesty alternative to the typically fruity

sweet soda fountain drinks of the day. He tried various mixtures of roots, barks, herbs, and berries.[7] Ingredients were selected for their flavor, but Hires also paid close attention to their
medicinal properties. He drew on his experience in preparing
medicines and extracts from herbs and other natural products.
He also sought advice from two professors whom he had come to
know while attending night classes at the Philadelphia College
of Pharmacy and Jefferson Medical College.

Hires envisioned his root tea not as a bottled beverage or a
soda fountain drink but as a home brew. He was bent on producing a "convenience food," although that term had not yet been
coined. He sought to relieve housewives of the labor of foraging
for roots, herbs, and bark with an easily prepared extract that
would yield a drink of consistent flavor and quality. The goal, as
Hires later described it, was "to produce a pure herb drink which
would be entirely neutral in its effects." The resulting beverage
would contain "the right combination of roots and herbs to produce flavor that would please at the moment and also send the
customer back for more."[8]

Hires had plenty of company in his efforts to make the lives
of the nation's housewives less burdensome. Improvements in
food technology and distribution were beginning to liberate
women from centuries of domestic drudgery. No longer would
they be required to roast and grind coffee beans or spend hours
producing soap, cheese, butter, or pickles at home. As the nineteenth century progressed, an increasing variety of prepared
staples was becoming available in stores. Innovators like Hires
rolled out a cornucopia of products that would become main-
stays of the country's diet. America was beginning to transition
from a nation of producers into a nation of consumers.[9]

Gilbert Van Camp's baked beans and Borden's condensed milk
had become favorites of Civil War troops during the 1860s.[10] Improvements in commercial canning were making soup and other
processed foods increasingly available. In 1869 Joseph Campbell
and his partner began producing preserves and canned vegetables
in Camden, New Jersey. Their business would become the Campbell Soup Co. following their introduction of condensed soups in
convenient cans.[11] Libby's precooked "corned beef" debuted in

1875 snugly packed in a trapezoidal container. Tomato ketchup, one of the earliest of H. J. Heinz's "57 Varieties," would be introduced alongside Hires Root Beer at the Centennial Exposition in 1876. Quaker Oats was registered as a trademark in 1877. The following year Dr. John H. Kellogg invented a multigrain biscuit that he crumbled and named "Granola." He also produced peanut butter to enable patients with poor teeth to consume nuts. By the end of the decade, Harley Procter of Cincinnati, Ohio, was marketing a buoyant white bar he would later brand as "Ivory Soap."[12] About the same time, Milton S. Hershey, who had prospered in the caramel business, branched out to produce chocolate in wrapped bars that retailed for a nickel apiece.[13]

The growing popularity of prepared food products is reflected in an analysis of magazine food advertising in the latter half of the nineteenth century. Ads for ready-to-use staples—soups, cookies, salad dressing, canned vegetables, and so on—increased significantly while the advertising of ingredients needed for cooking from scratch, such as flour and sugar, declined.[14]

No record exists, if indeed Hires retained one, of the ingredients and combinations he tested and discarded in his experiments. Finally the arduous trial-and-error process yielded a mixture of dried roots, herbs, and berries that when brewed in water with sugar and yeast (for carbonation) produced a beverage that met the young pharmacist's requirements. Its flavor was described as woodsy, minty, and a little medicinal.[15]

The final recipe for Hires' drink remains a mystery. But trade secrets aside, evidence supports an educated guess as to its main components. Hires noted "teaberry leaves (a source of wintergreen), sassafras bark and berries" as among the ingredients used by the New Jersey farmer's wife in creating the original brew. Hires added several others, including juniper, pipsissewa, wintergreen, sarsaparilla, hops, chiretta, and spikenard.[16] The finished product also contained ginger, vanilla, juniper berries, dog grass, and licorice root. Caramel coloring derived from burnt sugar was added to give the drink its characteristic brown hue.[17]

Later Hires ads and various company publications sought to entice would-be purchasers with summaries of the drink's ingredients accompanied by their exotic points of origin, which included Italy, India, Africa, Spain, Jamaica, and Brazil. Hires maintained through the years that Hires Root Beer contained precisely 16 roots, barks, herbs and berries.

The original makeup of Hires Root Beer apparently changed little over time. More than forty years later, Hires told an interviewer that his root beer formula remained unaltered.[18] Lacking the original recipe or a chemical analysis of its later ingredients, this assertion cannot be verified. Despite the consistency of its components, however, the formula proved to be quite malleable. After creating a popular concentrate for home brewers, Hires would later adapt his recipe to produce both fountain beverages and a line of bottled soda pop.

Hires sought out components of the highest quality, purity, and freshness, abjuring chemicals or anything "artificial." His pharmacy training and experience working with botanic commodities guided his selection. He maintained, for example, that roots gathered in the winter were more flavorful than those harvested in summer after their sap had ascended to the plant above.[19] In fact, Hires' insistence on the finest natural ingredients became the mantra of his business philosophy. It was noted that Hires complied with the strictest provisions of the pure food laws before such laws were conceived.[20] The Pure Food and Drugs Act of 1906 was intended to prevent the manufacture, sale, or transportation of adulterated, misbranded, poisonous, or deleterious foods, drugs, medicines, and liquors. It was the first of several consumer protection laws enacted by the federal government during the twentieth century. Although Hires Root Beer was unaffected by the 1906 law, its provisions forced makers of a number of patent medicines and even some food products to revamp their formulas.

What Hires clearly did not do, as some have suggested, is invent root beer. The drink had existed since Colonial times in America and earlier in Europe. Its origin can be traced to a family of beverages known as "small beers," introduced here by European settlers. These low-alcohol beers were brewed from mixtures of roots, berries, barks, and herbs. They typically contained a small amount of alcohol and were mildly carbonated as a result of fermentation, similar to hard cider. Their brief fermentation period limited alcohol formation and distinguished them from their more potent cousins served across the bar. Ingredients deemed to be healthful and the pleasant buzz induced by their mild alcohol content and carbonation heightened the appeal of these small beers.

A small beer brewed from spruce boughs proved popular among American colonists. General George Washington reportedly included a quart of spruce beer in his troops' daily ration.[21] More enduring variants included root beer and birch beer. These typically contained various combinations of sarsaparilla, vanilla, sassafras, and wintergreen.

Traditionally, small beers were produced at home; their recipes handed down across generations. Initially, they stood apart from the fizzy beverages sold at drugstores following the introduction of soda fountains earlier in the nineteenth century. However, by midcentury entrepreneurs had begun to explore the commercial potential of these humble home brews. In 1866 two New Hampshire residents applied for a patent to produce Smith's White Root Beer in stoneware bottles. The drink would be carbonated by fermentation and included sarsaparilla, life-of-man root, prince's pine, spruce oil, and sassafras among its ingredients. Whether this beverage was ever sold commercially is unknown.[22]

TRADITIONAL RECIPES

As he labored to perfect his beverage, Hires may well have been influenced by existing root beer recipes. For example, an 1860 handbook of household recipes offered a simple formula for common small beer. The authors advised combining "a handful of hops, to a pailful of water, one pint of bran, half a pint of molasses, one gill of yeast, and a spoonful of ginger." They also included a root beer recipe. It contained more ingredients but offered wide latitude to the home brewer. "Take a pint of bran, a handful of hops, some twigs of spruce, hemlock or cedar, a little sassafras, or not, as you have it; roots of every kind; plantain, burdocks, docks, dandelions, [etc.]; boil and strain, add a spoonful of ginger, molasses, to make pleasant, and a cup of yeast; this for one gallon."[23]

Dr. Chase's Recipes, published in 1864, contained a list of ingredients and directions for making a root beer similar in many respects to that developed a few years later by Hires:

> For each gallon of root beer to be used, take hops, burdock, yellow dock, sarsaparilla, dandelion, and spikenard roots, bruised, of each ½ oz.; boil about 20 minutes and strain while hot, add 8 or 10 drops of oils of spruce and sassafras mixed in equal proportions, when cool enough not to scald your hand, put in two or three table-spoons of yeast; molasses ⅔ of a pint, or white sugar ½ lb. gives it about the right sweetness. You can use more or less of the roots to suit your taste after trying it; it is best to get the dry roots or dig them and let them get dry, and of course you can add any other root known to possess medicinal properties desired in the beer. After all is mixed, let it stand in a jar with a cloth thrown over it, to work about two hours, then bottle and set in a cool place.[24]

The doctor's recipe contained eight active ingredients—about half the number in Hires' final formula—yet major components such as sarsaparilla, hops, and sassafras were identical. In any event, Dr. Chase had no problem with adding a few more ingredients, especially if they were reputed to be medicinal. Perhaps Hires took the good doctor at his word when concocting his own brew. Their recipes diverged when it came to the fermentation step, however. Chase, on the one hand, suggested that the drink be bottled two hours after the ingredients were mixed, then storing the bottles in a cool place. Presumably, this cooling would stop fermentation. Hires, on the other hand, directed that his root beer be bottled immediately. Both methods were likely to produce a drink with only a trace of alcohol.

Dr. Chase, as would Hires, extolled the health-giving properties of his homemade root beer without being overly specific. "This is a nice way to take alteratives, without taking medicine," the doctor advised. "And families ought to make it every spring and drink freely of it for several weeks, and thereby save, perhaps, several dollars in doctor bills." Modern herbalists classify alteratives as blood purifiers.[25]

Hires had sound business reasons for introducing his drink as an extract rather than a syrup to be mixed at soda fountains. He envisioned a bigger market for an extract. Soda fountains were not then as numerous as they would later become, driven by the marketing prowess of Coca-Cola, Moxie, Dr. Pepper, and other early soft drinks. And many households, especially those in rural areas, lacked ready access to a drugstore. Producing an extract also enabled Hires to standardize his ingredients and ensure a degree of consistency in the finished product, as long as the home brewer followed his directions. This was important to Hires. He would have no control over how a root beer syrup might be mixed or served at the soda fountain. Indeed, the substitution of bogus Hires for the real thing would later become an unending nuisance (see Chapter 4). While some enterprising pharmacists would purchase his extract to produce root beer for sale at their fountains, Hires' creation chiefly entered the market as a packaged product sold over the counter by pharmacists and grocers.

The yellow three-ounce box of pulverized roots, bark, and herbs was labeled "Hires' Household Extract" in bold black letters. The compact package retailed for twenty-five cents and was potent enough to flavor five gallons of root beer. But converting its contents into a palatable drink was anything but simple, at least by modern standards.

Home Brewers Beware!

The home brewer first had to assemble additional ingredients— five gallons of water, four pounds of sugar, and a quantity of yeast. Either a half pint of fresh yeast or a half cake of fresh compressed yeast would do. The process began by boiling the dried extract like tea leaves and carefully straining out the residual solids before adding the liquid to the heated water. Next, the sugar and yeast needed to be stirred into the mixture until dissolved. Hires advised that the concoction then be poured into "strong bottles or jugs, at once corking and tying the corks securely." The bottles were then to be set in a warm place to encourage fermentation. A minimum fermentation period of ten to twelve hours was recommended, but Hires suggested that greater effervescence might be achieved by aging the finished brew three or four days.[26]

Hires' instructions cautioned home brewers to avoid several potential pitfalls. For example, a failure to ferment could result from defective yeast or placing the filled bottles in a cool place, which would abort the fermentation process. Fresh baker's yeast was strongly advised over the dried variety. "If these simple hints are carefully borne in mind," buyers were assured, "the Root Beer is very little trouble to make successfully." However, a final precaution was included for the imprudent: "When we say 'yeast' we do not mean Baking Powder."[27] Unmentioned were unnerving "explosions" that might result if weak bottles were used and the corks were secured too tightly.

Although Hires original formula is no longer produced, similar products are available today for home brewers. These are liquids similar to the concentrate Hires would offer a few years after introducing his original package of dry ingredients. With some trepidation, this author tried his hand, closely following Hires' recipe but substituting Zatarain's Root Beer Concentrate for Hires' Household Extract. I also used dry champagne yeast instead of the fresh yeast recommended by Hires. The finished product seemed properly carbonated and had a pleasant root beer flavor. I must confess to using plastic bottles with snug screw caps, which are recommended to avoid possible explosions from over-carbonation. Also, as fermentation creates carbon dioxide, these flexible bottles harden, offering a rough gauge of carbonation. My home-brewed root beer surely contained some alcohol but in an amount too slight for me to measure using a hydrometer.

While Hires most certainly was aware that beverages produced using Dr. Chase's recipe and others had been called "root beers," the working name for his drink was "Hires' Root Tea." He may well have decided to market it as a tea out of deference to the temperance movement, which had been gathering strength as a social force in American life. Hires' personal life reflected his sincere religious beliefs and commitment to the temperance cause.

Serendipitously, a friend and fellow advocate of abstinence intervened to alter Hires' naming decision and—quite possibly—assure the success of his product. Reverend Russell Herman Conwell was an apt adviser for an aspiring capitalist such as Hires. The Baptist minister, who would found Temple College (later Temple University) in 1884, had carved out a niche as a motivational speaker and apostle of Gilded Age values. Conwell warmly embraced the Protestant ethic that stresses the values of hard work, discipline and frugality in the pursuit of economic success.

"I say that you ought to get rich, and it is your duty to get rich," he exhorted his audiences. "To make money honestly is to preach the gospel . . . The men who get rich may be the most honest men you find in the community."[28]

Conwell delivered his spellbinding lecture "Acres of Diamonds" thousands of times on the Chautauqua circuit and beyond.[29] In it he related the saga of Al Hafed, an ancient Persian grandee who owned a large and prosperous farm. After learning from an itinerant priest about the value of diamonds and the wealth they might confer, Al Hafed became convinced that the sparkling gems were a man's best friend. He found a buyer for his property and set off on an obsessive quest for diamonds. His futile search would lead him from the "Mountains of the Moon" to the Bay of Barcelona. There in utter despair, the now penniless wretch threw himself into a "tidal wave" and drowned. Meanwhile, back at the farm he had abandoned, fortune smiled. The new owner chanced to pick up and examine a curious looking rock. Lo and behold, it was a diamond in the rough! The entire farm, it seemed, was sitting atop acres of the gemstones.[30]

The moral of Conwell's tale was clear. Opportunity lies at home, literally under our feet, if we would but recognize it. There is no need to rush off in search of greener pastures. "Friends, never in the history of our country was there an opportunity so great for the poor man to get rich as there is now and in the city of Philadelphia," Conwell declared. "The very fact that they get discouraged is what prevents them from getting rich. That is all there is to it. The road is open, and let us keep it open, between the poor and the rich."[31]

Do Not Call It "Tea"

Conwell's beguiling bombast may have inspired his idealistic young friend as he plotted his own route to riches. One day in 1875 the two men discussed Hires' plans to launch "Hires Herb Tea."[32] As the story goes, Conwell had sampled the drink and found it delicious. But he was less than enamored with the name Hires proposed for his product. "Why not call it root beer?" Conwell demanded. At first Hires recoiled at Conwell's suggestion. He feared the word "beer" would degrade what he envisioned as a temperance beverage. But the preacher persisted. "Our hard-drinking miners in central Pennsylvania will never touch a drink labeled 'tea,'" Conwell insisted. "Call it 'root beer' and beat the anti-temperance crowd at their own game."[33] Conwell's logic prevailed. We cannot know how successfully Hires might have marketed an "herb tea"— would we still be drinking "Hires Root Tea" today?

Hires and Conwell would remain close friends throughout their lifetimes, with Hires later becoming a generous benefactor of Conwell's charitable causes. In 1893, for example, the then prosperous Hires would contribute $1,000 toward the construction of a classroom building that Conwell was erecting at his emerging university in north Philadelphia.[34] On Conwell's seventy-fifth birthday in 1918, the reverend received a $2,000 check from his old friend to further his work at Temple University. Hires termed it "a slight token of my love and appreciation for your friendship and the splendid work that you have done and are still doing . . . Your talks and writings have enthused many thousands of young men and women to see more in life and [given them] the opportunity to grow and enjoy a broader interpretation of all that is true and beautiful in life."[35]

The twenty-four-year-old entrepreneur began selling his newly named extract in 1875 with high hopes but modest means. Hires offered packages of his extract over the counter at his store, where they sold "pretty well," as he recalled. Hires continued to pursue his day job selling botanical drugs and flavoring extracts while finding time to methodically introduce his drink to wholesalers in the Philadelphia area. Hires could not afford to hire salesmen, so he did the legwork himself. The local response to Hires Root Beer Extract was positive if not overwhelmingly favorable. But this was sufficient evidence to convince the optimistic druggist that his drink had a future—if only enough people could be induced to try it. Eventually, he managed to recruit a pair of salesmen who shared his enthusiasm to take his root beer on the road.

"Finally, I found two young men who were willing to tackle the proposition on the chance of making enough cash sales to pay their traveling expenses," Hires recalled. "They were the first salesmen I ever hired. They travelled through the South and clear up into the Northeast on this rather precarious basis, getting enough cash from the dealers in a town to carry them on to the next stop. Sometimes they came pretty close to being stranded, but they made the round trip to Philadelphia all right, and many trips after that."[36]

Yet the efforts of audacious young men alone were not enough to propel Hires' home brew onto a larger stage. It needed a harder push. Fortuitously, the granddaddy of American trade shows to that time—popularly known as the Centennial Exposition of 1876—was preparing to open in Hires' backyard.

Public attention in the United States and abroad was focused on Hires' adopted hometown in 1876. Asserting its claim as the nation's birthplace, Philadelphia had won its bid to host a grand centennial exhibition. The exhibition, of course, was intended to commemorate the nation's founding and to celebrate its century of accomplishments and growing world stature. But the event's formal title—*The International Exhibition of Arts, Manufactures and Products of the Soil and Mine*—hinted at a more practical and commercial purpose. The exhibition provided an epic showcase for the advances achieved by science, industry, and agriculture during the preceding hundred years. Yankee ingenuity at its most fecund would be on glorious display.

A Fair to Remember

The size and scope of the Centennial beggared superlatives. Extensive exhibition buildings, including the Main Exhibition Hall, Machinery Hall, Agricultural Hall, Horticultural Hall,

Memorial Hall, and a Woman's Pavilion rapidly took form on a 284-acre fairground carved out of the city's Fairmount Park. The Main Exhibition Hall, which sprawled over 22 acres, was reputed to be the world's largest building. In addition, twenty-four states constructed buildings, some of which housed dignitaries and visitors rather than exhibitions. Fifteen nations hyped their native products and achievements in individual pavilions. The Pennsylvania Railroad built a spur from its main line to bring visitors directly to the Centennial's gates. Nearly ten million visitors attended throughout the event's six-month duration, with admissions on some days exceeding a hundred thousand.[37]

A reputed throng of seventy-six thousand visitors plodded across the unfinished expo's muddy grounds to purchase fifty-cent admissions on opening day, May 10, 1876. Philadelphia's Liberty Bell rang for half an hour. A chorus of eight hundred voices accompanied by an orchestra of a hundred and fifty musicians performed Richard Wagner's opening festal march in resounding fashion. *Grand Festival March* was later judged one of the worst pieces the renowned composer ever wrote. By contrast, President Grant's brief opening remarks were inaudible to those more than a few yards away.[38]

Hundreds of inventers, manufacturers, horticulturists, artists, and assorted hucksters regaled the Centennial crowds with marvels ranging from the right arm and torch of the unfinished Statue of Liberty to the massive Corliss steam engine that powered displays throughout Machinery Hall. Some products and inventions introduced at the Centennial would radically alter the lives of millions over the next hundred years. These included Alexander Graham Bell's telephone, Eliphalet Remington's typewriter, and the dynamo-powered precursor to the electric light. Others that debuted there, such as Heinz Ketchup, Hires Root Beer, and the banana, would also achieve wide popularity although their impact on society was admittedly less profound.

By 1876 Hires felt confident that his root beer concentrate was ready for prime-time exposure. He had test-marketed it for the past year over the counter at his drugstore. Consumer response had been encouraging. Hires recognized the Centennial as a unique opportunity to introduce his drink to a larger audience. He somehow wangled a space in one of the vast exhibition halls.[39] Just how he accomplished this feat and under what circumstances he presented his root beer there are unclear. A search of Centennial guides and catalogs reveals no reference to Hires as a formal exhibitor.[40] Exhibitors of commercial food products at the Centennial tended to be established firms such as Whitman and Son, Philadelphia, confectioners; American Condensed Milk Co., condensed milk; George V. Hecker and Co., New York, flour; Crosse and Blackwell, London, pickles, sauces, preserved fruit; and Rumford Chemical Works, Providence, Rhode Island, baking powder.[41] Perhaps small-scale producers such as Hires lacked the wherewithal required to mount a formal exhibit.

An unattributed note in the Hires Family Papers raises the possibility that Hires may not have introduced his root beer at the Centennial but instead represented a British chemical firm. The family papers also include a Centennial pass identifying Hires as a representative of the United Kingdom, which as the largest foreign exhibitor occupied three buildings at the expo.[42] Nevertheless, a preponderance of evidence supports the conclusion that, however he may have gained entry to the Centennial, Hires promoted his drink there. Numerous sources lend confirmation. For example, in his history of the exposition, William Pierce Randel states:

> Charles E. Hires not only displayed his root beer but gave demonstrations of how he made it, with dried roots and spices. The standard price of a soft drink was three cents, handy enough because the three-cent piece was one of the standard coins.[43]

An article describing the Centennial in *Nation's Business* offers additional verification. "Charles E. Hires once told me that the Centennial contributed much to his success in putting over Hires Root Beer," its author attests.[44] Yet another source postulates the plausible explanation that Hires introduced his root beer at a "friend's booth" at the Centennial.[45]

The installations of well-endowed soda fountain manufacturers would have dwarfed Hires' modest root beer station at the Centennial. Two companies, Lippincott of Philadelphia and Tufts of Boston, paid the eye-popping sum of $50,000 (more than $1 million today) for the expo's exclusive soda fountain concession.[46] Several of their ornate fountains adorned the exposition halls. As examples of nineteenth-century ingenuity, these fountains explored "the whole range of art . . . to furnish designs and ornamentation of the marvels of taste and skill," replacing "the crude designs of former years," an exhibition program gushed.[47] The extravagance of Tuft's main fountain astonished fairgoers. They gaped in admiration at the company's centerpiece, an elaborate three-story, seven-ton creation that dispensed no fewer than twenty-eight types of soda water and six flavoring syrups. It was capped with hanging ferns, a chandelier, and a device that sprayed perfume over the awe-struck throngs below.[48]

Fountain drinks proved extremely popular with fairgoers during the unusually hot summer. "The business done was enormous," exhibitor James Tufts allowed, "and although not profitable in itself (the fountain), proved a valuable advertisement."[49] Hires handed out free samples of his root beer and packets of his powdered concentrate. He also demonstrated its preparation and sold glasses of the beverage for three cents.[50] Fairgoers unable to afford this price could obtain a free glass of water at a huge fountain erected by the Catholic Total Abstinence Union, topped by a sixteen-foot figure of Moses.[51] Visitors who tried Hires' beverage seemed to like it. Among them, he later recalled, were druggists from across the United States, many of whom had concocted similar drinks for their own customers. Hires lavished attention on this group and encouraged them to take home samples of his product. Many would later place orders for Hires' extract to sell at their own pharmacies.[52]

Thus the Centennial helped Hires "attain a spotty but semi-national distribution. Druggists and (other) visitors told the folks back home about the sensational new drink—absolutely temperance—which they could make and bottle at home," a trade journalist later wrote.[53]

His positive experience at the Centennial convinced Hires that his drink had popular appeal, but an additional "ingredient" would be needed to broaden its market. Hires could scarcely have imagined the potential power of advertising to increase root beer sales. Fortuitously, around this time a visionary newspaper publisher would make Hires a proposition that was destined to change his life (see Chapter 4).

Meanwhile, technological innovation was transforming the soda fountain industry. Improvements in production and delivery systems increased the popularity and profitability of fountain beverages, while attracting scores of inventors and entrepreneurs. Hires would need to alertly tweak and reposition his original formula to compete in this dynamic marketplace.

3

BUBBLY WATER BEGETS
AN INDUSTRY

C HARLES HIRES HAD the good fortune to live during the era of remarkable technological innovation that heralded the emergence of industrial America. Inventions including the telephone, typewriter, elevator, sewing machine, light bulb, and internal combustion engine replaced centuries' old customs and practices and shaped the future in surprising and dramatic ways. Often overlooked in inventories of nineteenth-century achievements is the invention and evolution of the soda fountain. Like other progressive pharmacists of his day, Hires recognized the profit-making potential of this ingenious countertop drink dispenser. He installed the finest one he could afford—Tennessee marble with a gas light on top—when he opened his first drugstore in 1872. Yet he could not have envisioned the critical role the soda fountain would play in shaping his future.

This initially crude device for dispensing carbon dioxide–infused water grew rapidly in efficiency and sophistication throughout the century. It would spawn soda fountain and soft drink industries while transforming the neighborhood drugstore into a social institution. Its impact can be traced in diverse historic movements, including urbanization, the rise of a consumer economy, temperance, and Prohibition.

By the second half of the nineteenth century, soda water was on its way to becoming the nation's drink of choice. Widely advertised beverages, such as Moxie and Coca-Cola, the spread of newfangled "ice cream parlors," and a growing temperance movement encouraged Americans from coast to coast to meet at the soda fountain. Steady technological improvements including Jacob Baur's patented process for liquefying carbon dioxide and compressing it into portable tanks improved efficiency and opened new venues.[1] A contemporary observer described the soda water phenomenon in fanciful fashion:

> Man is born thirsty. His first cry is for drink. The natural sources of supply are the kindly milk and the abundant water. But the allotted years of his life are three-score years and ten. In this stretch of time both milk and water become monotonous. To prevent this, the arts, the sciences, the industries have largely been directed. The consequences, industrial and social, are among the most conspicuous features of our civilization, which they have helped both to promote and retard. According to the formulae of the purveyor of drinks the world marches. In this light the most important date in the history of events was that on which carbonic acid gas was discovered. Yet to this day no one has erected a statue to Van Helmont.[2]

Jean Baptiste Van Helmont, a Flemish chemist, isolated carbonic acid gas produced by fermentation in the early seventeenth century. He determined it to be distinct from the ordinary atmosphere and coined the word "gas" to describe it.[3] Unflavored soda water is a pleasant enough drink. But a group of inspired nineteenth-century entrepreneurs—frequently pharmacists—resolved to raise the bland bubbly to another level. They began mixing it with fruit syrups and more exotic ingredients, including birch bark, dandelion, and sarsaparilla, to create tempting soft drinks. Hires, an early member of this fraternity, painstakingly perfected his root beer formula at his drugstore soda fountain.

Hires initially marketed his creation as a convenient concentrate for home brewers. Later, as the beverages created by his rivals stimulated the soda fountain trade, Hires prudently opted to also offer his root beer first as a bottled drink and eventually in the form of a syrup base for soda fountain beverages.

AN AFFINITY FOR SODA WATER

The distance between prescription counter and soda fountain was not as great as may first appear. Pharmacists' affinity for soda water grew out of their role as purveyors of healthful remedies. Naturally carbonated mineral water from spas such as Vichy and Saratoga Springs had long been prized for their reputed health benefits. In 1784 George Washington, a patron of mineral springs, received a letter commenting on the high carbonation of Saratoga's waters. "Several persons told us they had corked it tightly in bottles and that the bottles broke," Colonel Othy Williams wrote the general.[4]

Early drugstores supplemented their inventories of chemicals, proprietary remedies, paints, and sundries with bottles of effervescent waters from native and foreign springs. These spas, often claiming restorative powers bordering on the miraculous, were popular among well-to-do patrons seeking therapies and cures. Those who could not afford the luxury of a spa visit might secure the purported benefits of natural springs at their local drugstore.

Ever since the ancient Greeks used them to treat disease, effervescent waters had fascinated healers and scientists. In 1684, following up on Van Helmont's discovery, English chemist Robert Boyle speculated about how mineral waters might be reproduced by chemical means.[5] Interest in effervescent drinks bubbled to new heights in 1767 when Joseph Priestley, an English clergyman and chemist, invented a method for carbonating still water by infusing it with carbon dioxide (CO_2). He called the gas he captured above fermenting vats at a Leeds brewery "fixed air." Priestley's countrymen refined his process. They discovered that the gas could be produced more reliably by using dilute sulfuric acid to dissolve the calcium carbonate in powered chalk or marble. By the end of the eighteenth century, artificially carbonated water began to appear in London apothecary shops. A

British patent for impregnating water with carbon dioxide was issued to Henry Thompson in 1807.[6]

Priestley's discovery stirred scientific interest across the Atlantic as well. American physician Benjamin Rush, for example, was convinced of the curative powers of natural mineral waters. In 1773 he published papers on the nature and consumption of such waters in the Philadelphia area.[7] His colleague, noted surgeon Dr. Philip Syng Physick, is credited with creating flavored carbonated soft drinks as early as 1807. He had been prescribing artificially carbonated water to relieve his patients' gastric disorders. While instructing a pharmacist how to produce such waters, Physick suggested adding fruit syrup to make it more palatable.[8]

In 1806 Benjamin Silliman, a Yale chemistry professor, purchased a British inventor's soda apparatus and began producing artificial mineral water for sale at a New Haven pharmacy.[9] He had difficulty finding suitable bottles for the drink. "I cannot procure any glass bottles which will not burst, or any stone ones which are impervious to the fixed air," Silliman wrote.[10]

An 1819 British visitor to Philadelphia reported: "During the hot season mineral waters (chiefly soda), sometimes mixed with syrup, are drank [sic] in great abundance—the first thing any American who can afford five cents (about three pence) takes on rising in the morning is a glass of soda water: many houses are open for the sale of it, and some of them are fitted up with Parisian elegance."[11] At one such establishment, the Shakespeare Gallery, patrons might find soda water on tap and peruse the latest novels, newspapers, and pamphlets. The gallery styled itself as "not only conducive to the health of the city, but an elegant and fashionable lounge for ladies and gentlemen throughout the day."[12] The term "soda water" may have derived from the European practice of adding sodium bicarbonate to such drinks to ease indigestion.

Elias Durand, who had been an apothecary in Napoleon's army, opened one of America's first "modern" drugstores at the corner of Sixth and Chestnut Streets in Philadelphia about 1825. The store featured mirrors, French glassware, mahogany display cases, and an unpretentious urn-like apparatus that dispensed carbonated water. His establishment became a social hub for

local scientists, physicians, and literati.[13] Another French immigrant to the Quaker City may have been the nation's first
commercial soft drink bottler. Around 1843 Eugene Roussel
added lemon flavoring to bottled soda water to create a popular
beverage that he sold at his perfume shop on Chestnut Street.[14]

A British immigrant who arrived in America in 1832 may
fairly lay claim to the title of Father of the American Soda Fountain Industry.[15] John Matthews learned to build soda-generating
equipment while working as an apprentice in England. After
opening a soda fountain at 55 Gold Street in New York, Matthews began to market his version of a soda-making apparatus.
The process started in a "generator," consisting of a cast-iron box
lined with lead, where carbonic acid gas was formed by mixing
sulfuric acid (oil of vitriol) with marble dust. The gas was then
purified by passing it through water and conducted into a tank
partially filled with cool water. An employee rocked the tank for
as long as half an hour, until the water was impregnated with
bubbles.[16] Matthews's firm would later purchase the scrap marble created during the construction of St. Patrick's Cathedral in
New York City. The marble, once pulverized, was said to have
generated some twenty-five million gallons of soda water.[17]

AN EXPANDING INDUSTRY

These early rudimentary soda fountains spurred the growth of
an industry for their manufacture. Matthews's company would
become one of its leaders. But it was not alone. Several strong
competitors entered the field, including companies started by
Charles Lippincott of Philadelphia, William Gee of New York,
and A. D. Puffer and James W. Tufts, both of Boston.[18] Drugstore
owners began supplementing their stocks of natural mineral waters with artificially carbonated still water.

Within a few years, soda fountain manufacturers were incor-
porating an arsenal of syrup pumps into their increasingly elaborate designs. Firms bottling flavored soda also were springing
up around the country. The race to discover new flavors was
on.[19] Simple early fountains—countertop boxes with taps for
dispensing soda water generated by works under the counter—

grew more ornate as manufacturers strove to outdo their competitors. Fanciful edifices of multihued marble and onyx with soaring fixtures found a ready market among pharmacies and other soda sellers.[20]

Even the smallest fountains were as ornate as wedding cakes. Larger ones sporting silver-plated spigots, gilded piping, Grecian columns, and miniature statues of scantily clad goddesses evoked gasps of awe—so did their prices, sometimes in the tens of thousands of dollars.[21] For example, a drugstore on New York's West Side dazzled patrons with a "temple of marble and silver. On top, under a crystal dome, a marble goddess in a continuous shower bath is surrounded by four nymphs. These are in turn guarded by four bronze knights in armor upholding gas jets."[22] Producing such works of popular art had grown so lucrative that by 1876, as noted in Chapter 2, two large manufacturers, Lippincott and Tufts, ponied up the then staggering sum of $50,000 for the exclusive right to vend soda water from their fountains at the Centennial Exposition.

Initially, some pharmacists dismissed the soda fountain as an intrusive nuisance. However, they soon grasped its potential benefit for their bottom lines, as a trade journal observed:

> Retail druggists, who operate the greater fraction of the fountains, have for generations been sick of penny-a-sale profits and credit purchases which have barely enabled many of them to eke out a living. They have naturally hailed the soda fountain business with glee. A properly managed fountain business can be made to show a profit of 100 percent.[23]

The article pointed out some additional advantages of operating a drugstore soda fountain:

> The fountain business is a cash business. It advertises a store and induces the purchase of much [sic.] other goods. Fountains do not get out of date. There is no price cutting, no wrapping and tying, and no delivery expense. Little extra help is required, if any. And finally . . . the fountain business has an all-the-year-round season.[24]

Soda fountains helped to sustain pharmacies following the Civil War when the cheaper products of drug manufacturers began inexorably to displace pharmacist-prepared remedies. As fanciers of effervescent beverages increased soda fountain revenues, the neighborhood drugstore became a community meeting place for young and old alike. Enhancements such as ice cream and, later, luncheonettes further contributed to their profitability.

Unlike taverns, almost exclusively a male domain, soda fountains afforded a pleasant social experience for all members of the family. Going to the soda fountain was an event. The marble counters and gleaming apparatus fostered a sense of wonder. "Soda jerks" in crisp white jackets played to their audience, skillfully mixing drinks while bantering with customers:

> Swift of hand, nimble of mind, dashing in appearance and charming to boot, the soda jerk came into his own as the big-city and small-town answer to the cowboy or the lumberjack. True, he (only occasionally, she) referred to manuals called "formularies" for the recipe of a Bonnie Belle Cream, Catawba Frappe or whatever happened to be in vogue that week, but still, soda jerking was high craft.[25]

Soda fountains at first appeared mainly in drugstores, but they soon popped up in ice cream parlors, department stores, and train stations. Large cities boasted freestanding fountains in public spaces.

"AN AMERICAN DRINK"

"Soda water is an American drink. It is as essentially American as porter, Rhine wine and claret are distinctively British, German and French," *Harper's Weekly* declared. "But the crowning merit of soda water, which fits it to be the national drink, is its democracy. The millionaire may drink champagne while the poor man drinks beer, but they both drink soda water. There is no quarter of this great town so poor that the soda fountain, cheaply but ostentatiously erected in marble and plate, does not adorn the street corners, and is not liberally patronized."[26]

Advertising trade journal *Printers' Ink* attributed America's growing passion for soda fountain beverages to several factors:

> One of these has been the widely reputed American love of ice-cold drinks. Another has been the proverbial sweet tooth of Americans. A third has been the gradual and insistent growth of Prohibition in this country. A fourth has been the pure food laws which resulted in purer ingredients. Some fountains, before pure food restrictions went into force, were deadly and dirty chemical kitchens. And perhaps more important than all, has been the widespread advertising of the trade-marked drinks.[27]

Pharmacists had become creative mixologists by the time Hires opened his Philadelphia drugstore in 1872. However, inventing novel quaffs to please the tastes of drugstore patrons was not their only goal. They were at root medicine men living in an age when patent medicine purveyors reaped fortunes peddling nostrums to a credulous public. Thus it is not surprising that pharmacists labored to produce drinks for which they might claim palliative powers—real or illusory.

Many inspired local druggists attributed fanciful, if not outlandish, health benefits to their soda fountain creations. In fact several drugstore-invented drinks whose brand names would join the popular lexicon—Coca-Cola and Moxie, for example—were initially marketed as "nerve tonics." Scarcely a paragon of modesty in this regard, Hires could not resist ascribing extraordinary health benefits to his formulation. He trumpeted his root beer as "the greatest health-giving beverage in the whole world" and "a temperance drink of the highest medicinal value." This "natural tonic," Hires promised, is "full of health. The blood is improved, the nerves soothed, the stomach benefitted by this delicious beverage."[28]

The latter half of the nineteenth century marked a period of rapid growth for an amazing variety of soft drinks. Dozens of new beverages, often concocted by creative pharmacists, debuted in local markets. Several would later achieve household name recognition and become Hires' competitors on the national scene. In addition to Hires Root Beer, first sold in 1875, these included Vernors Ginger Ale (1866), Moxie (1876), Dr. Pepper (1885), Coca-Cola (1886), and Pepsi-Cola (1898).

The earliest of this group was Vernors Ginger Ale. According to legend, Detroit pharmacist James Vernor had been mixing fountain flavors in an effort to replicate a popular imported ginger ale when he was called to duty in the Civil War. He prudently stored the drink's syrup base composed of nineteen ingredients, including ginger, vanilla, and other natural flavorings, in an oak cask. When Vernor returned after being discharged in 1865, he opened the barrel and was pleasantly surprised. The venerable syrup produced a drink with a zesty, sweet, gingery flavor, accentuated by the aging wood. Vernor sold the beverage exclusively at his own soda fountain for several years, but as demand grew, he began to distribute his ginger ale commercially.[29]

A Competitor with Moxie

The Moxie Nerve Food Co. began to produce its distinctive drink commercially in 1885.[30] Its inventor was Dr. Augustin Thompson, a Maine native. About 1876 the homeopathic physician dreamt up a concoction consisting of sugar water mixed with a variety of flavorings, the main one being gentian, a flowering plant grown in the Pyrenees Mountains. Moxie also had a Civil War connection, although of dubious legitimacy. Thompson said "Moxie" was the name of his West Point classmate, Lieutenant Moxie, who had discovered the drink's main ingredient. Thompson, however, had never attended West Point, and, coincidentally, a tribe of Moxie Indians was native to his home state.[31]

To boost sales of his dark acerbic potion, Thompson added carbonation and reintroduced it in 1888 as a bottled soda and fountain syrup. He claimed the bitter brew would cure a catalog of ills, including nervous exhaustion, paralysis, insanity, and impotence. In addition to adding a new word to the English vocabulary, Thompson was a masterful promoter. To supplement a plethora of print advertising, he took his drink on the road. Eight-foot-high replicas of the Moxie bottle were hauled throughout New England on horse-drawn carts. A pitchman sold Moxie to awestruck locals through a hatch in the bottle. The advent of motor vehicles led to an even more outrageous promotion, the patented Moxie Horse Car. This consisted of an open touring sedan with seats removed and replaced by a horse dummy. The car's steering column was extended and its driving controls modified to allow the vehicle to be operated by a Moxie salesman astride the horse.[32]

As late as 1920 Moxie actually rivaled Coca-Cola in popularity. But it lost momentum due to its decision to slash advertising in an effort to cut losses incurred in the postwar sugar crisis.[33] Nevertheless, a version of Moxie continues to be produced today by several bottlers.

The beverage that would become the juggernaut of the soft drink industry was introduced at an Atlanta drugstore in 1886, ten years after Hires handed out samples of his root beer at Philadelphia's Centennial Exposition. Its originator, John Pemberton, a pharmacist and dabbler in Atlanta's thriving patent medicine scene, had been profiting nicely from the sale of a nostrum he called French Wine Coca. The drink consisted of wine laced with extract of South American coca, a potent stimulant.[34] It was one of numerous knockoffs of Vin Mariani, a drink composed of Bordeaux wine with an ample infusion of coca leaf. Invented by Corsican Angelo Mariani, that drink became popular in the United States, where its tonic properties were acclaimed by devotees including Thomas Edison, President William McKinley, Sarah Bernhardt, and Buffalo Bill Cody. Former President Grant, suffering from terminal throat cancer, relied on Mariani's concoction to ease his pain while eking out his widely admired autobiography.[35]

Pemberton, who had been wounded in the Civil War, might have sought out coca leaf to alleviate his own morphine addiction. Many veterans who received medical treatment during the war returned home with this condition. Cocaine, a derivative of coca, was believed to relieve "morphinism."[36]

Pemberton was inspired to change the formula of his beverage when Atlanta and the rest of Fulton County voted to go dry in 1885. Although the law applied only to saloons, Pemberton prudently decided to remove the alcohol from his French Wine Coca. He retained the coca leaf and added an extract of the kola nut, an African-grown stimulant that was gaining medical attention. He also experimented with flavoring agents, including citric and phosphoric acids, vanilla, lemon oil, and nutmeg. Eventually, he added sugar and largely replaced the bitter kola nut concentrate with synthetic caffeine.[37]

The formula for Coca-Cola has changed over time but remains a jealously guarded secret. Significantly, the drink was developed as a soda fountain syrup as opposed to the home brew extract originally produced by Hires. Also in contrast to Hires Root Beer, long guided by the firm hand of its founder, Coca-Cola's early history was shaped by several actors in addition to Pemberton. Frank Robinson, a transplanted Yankee and aspiring adman, became one of Pemberton's partners and supervised the drink's marketing. He coined the name "Coca-Cola" for the reconstituted drink and penned its distinctive trademark in Spencerian script. Robinson's first ad, published in 1886, clearly conjured up a beverage with a dual personality, part brain tonic and part temperance tempter:

> COCA-COLA SYRUP AND EXTRACT for Soda Water and other Carbonated Beverages. This Intellectual Beverage and Temperance Drink contains the valuable Tonic and Nerve Stimulant properties of the Coca plant and Cola (or Kola) nuts, and makes not only a delicious, exhilarating, refreshing and invigorating Beverage (dispensed from soda water fountains or in other carbonated beverages), but is a valuable brain tonic and a cure for all nervous affections—Sick Head-Ache, Neuralgia, Hysteria, Melancholy, etc. The peculiar flavor of COCA-COLA delights every palate.[38]

SOFT DRINKS PROLIFERATE

Prior to his death in 1888, Pemberton endeavored to sell his interest in Coca-Cola and its formula to raise money. After a series of convoluted and at times legally questionable transactions involving several individuals, the rights to Coca-Cola wound up in the capable hands of Asa Candler, a prominent Atlanta druggist, who would by the 1920s make it America's most popular soft drink.[39]

Dr. Pepper, like several of its contemporaries, was formulated by a druggist and first marketed as a curative quaff. In 1885 Charles C. Alderton, who worked at Morrison's Old Corner Drug Store in Waco, Texas, came up with a blend of fruit-based flavors that patrons apparently could not get enough of. Alderton was a transplanted New Yorker who had earned a medical degree at the University of Texas. So who was Dr. Pepper? He may have been the owner of a pharmacy where Morrison once worked or merely an invention. Formulas for patent medicines of the day were often ascribed to doctors, real or imagined.[40] Promotions for Dr. Pepper presented fanciful medical claims akin to those of Hires, Moxie, Coca-Cola, and other soft drinks of the era. They proclaimed Dr. Pepper "bracing and invigorating," a tonic "for nerve, brain and blood," an "antidote for nicotine," and a restorer of "vim, vigor and vitality."[41]

Coca-Cola's success spawned a host of cola imitators. The drink that would prove Coke's strongest and most enduring copier was conceived in a North Carolina drugstore in 1896.[42] New Bern pharmacist Caleb D. Bradham, an erstwhile medical student, served dyspeptic customers a drink he had created to calm their stomachs. To his surprise it became a hit with his other patrons, who would ask for "Brad's drink." Forfeiting his opportunity for immortality, Bradham rechristened the drink "Pepsi-Cola." The name suggested two of the drink's ingredients, the digestive enzyme pepsin and the kola nut, in a form and cadence suggestive of Pepsi's Atlanta competitor.

By no means did Charles Hires have the root beer market to himself. Champion Root Beer Extract, curiously similar to Hires' product, was advertised in a grocery trade journal in 1893. A single bottle was said to produce "five gallons of delicious, health-giving, non-intoxicating beverage in five minutes." The resulting drink was proclaimed a blood purifier "refreshing to the tired, thirsty man or woman who without it would consider life a burden." The manufacturer was Finnerty, McClure and Co. of Philadelphia. The grocery journal also carried a competing ad for Hires Root Beer extolling its pure, nonchemical nature and boasting that it outsold all other root beer extracts combined.[43]

Bean and Brother had entered the Philadelphia market about 1880 with their "Beans' Great American Root Beer." Another Philadelphia brew was "O.K." root beer produced by C. L. Heinle Co. Allen's Root Beer Extract, produced by Charles H. Allen of Lowell, Massachusetts, competed with Hires during the 1890s. It sold for twenty-five cents, the same price as Hires', but would yield an additional gallon of root beer. A company trade card promised a pleasant and healthy beverage "perfectly safe for children and much preferable to ice water."[44] Other brands of root beer were being sold as extracts or over the counter in local drugstores, and at least one had entered the national market by the turn of the century.[45]

Canadian-born Dr. George W. Swett operated wholesale and retail pharmacies in Boston and New York during the late nineteenth century. Like Hires, Dr. Swett sold his eponymously branded root beer in small packets of dry extract for home brewers and later as a fountain syrup and bottled drink. Dr. Swett's extract contained many ingredients similar to those used by Hires with the exception of yeast. Produced without fermentation, Dr. Swett's root beer could credibly claim to contain not a trace of alcohol. Just when the doctor began marketing his "original root beer" is uncertain. Advertisements placed the date at 1845, which seems unlikely because Swett would have been eleven years old at the time. By 1885 he had begun to advertise his drink as an extract comparable to Hires. A twenty-five-cent packet containing sarsaparilla, life-of-man, wintergreen, juniper, and so on, would make five gallons of root beer. "Health and pleasure" might ensue as the drink acted "mildly and beneficially on the stomach, liver and kidneys." Bottled Dr. Swett's was introduced in 1890 and later produced by franchised bottling companies.[46]

BARQ'S IS GOOD

Barq Brothers Bottling Company was founded in 1890 in the French Quarter of New Orleans by Edward Charles Edmond Barq and his younger brother, Gaston. Edward Barq moved to

Biloxi, Mississippi, in 1897 and opened the Biloxi Artesian Bottling Works. In 1898 he began producing a beverage that would become Barq's Root Beer. At first, Barq's was not marketed as a "root beer" in part to avoid a legal conflict with Hires over the term and in part because it differed from other root beers at the time. The basic sarsaparilla soda contained caffeine but had a less foamy head than similar brands. It also used less sugar but was more highly carbonated than others.[47] The drink was marketed simply as Barq's; its slogan: "Drink Barq's. It's good." The Barq's brand was later purchased by Coca-Cola.

Many of these soft drink pioneers started out by producing syrup for the soda fountain trade. Soda fountains were becoming multipurpose appliances able to generate, chill, and dispense carbonated water as well as flavored syrups. Hires Root Beer remained largely an exception to the soda fountain trend. Although some operators used Hires Root Beer extract to produce soda fountain drinks, Hires seemed content to fulfill the booming demand for his home brew extract. Notwithstanding his drink's soda fountain roots, Hires did not make a serious effort to nationally market a fountain syrup until 1905. Coming tardy to the party almost proved a costly mistake for Hires (see Chapter 7).

Jacob Baur of Terre Haute, Indiana, was another inspired druggist who pushed the envelope of carbonated beverage technology. In 1888 he founded the Liquid Carbonic Acid Manufacturing Company of Chicago, which pioneered the production of liquefied carbonic acid in steel cylinders.[48] With this innovation the liquid gas could be bubbled through a water mist until it dissolved to create the soda water. Soda fountain proprietors no longer had to make their own carbonic acid by mixing acid and marble dust.[49] Both fountain operators and bottlers began to order compressed carbon dioxide in portable cylinders from suppliers. A few years later Baur's company would also pioneer the development of the iceless soda fountain. This device kept soda water cool by circulating salted brine from the melting ice used to chill ice cream.[50]

Harper's Weekly marveled at the high technology that had taken soda water production from makeshift devices concealed beneath drugstore counters to the factory floor within fifty years:

The most interesting fact in the manufacture of soda water is that it contains no soda. The prominent ingredients are marble dust and sulphuric [sic] acid neither of which are regarded as healthful or palatable when take separately. Moreover, to render them so in combination requires a pressure of at least 150 pounds to the square inch—a condition dangerous to life and limb except under proper safeguards and with the strongest machinery. . . . Surely in all the history of fairyland there is nothing more marvelous than the escape of this sparkling, bubbling, foam-crested liquor, like an enchanted prince from the gloomy death chamber, to delight and refresh the world.[51]

Throughout the latter half of the nineteenth century, bottled soda water producers had been offering an alternative to beverages mixed at the soda fountain. Philadelphians Joseph Hawkins and Elias Durand, who marketed bottled soda water about 1835, were recorded among its earliest producers. Writers praised bottled soda and seltzer drinks for their bracing flavor and stomach-calming properties. The tendency to consider carbonated beverages as health drinks led bottlers to adopt such fanciful names as Sparkling Phosphate Ferrozodone, Phosphodone, Voldat, Hedozone, Quinada, and Vigorine. Soda water producers, initially numerous only in metropolitan areas of the East and Midwest, variously described their products as "aerated water," "mineral water," and the onomatopoeic "pop," the sound of a cork being withdrawn from a soda bottle.[52] However, their efforts to expand the market for bottled drinks were hindered by technical problems with bottles and seals that would not be fully resolved until the end of the century.

THE SEARCH FOR A SEAL

Devising an airtight bottle seal that would prevent carbon dioxide gas from escaping proved especially vexing. Approaches ranging from corks to various cleverly conceived devices turned out to be less than satisfactory. About fifteen hundred kinds of stoppers had been patented by 1892. Most were complicated and cumbersome and few provided a tight or lasting seal. They also tended to be unsanitary since they were seldom sterilized between uses.[53] Corks were prone to leak gas or pop from their bottles prematurely under excessive pressure. Other closures including glass balls and spring-loaded rubber seals were unreliable or hard to keep clean. For many years the Hutchinson spring stopper predominated. It consisted of a hook attached to a rubber gasket that was sealed by the pressure of carbon dioxide within the bottle. The stopper was low cost, relatively simple, and readily adapted to bottles of irregular shapes.[54]

This lack of uniformity in the handblown glass bottles then in use compounded the industry's sealing problem. But this was an era of inspired tinkerers and inventors. Two ingenious devices emerged in the century's final decade that would lead to a mass market for bottled carbonated beverages. In 1892 William Painter, a Maryland machine shop operator, received a patent for his crown cork bottle cap. This invention revolutionized the bottling industry. It consisted of a cork seal inside a metal cap that when crimped around the bottle's lip created an airtight closure.[55]

For Painter's seal to perform consistently, however, a bottle with a standardized glass lip was needed. This obstacle was overcome in 1894 when Michael J. Owens, who at age fifteen had worked as a bottle blower, obtained patents for a machine that would produce uniform glass bottles.[56] Owens's bottles combined with Painter's crown cork seals led to the manufacture of automated bottling machines capable of filling and capping up to one hundred bottles per minute. However, the industry's transition to crown caps took several years as bottlers were required to refit their operations. Serious production of bottled soft drinks using the new technologies did not begin until the turn of the twentieth century. Ginger ale was the leading bottled soft drink at that time, but sarsaparilla, root beer, cream soda, and lemon- and strawberry-flavored drinks were also popular.[57]

"Hires Carbonated" Sold in Bottles

Hires entered the bottled soft drink market in 1893, selling ready-to-drink root beer through his Crystal Bottling Company and offering it to other bottlers.[58] Hires bottles originally sported a paper label and contained fourteen ounces. They were sealed with Hutchinson spring stoppers. An 1896 ad offered "Hires Carbonated, ready to drink except for the cooling" at the company's store at 1016 Chestnut Street in Philadelphia. Pint bottles retailed for two dollars per twenty-four-bottle case, with a thirty-cent refund paid for return of the empties.[59]

In an 1896 pitch to prospective investors, Hires boasted of plans for "the most complete plant in the world for bottling carbonated beverages" with a production capacity of 3,500 dozen bottles of Hires Root Beer Carbonated a day.[60] During the following years Hires became one of the first soft drink bottlers to use Painter's new crown seals.[61] In 1897 a full-page advertisement in the *Ladies' Home Journal* featured the familiar Hires Boy in a bolero-style jacket holding a bottle of Hires Root Beer with a crown seal cap in one hand and a package of Hires extract in the other.[62] By then Hires Carbonated was marketed in pint bottles embossed with the brand's name. A dozen bottles of root beer could be purchased for $1.10 or a twenty-four-bottle case for $2.00.[63] To introduce the product nationwide, Hires offered attractive discounts to retailers who ordered one dozen or more pints of Hires Carbonated along with their regular purchases of root beer extract. However, Hires' centralized bottling scheme proved impractical in the long run.[64]

"The experiment was not a success because of the price we [were required to] put on the bottled goods," Hires later explained. "Transportation charges were too heavy, and we found it more economical to license the bottling privilege to local concerns, as we are doing today."[65] Such licensing or "franchising," as it came to be known, was indeed a more efficient and profitable system for distributing bottled soft drinks.

Coca-Cola is credited with developing, albeit inadvertently, one of the industry's earliest franchising systems. The company showed little initial interest in bottles, preferring to market its signature libation as a soda fountain drink. Thus Coca-Cola president Candler in 1899 gave a pair of entrepreneurs the right to bottle the beverage in much of the United States with the proviso that they purchase the company's syrup and adhere to its quality standards.[66] After encountering economic reality while trying to establish a centralized bottling plant, Benjamin Thomas and Joseph Whitehead were forced to rethink their business plan. Ingeniously, they decided to carve up their allotted territory into smaller pieces and sell the exclusive rights to bottle and sell Coca-Cola in these areas starting in 1901. Local bottlers were required to purchase the company's beverage syrup and abide by strict rules regarding production and distribution. This scheme ensured the parent company's continuing profits from franchise fees and syrup sales while shifting start-up and transportation costs to the local bottler.

The economic benefits of this model were not lost on Hires and other soft drink makers.[67] However, bottled soft drinks would not fully hit their stride until motor trucks began to replace horse-drawn delivery wagons in the second decade of the twentieth century.[68] The more efficient delivery system expanded the market for soft drinks, making them widely available in grocery stores, bars, gas stations, and other venues without soda fountains.

As bottles achieved wider use, soft drink makers expressed concern regarding their unauthorized reuse. The makers of Clicquot Club beverages, founded in Millis, Massachusetts, in 1881, discovered their bottles being "recycled" by manufacturers of products ranging from ketchup to ammonia. Hires halted the sale of bottles embossed with his company's logo to prevent their reuse by purveyors of bogus root beer. Instead, he reintroduced plain bottles with pasted labels, similar to those the company had originally used. It was hoped that the paper label would become sufficiently defaced after the bottle's initial use to discourage rogue refillers. The company acknowledged, however, that even this solution was not foolproof. "A certain adventurous few will succumb to the temptation and print labels, if it is necessary, to sell the refilled bottles," Charles E. Hires, Jr. told an interviewer.[69]

The 1889 U.S. census counted 1,377 bottlers of carbonated beverages, many of them one-person operations.[70] Per capita annual consumption was less than seven twelve-ounce-equivalent bottles per person that year. The rate would rise to eight bottles in 1899 and to eleven in 1909. Advances in bottling technology and transportation would push that figure to nearly twenty-six bottles per capita in 1919.[71] Meanwhile, the soda fountain trade continued its impressive growth. By 1911 a hundred thousand soda fountains were in operation across the United States.

Over the years, Hires kept abreast of the technological innovations roiling the soft drink marketplace and adapted his products accordingly. At the same time, robust botanical products sales and, later, the success of his root beer extract allowed the curious and inventive druggist to explore other sidelines, both professional and personal.

4

FROM SIDELINE TO MAIN LINE

CHARLES HIRES ONCE CONFESSED his lifelong fondness for pursuing sidelines to his full-time business. The earliest of these diversions sprang from his discovery of "gold" in the hills of excavation spoils at a neighborhood construction site. Converting humble fuller's earth into a profitable branded stain remover earned Hires the capital he needed to assure his drugstore's success. When competition depressed prices of "Hires' Special Cleaner," he deftly moved on, leaving the sale of knockoff spot removers to a gaggle of greedy imitators.

Hires' next gainful digression involved a pair of patented cough remedies—Hires' Cough Cure and Hires' Cough Candy. The former was an elixir designed to soothe the throat and suppress the cough. "Fast, safe and always reliable," early advertisements promised, "in coughs, colds, croup and whooping cough." The so-called cure contained white pine balsam, gum Arabic, sarsaparilla root, birch bark, and wintergreen. Not only were these ingredients similar to those of his root beer, but Hires also distributed his "Cough Cure" in a package that closely resembled his root beer extract box, and for the same price, twenty-five cents. Indeed, Hires frequently promoted his root beer and cough cure together in the same ads. While hyping the nostrum as the "greatest remedy for coughs and colds ever prepared," he assured buyers that Hires' Cough Cure included "neither opiates nor narcotics." Several other patented cough medications in this era before government regulation contained cannabis, morphine, heroin, and healthy amounts of alcohol.[1]

Hires concocted his cough candy to compete with the hirsute Brothers Smith, "Trade" and "Mark," and other cough drop marketers, but he promoted it less outlandishly than his elixir. Rather than a cure, Hires promised merely relief for a dry hacking cough. A package sold for five cents over the counter or for seven cents' worth of postage stamps by mail.

Yet another sideline, root beer, would become Hires' lifework. He refined the formula for the drink while earning a living as a pharmacist. In 1875 Hires sold his retail business and opened a wholesale house in Philadelphia's Old City area specializing in flavoring extracts and botanical products such as vanilla beans. He nurtured this new enterprise while continuing to prepare and distribute his proprietary sidelines—root beer extract, Cough Cure, and Cough Candy.

The enthusiastic response of visitors to the 1876 Centennial Exposition had convinced Hires that a wider market existed for his beverage. He also understood that advertising might be that one additional "ingredient" that could help him break into that market. But with little cash to spare, Hires was naturally hesitant to place ads that he could not afford. That's when an acquaintance who had sampled his root beer, perhaps at the Centennial, supplied a fateful nudge. One morning while Hires commuted to his store on the Market Street cable car, a distinguished-looking gentleman boarded and sat down beside him. George W. Childs was the proprietor and editor of the *Public Ledger*. Their conversation, as Hires recalled it, turned to his fledgling drink.[2]

AN OFFER TOO GOOD TO REFUSE

"Mr. Hires, why don't you advertise that root beer extract of yours?" Childs asked. "It is good stuff."

I told Mr. Childs that I hadn't seriously considered advertising it and that, in any event, I hadn't any money to spend for advertising.

"I'll tell you what to do," said Childs. "You advertise in the *Ledger* beginning right away, and I'll tell the bookkeeper not to send you any bills until you ask for them."[3]

The *Public Ledger* was a prominent Philadelphia newspaper. But Hires did not immediately share its editor's confidence in the power of newspaper advertising. He mulled over Childs's offer for several days before walking the few blocks from his store to the imposing six-story Public Ledger Building at Sixth and Chestnut Streets. The newspaper's advertising department prepared the copy. The first ad was published September 1, 1877. It would run daily thereafter in a one-inch by one-column space. The ad read:

Five (5) Gallons of Delicious Root Beer
Made from Hires Root Beer Package, only 25c.
Chas. E. Hires, Wholesale Botanic Druggist,
No. 9 Letitia Street.[4]

"Sales increased slowly at first," Hires recalled, "and then more rapidly until I felt justified in asking the *Ledger* for a bill." Although his ad had been running for nearly six months, Hires was shocked by the amount of the bill—$700. "I nearly had heart failure," he said. "While I knew that advertising cost money, I had no idea that it would cost *that much!*"[5]

Far from being deterred by this expensive initiation to newspaper advertising, Hires determined to persevere. "I found courage enough to let the advertising go on running while I was paying off the $700," he said. "For the next 10 years I put every penny of profit from the root beer business back into advertising."[6]

Hires' trade in wholesale botanicals and flavorings would continue to expand and prosper. Indeed, it would generate dollars for root beer ads and provide a livelihood for the growing Hires family over the next several years. But this business—a fulfilling career for many—would eventually be shouldered to the sideline as demand for Hires Root Beer accelerated.

At first the public seemed in no hurry to sample Hires' latest creation. Exactly 876 packages of Hires' powdered root beer extract were purchased for twenty-five cents each in 1878, the year after the first advertisements appeared. But like a nineteenth-century locomotive straining from the station, root beer sales volume began to gather steam at a surprising rate. The momentum was stoked by Hires' aggressive advertising campaign. Persuaded of the power of ads by the impact of his early single-inch newspaper insertions, Hires relentlessly increased their scope and volume. The magnitude of this promotional push was, as explained in Chapter 5, unprecedented for a consumer product. Savvy business decisions that made his root beer mixture more user-friendly and increased its footprint at drugstore soda fountains also contributed to the sales surge.

Liquid Extract Proves a Winner

Hires' decision in 1880 to market a three-ounce bottle of liquid extract, in addition to his original powdered concentrate, greatly enhanced the product's appeal. No longer would busy housewives and other root beer fanciers have to endure the messy ritual of boiling and straining dry ingredients to create their own liquid extract. As the company later observed: "This change removed the last obstacle to popular favor, and from that day, Hires Root Beer became the home drink of America."[7] Company sales more than doubled the following year. However, Hires would continue to offer his original mixture of dry ingredients until 1918.[8]

Although Hires Root Beer was marketed primarily to home brewers, a lesser amount was sold as a soda fountain beverage. A number of pharmacists had been preparing Hires Root Beer for sale at their fountains, using the three-ounce bottles of extract marketed for home consumption. To capture additional soda fountain sales, Hires began to offer the liquid extract in a pint size as well. Druggists could now prepare root beer in larger batches for fountain sale. Although the new size container proved a winner, Hires failed to fully appreciate the vigorous growth of the soda fountain trade. He would not distribute a fountain-ready root beer syrup for more than twenty years (see Chapter 7).

Table 4.1 traces the dramatic growth in unit sales of "Hires Improved Root Beer Package" from 1879 to 1894. The 135 percent

Table 4.1 Unit Sales of Hires Root Beer Packages, 1879–1894		
1879 → 3,024	1885 → 55,728	1891 → 1,941,319
1880 → 5,804	1886 → 83,728	1892 → 2,880,278
1881 → 13,680	1887 → 191,808	1893 → 2,669,579*
1882 → 18,464	1888 → 394,560	1894 → 3,134,947
1883 → 28,512	1889 → 578,048	*Decline attributed to
1884 → 45,216	1890 → 1,296,000	financial panic.

Note: The root beer package contained either the original powdered root beer extract or the three-ounce bottle of concentrate, which Hires began to market in 1880.

Source: Unit sales figures for 1879–1891 derived from "As Others See Us," *Philadelphia Daily News*, February 14, 1891, and 1892–1894 from "Hires Rootbeer," a company flier issued in January 1895 (Warshaw Collection of Business Americana, National Museum of American History, Smithsonian Institution.)

jump between 1880, the year Hires introduced his liquid extract, and 1881 is striking. Within the next five years, sales increased another sixfold to some 84,000 packages. While this rate of increase was clearly unsustainable, Hires sales would continue their explosive growth over the next eight years with one exception: Sales declined slightly in 1893. The company attributed this slippage to the national recession induced by a financial panic that year.

This sales tsunami surely gratified the young entrepreneur, but it also presented him with daunting strategic and logistical challenges. Hires had captured a sweet spot in the soft drink market with his home-brewed drink, but that marketplace was continuing to evolve. Consumers were increasingly choosing ready-made beverages from among a large variety offered at soda fountains. Nationally branded competitors such as Coca-Cola, Moxie, and Dr. Pepper were emerging. Marketed as syrups for soda fountain use, several of these drinks would soon be offered in bottles for home consumption as well. While positioning his product to compete in this changing marketplace, Hires needed to rapidly expand his manufacturing capacity, workforce, and distribution network to keep pace with the growing demand for root beer extract.

It has been observed that the talents of the innovator differ markedly from the skills needed to assure the commercial success of his or her discovery. History abounds with cautionary tales of brilliant inventors whose business skills proved less than stellar. Hires, however, combined a talent for innovation with the ability to execute in the commercial arena. His journey from entrepreneur to business dynamo, notwithstanding a few missteps along the way, was generally assured and productive.

Philadelphia city directories trace a series of Hires' business relocations. During the 1880s, his firm occupied four different sites, the last at 215 Market Street, the city's main commercial thoroughfare. In 1890 unit sales of root beer extract more than doubled those of the previous year. It was time for Hires to incorporate his business and move it into a new headquarters and manufacturing facility spacious enough to meet the public's seemingly insatiable thirst for his root beer.

The Charles E. Hires Company was chartered in 1890 in Pennsylvania as a stock corporation with a capital of $300,000. The stock carried a par value of $50 a share and offered a 15 percent dividend.[9] Incorporation allowed the thirty-nine-year-old to raise the capital he needed to expand his company. It also enabled him, as he remarked, to give "an interest to those who have been closely connected to me for years." Hires grandly predicted a bright future for the new corporation. "The knowledge and the value of Hires Root Beer will be pushed with even greater energy, until every inhabitant of the globe shall know of its delicious and health-giving properties," he declared.[10] In pursuit of this goal, the company contracted with agents in London, Copenhagen, Montreal, and Australia to promote the sale of its products abroad.[11]

In 1890 Hires moved his manufacturing operations into a four-story commercial building at 117–119 Arch Street in Philadelphia. It had a 28-foot frontage and a depth of 115 feet with a basement extending 15 feet beyond the bricks and mortar above. The building provided the production and warehouse space the growing business required. Hires methodically organized the interior to facilitate his manufacturing and distribution activities.

Root beer extract was brewed on the top floor, which Hires designated as the "laboratory." Here the roots, barks, herbs, and berries of Hires' formula—over fifty thousand pounds a year— were assembled, weighed, and pulverized before being steeped in warm water for several hours in one-hundred-gallon cauldrons. The dregs were pressed and percolated again to capture any remaining flavor. The finished extract was stored in reservoirs awaiting gravity-powered transfer through a network of pipes to the floor below. Compounded alongside the root beer extract vats was Hires' Cough Cure. As noted, the two products shared a number of ingredients.[12]

The liquid root beer extract was bottled, corked, and packaged on the third floor. An observer during the factory's peak season in July found "one hundred nimble-fingered girls working both day and night" to fill orders for the extract. They sat at a long table, dexterously manipulating patented tin dispensers to fill the extract bottles before pounding home their corks with wooden mallets.[13] Once filled, the boxes were sealed before their transfer to the first floor for shipping. A large workforce had labored through the previous winter at these tasks, piling the filled boxes high in the storeroom, yet this stockpile had been exhausted before June.[14]

PRINTING PLANT BUTTRESSES SALES PUSH

The work performed on the factory's second floor was crucial to Hires' success. Dedicated not to production but to promotion, the floor housed a full-time printing plant described as "a marvel of completeness."[15] Steam-powered printing presses churned out stacks of trade cards, circulars, and other advertising materials. The plant's annual output included four million ten-color trade cards and millions of circulars, point-of-sale "hangars," and signs for distribution to dealers. Behind the print shop, boxes of lithographic images and other advertising materials were marshaled, ready for shipping to any part of the country. But as extensive as it appears, this in-house production capacity did not fully meet Hires' needs. He spent another $25,000 in 1890 on outside printing jobbers. The company's postage bill that year was reported to exceed $6,000.[16]

On the ground floor, the company's business offices shared space with a rear loading dock. A corps of clerks worked in the office addressing letters, folding circulars, and mailing information requested by distributors, merchants, and the public. Hires' private office occupied an enclosure to the rear of the clerks' space. It was sparely furnished with the proprietor's wide pigeonhole desk, a few straight-backed wooden chairs, and a divan. Hires would pull open a desk drawer to show visitors a cache of exotic currency and stamps he had received from residents of far-off lands requesting extract samples. A collection of advertising lithographs, mainly of smiling babies, adorned the walls. The only sign of clutter was a stack of unfilled orders on the desk.

Another first-floor enclosure held Hires' supply of precious vanilla beans. He kept a close watch over this commodity. No one was permitted to smoke in the vicinity, an employee recalled.[17] The beans were used as a root beer ingredient and brokered to dealers as part of Hires' wholesale trade.

STALKING AN EXOTIC BEAN

While focusing his attention on root beer, Hires did not neglect what had developed into a thriving business in flavoring extracts and botanicals. Indeed, the vanilla bean held a special attraction for Hires. He would become recognized as an expert on this exotic flavoring and remain a major East Coast importer, even after the success of his soft drink.

Hires' fascination with vanilla extended to its source—the jungles of eastern Mexico. He traveled there to study the cultivation and processing of the vanilla bean in its native habitat. On his return, Hires regaled an audience at the Philadelphia College of Pharmacy with an absorbing account of his sometimes perilous trek and his insights regarding *vanilla planifolia*[18]: He explained his passion for the object of his journey:

> After 20 years of active experience in handling vanilla, after a long and careful study of it as an article of commerce, and an intimate acquaintance of its various uses, and its growing value as an article of import, I became possessed with a desire to see it in its natural state, to ride beneath the forests where it grew, to pluck it by my own hands from its natural branch; to enjoy its sweet and delicious aroma in the land of

its birth, and . . . to familiarize myself with the growth and preparation of this wonderful product, which is so rapidly growing in favor as one of our nineteenth century luxuries.[19]

Hires invited his audience to share the journey with him:

Take down your map of Mexico and locate the city of Vera Cruz in the state of Vera Cruz situated on the western side of the Bay of Campeche. Go north from Vera Cruz a distance of some 300 miles to Tuxpan. Equip yourself there with a retinue of mustangs, servants, guide and interpreter, and start to the southwest on a three days' journey over mountains, through impenetrable forests, over dangerous and treacherous morasses and through tropical jungles to the city of Papantla, situated about 75 miles from the coast, inaccessible by railroad or water, and in the heart of as wild and lawless a country as you would care to visit, you have reached the heart of the vanilla growing district; only a few hundred miles by actual measurement, but requiring more time, toil, privation and danger than to make a trip to the Orient. The journey southward was one to me of absorbing interest and constant danger.[20]

Hires entered Mexico from Laredo, Texas, and traveled south 170 miles to the city of Monterrey on his way to Mexico City. After spending nine days in the Mexican capital, he proceeded to Veracruz, where he boarded a steamer for a thirty-hour voyage north to Tuxpan. It seems likely that Hires contracted yellow fever during this trip. In applying for an insurance policy some years later, he reported having a case of the mosquito-borne disease lasting for thirteen days at about the time of his expedition.[21]

A Sensual Experience

Hires described his initial encounter with the reclusive vanilla pod in its native habitat as an experience bordering on the sensual. His party reached the actual vanilla field only after abandoning their mustangs and advancing stooped through heavy underbrush. They paused at a clearing. Ahead, a stand of Mexican cedars supported a tangle of interlaced vines:

> Tree after tree in this vast forest is covered with these vines, peeping from which, in all the glory of tropical luxuriance, are countless hundreds of the long, luscious, tapering vanilla beans; in circumference almost equal to a banana and from two to three inches longer. Some of a dark green and others of a bright yellow, and sometimes where they grow most luxuriantly resembling bunches of bananas, apparently growing upon the native trees of the forests. The remoteness from civilization, the total absence of everything indicating care or cultivation, and the strange juxtaposition of this wealth of ripened fruit to the wild and unbounded woods made the scene one of the most strange and marvelous upon which the eye ever rested.
>
> Vast areas containing hundreds of square miles of contiguous territory in this province are devoted to the growth of this plant: wherever you look and wherever you travel you are confronted with this overhanging vegetation. You behold the primeval forest utilized by the half civilized natives as a natural garden for the growth of this delicious aromatic plant.[22]

Hires' presentation included more than a colorful, impressionistic tale of his expedition. He had queried vanilla growers and carefully observed the region's ecology and the propagation of the plant itself. According to Hires, the vanilla pods were most prolific in areas where streams and brooks abounded with somewhat sandy soil that retained moisture during the dry season. He noted that the plants seemed to thrive in areas where sunlight could reach them and that the largest growers had trimmed away some of the vegetation around their trees. He provided detailed descriptions of the different varieties of vanilla vines and their yields. He also endeavored to correct misconceptions about the plant, including those he himself had held prior to his journey.

Hires' treatise on vanilla was copyrighted by the company in 1897 and issued as a twenty-four-page pamphlet.[23] His contribution to the field was recognized in academic circles, including the Botanical Society of Pennsylvania, which invited Hires to give a talk on his observations.[24]

PANIC AND PERSISTENCE

The nation was entering a new era when Hires opened his Arch Street factory. The Gay Nineties were anything but for many Americans. The nostalgic term itself would not be coined until decades later. Gilded Age excesses contributed to a stock market crash and financial panic in 1893. Locally, the collapse of the Philadelphia and Reading Railroad provided an ominous warning. A depression spanning four years, marked by bank failures and high unemployment, would follow.[25]

The Charles E. Hires Co., however, began the decade on a decidedly optimistic note. Sales were booming, and employees in the new factory were working double shifts to meet the demand. The upward sales trajectory would be briefly interrupted by the Panic of 1893. Far from being discouraged by this economic adversity, Hires accelerated his promotional campaign. During a three-month period in 1893, the company spent more than $200,000 ($5.3 million in current dollars) on advertising, a mind-blowing amount at the time. By then the firm's workforce had grown to approximately two hundred. This number included over one hundred workers employed in mixing, bottling, and packaging root beer extract, seventy-five in the office and shipping department, and eight in the printing plant. An additional team of salesmen was deployed across the country.[26]

The 1893 World's Columbian Exposition in Chicago gave Hires another marketing avenue. He rented a booth in a pavilion and installed an elaborate soda fountain to dispense free samples of his product.[27] The company captured the fair's highest prize for root beer.

Demand for twenty-five-cent packages of Hires' Improved Root Beer Extract resumed its upward thrust in 1894. The previous year's decline was more than erased by a 17 percent increase as 3,135,000 packages of concentrate were sold.[28]

COUNTERFEITERS AND COPYCATS

Nettlesome problems as well as profits accompanied Hires' business success. His root beer's prominence in the marketplace attracted a succession of imitators who attempted to exploit its popularity by selling drinks with similar sounding names or knockoff formulas. An even greater scourge than the copycats was posed by the substitutors. Typically, these were sleazy soda fountain operators with no qualms about passing off a counterfeit draft of their own making or an inferior version of root beer under the name "Hires."

"Cheap coal tar products and a little citric acid may quite easily be turned into a concoction that looks and tastes something like root beer," an N. W. Ayer company representative explained. "Naturally it costs far less than the genuine article, made from selected herbs, roots, barks and berries."[29] Hires took immense pride in his use of only the purest and most natural ingredients. Despite what his accountants may have suggested, he stubbornly refused to compromise quality or cheapen his product to combat his cut-rate competitors.

Imitation may be the sincerest form of flattery, but for Hires it proved an unending source of frustration. The deceptions multiplied as Hires Root Beer gained popularity. They infuriated Hires. Not only did imitation and substitution capitalize unfairly on Hires' unprecedented advertising expenditures, they also damaged the reputation of the beverage that he had so zealously nurtured. He waged an interminable battle with the pretenders. "It is doubtful if any modern commodity, excepting money, has been counterfeited more than Hires Root Beer," the *Philadelphia Times* observed. "Its wide popularity and immense sale having proved an irresistible attraction for the unscrupulous imitator."[30]

Ironically, the term "root beer" aggravated Hires' dilemma. An 1879 law prohibited the registration of generic words and phrases, such as "root beer," as trademarks.[31] Although Hires would later register his last name as a trademark, the law precluded protection of the very term that described his product and that he had popularized at considerable expense.

"The greatest problem of this business has been that of substitution," Hires declared. "Anybody could make root beer, and sell it as root beer." Looking back at his experience with substitutors and scammers, Hires rued his unwitting failure to christen his drink with a proprietary name such as Coca-Cola that could be better protected under the law. "Another advantage of starting in this day and age," he opined in a 1913 interview, is that "there will be plenty of people to advise you to choose a fanciful name which can be protected instead of a descriptive name which anybody can use."[32] Hires fought tirelessly to protect his brand, frequently going to court and swallowing the resulting legal fees as a necessary business expense.

In taking action against one egregious copycat in 1896, Hires demanded that the sale of Heyers Root Beer be restrained. The homophonic counterfeit was marketed in a package closely resembling Hires' at the price of ten cents, fifteen cents cheaper than Hires Extract.

Hires on the Offensive

The following year, in 1897, Hires went to court again to enjoin a member of his own family from selling a knockoff product. George Hires, who had been employed by Charles, left the company to join forces with two willing accomplices. Their plan was to market a root beer remarkably similar to the original in content and packaging. In granting the injunction, the court observed that the defendants' "sole and only purpose was to fabricate an article of trade which, in shape, color . . . name and general appearance, should . . . deceive and mislead the public and purchasers generally."[33]

Company sleuthing detected widespread soda fountain fraud in its own backyard. Suits pending against two local druggists for substituting inferior root beer for Hires prompted the Philadelphia Association of Retail Druggists to intervene. The association pledged to call these members to account along with "eight to 10 others" against whom Hires was preparing to act.

The association noted that Hires did not object to a dealer selling his own root beer as long as he sold it as his own and not as "Hires." However, a customer who asks for "Hires," the company insisted, must either be served with the genuine product or be plainly told that it is not handled at that store.[34]

Substitution and trademark infringement took many forms. None were too trivial to escape Hires' attention. For example, he sued one Nicholas John Xepapas, who shamelessly used Hires Household Extract as the base for his own fountain syrup. After purchasing the extract from his retail supplier, Xepapas ignored Hires' directions for its preparation. Instead of fermenting the brew with yeast, he combined the raw extract with homemade sugar syrup. After mixing the syrup with carbonated water, Xepapas sold the resulting drink as "Hires Root Beer." In ruling for Hires, the South Carolina Circuit Court concluded that the defendant's beverage was "an article entirely distinct from the extract used in making it."[35]

Hires responded proactively to discourage would-be fakers. His company purchased ads in trade journals sternly cautioning pharmacists about the perils of substitution. "Substitution is Dangerous," warned an ad in *The Spatula* in 1896. "If it is ever discovered you are apt, in the first place to lose a customer; and in the second place you make yourself liable to more serious consequences." The ad was illustrated with an overtly racist image. A black woman, ostensibly a nursemaid with kerchief on head, is depicted removing a white infant from the cradle and replacing it with a black baby.[36]

A compendium of opinions rendered by courts against Hires' substitutors was distributed among purveyors of the company's products. The introduction, titled "The Law on Substitution," soberly presented the company's position:

> One dealer substituting his "own make" when a well-known and expensively advertised article is called for will not ruin a business, but when substitution becomes a common practice ... the manufacturer is compelled as a matter of self-preservation to stop the drain or lose his business. It has cost us hundreds of thousands of dollars and years of labor to establish "Hires" as

a trademark . . . before the public and create a demand for the beverage "Hires" among consumers.

Some unscrupulous dealers have taken upon themselves to serve a beverage made from their own extract for a beverage made from HIRES' HOUSEHOLD EXTRACT when Hires was called for. This has forced us, reluctantly, to bring many suits to prevent this wrong and to establish our rights by conclusive adjudications and herein we print copies of opinions and decrees of the courts in these matters.[37]

Newspaper reports of Hires' legal victories may have deterred some would-be substitutors and imitators. An article headlined "Hires Gets Heavy Damages for Root Beer Substitution" reported a $1,000 penalty levied against a fountain operator by Philadelphia's Court of Common Pleas for selling ersatz Hires. Pennsylvania law allowed $200 in damages for each act of substitution that could be proven.[38]

Although the rip-off artists undoubtedly syphoned some sales away, their schemes failed to impede the company's growth. By 1894 Hires' Arch Street facility, which seemed spacious four years earlier, had become cramped. The press reported plans to relocate the plant to a larger building. The year was exceptionally profitable for Hires. Sales rebounded from the recession-induced decline of the previous year. The company proudly announced the sale of more than 3.1 million packages of extract, placed an additional thirty "men on the road" to canvass areas beyond its previous sales territory, and established a regional office in Chicago.[39]

Hires gained some elbow room in 1895 by moving his corporate office from the root beer plant to a more prestigious location in the Philadelphia Bourse. This nine-story building, one of the country's earliest steel-frame structures, had recently been completed near Independence Square. The pride of the city's business community, its six-story atrium housed stock and maritime exchanges surrounded by several floors of office space. The Philadelphia Drug Exchange, a trade association of drug manufacturers and wholesalers, was another Bourse tenant. Hires would be elected president of the exchange two years later.[40]

A GIFTED ORATOR AND A BIT OF A HAM

About 1882 Charles, Clara Kate, and Linda, their four-year-old daughter moved from Philadelphia to 416 Linden Street in Camden, New Jersey. It was a brief commute by Delaware River ferry to Hires' business in central Philadelphia. The family would later move from Camden to nearby Haddonfield, New Jersey, before eventually returning to Philadelphia.[41]

Although his business had become increasingly demanding, Hires did not allow it to consume him. His natural wit and curiosity combined with a flair for the dramatic made him a welcome speaker and presenter at civic and religious events.

Hires journeyed to rural southern New Jersey to participate in a fund-raising benefit for the Sunday school of the Cohansey Baptist Church of Roadstown, which he had once attended. The program consisted of "dramatic, pathetic and humorous readings and recitations, as well as selections introducing the German, Irish and Negro dialects."[42] He again displayed his vernacular dexterity in reciting "Coney Island Down Der Pay," a humorous poem about a German immigrant's first visit to the beach, before an audience at the Second Presbyterian Church of Camden.[43] Later in that performance he switched gears to read the "instigation scene" from Shakespeare's *Julius Caesar*. Hires recited "Smiting the Rock" as part of a "Grand Literary and Musical Entertainment" at the Broadway Methodist Episcopal Church of Camden in 1884.[44] The poem, by an unknown author, relates the tale of a steely trial judge moved to release a young miscreant who emotionally reveals "a shadow of shame" for his criminal actions in his quick defense of his mother.

Hires won applause for his lecture "Orators, Ancient and Modern" at the Wagner Free Institute of Science in Philadelphia in 1883, assisted by three students from the National School of Elocution and Oratory.[45] The institute, at Seventeenth Street and Montgomery Avenue, was founded in 1855 by William Wagner, a merchant and philanthropist, to offer free educational courses on natural science. Today it is a National Historic Landmark. In 1894 Hires delivered a memorial lecture to honor the late Philadelphia *Public Ledger* publisher, who had encouraged him to place his first root beer advertisement seventeen years earlier. It was titled "George W. Childs' Life Work an Inspiration to Struggling Young Men."[46]

Hires also found time to indulge a thespian bent. For example, a drama titled *Dearer Than Life* featured Hires in the role of Michael Garner, a hardworking but harried tradesman forced to cope with the misadventures of a dissolute son. The play was presented at the Haddon Lawn Tennis Club in 1886. A reviewer declared the play to be the best entertainment ever presented to a Haddonfield audience.[47] Another production of the tennis club featured Hires as a linguistically challenged innkeeper seeking to attract distinguished foreign guests in the farce *Ici on Parle Français*. The innkeeper's efforts after enrolling in a course titled "French before Breakfast" and moving his family to the attic led to hilarious complications.[48]

Hires kept a scrapbook containing programs, announcements, and reviews pertaining to his extracurricular activities. Among these memorabilia, a handwritten note begs the forbearance of an unspecified audience:

> *Ladies and Gentlemen:*
> *An earnest desire to advance the interest and contribute to the funds of a noble and worthy charity has prompted me to appear before you. . . . This is the first time I have attempted the ambitious task of appearing in a public hall before [such] a large and cultivated audience. I trust the motive thus explained and the worthy cause in which we are all engaged will be remembered should the temptation to criticize arise during the evening's performance.*[49]

Hires relished more competitive pastimes as well. A harness driving enthusiast, he raced Standardbred horses for sport on both track and street. His sleek pacing mare Ettie held a record for the best time over a half-mile oval. It seems likely that such racetrack contests may have been run with a professional driver in the sulky. However, Hires competed avidly in road races against other amateur drivers. An 1886 newspaper account described the scene as "some well-known trotters" sped down the main street of Camden:

> Feathery clouds of snow dust marked the flight of some of Camden's fleetest horses as they dashed down Cooper Street yesterday afternoon and merrily jingled the silvery sleigh bells with which they were decked. It was the first good day for sleighing this season and although the snow was rather loose, the horses and their drivers were full of the glow of a sharp winter's day . . . Charles Hires' bay pacing mare took the lead in many friendly contests, although William Dayton's dappled gray pushed her as a sharp second . . . the crowd urged their respective favorites with encouraging shouts as they came flying down the street together.[50]

Hires' passion for harness racing remained strong even after relocating his family to an estate in suburban Merion several years later. There on occasion he would challenge other suburban gentlemen in daredevil sleigh races across Philadelphia's Fairmount Park on the way to their businesses in the city.[51]

FAMILY JOINS MAIN LINE EXODUS

By 1890 the Hires family had settled into a three-story brownstone at 1712 Mount Vernon Street in the Fairmount section of Philadelphia just north of the city center.[52] However, growing profits from his burgeoning root beer business encouraged the usually frugal entrepreneur to seek more spacious living quarters. In 1894 he advertised the fourteen-room Mount Vernon Street property for sale: "all modern conveniences, two baths, electric lights, etc., in perfect order."[53] The Hires clan joined the exodus of other prosperous Philadelphians to the upscale Main Line suburbs that flourished following the extension of passenger service by the Pennsylvania Railroad.[54]

The Main Line was becoming a bastion of Philadelphia's elite families. Many possessed inherited wealth or, like Hires, had made fortunes as industrialists, entrepreneurs, or investors.

They had the capital to build homes that confirmed their social status and to support a network of exclusive private schools, clubs, and churches. The initiation of convenient commuter rail service made moving to this semipastoral locale, away from the city's poverty, grime, and congestion, all the more attractive.[55] A best-selling author expressed a jaundiced view of the community that evolved. He described it as "an oligarchy more compact, more tightly and more complacently entrenched than any in the United States . . . one of the few places in the country where it doesn't matter on what side of the tracks you are. These are very superior tracks. . . . What does the whole Main Line believe in most? Privilege."[56]

Hires purchased a large Gothic-style mansion known as Rose Hill situated on twenty acres in the community of Merion. The house had been designed for Lincoln Godfrey, a textile magnate, by Theophilus P. Chandler, noted architect of churches and Main Line houses.[57] Curiously, two years earlier Hires had purchased several lots near the railroad station in Devon, another Main Line community. Architect William Price drew up plans for a grand half-timbered house on the property. The drawings were published in 1894, but the house was never built. Hires later sold his Devon lots to Godfrey from whom he had purchased the Merion estate. It is not clear why Hires reversed his decision to build in Devon.[58]

Melrose, as Hires renamed the Merion property, rose three stories behind its ivy-covered front turret.[59] It featured stained-glass windows and an extended second-story terrace. The home offered ample space for the still growing family, which included Charles, Clara Kate, and their four children—Linda, John Edgar, Harrison, and Charles Jr. Another daughter, Clara, would be born three years later. The estate included a five-acre lawn. Trimming this expanse in the age before power mowers must have been expensive, but the price was one that Hires could well afford by then. Neighbors recalled seeing the Hires boys riding to the private and selective Haverford School on horseback.[60]

While building his root beer empire, Hires had also found time to indulge his inner chemist by dabbling in the creation of flavoring extracts for the candy trade and colognes. Based on these experiments, he compiled a "cookbook" for pharmacists in 1894 titled *Recipes for the Manufacture of Flavoring Extracts, Handkerchief Extracts, Toilet Water, Cologne, Bay Rum, etc., etc.* The publication was advertised to the trade and sold by mail for a dollar a copy. The book reflected its author's commitment to using the finest ingredients available. Under no circumstances buy cheap material in order to make cheap goods, Hires reminded readers, inferior and cheaper crude material can never make "good goods." Producing directly from fruits and plants is not only the truest to nature but is the most wholesome as well, Hires added.[61]

Hires' trade as an importer and dealer in botanicals and flavoring extracts, by now a "sideline" business, remained brisk. For example, he reported the sale of $3,000 worth of vanilla beans in a single transaction with a New York firm in 1896.[62] In 1898 the trade journal *National Druggist* hailed the Charles E. Hires Co. as "one of the few very large houses importing and dealing in vanilla beans. They have been in the front ranks for the last quarter century, and their business increase of fifty percent during 1898 is only in keeping with their persistent progressiveness. They carry a very large stock of both Mexican and Bourbon vanillas."[63]

By the mid-1890s, Hires' varied enterprises had succeeded beyond the wildest dreams of the young druggist who had discerned the commercial potential of a rude root tea. Sales and profits escalated dramatically in the two decades following the drink's debut at the Centennial Exposition. Hires had invented a product of acknowledged quality and created a national demand for it through an audacious advertising campaign. He had also waged a spirited and largely effective battle against the imitators and substitutors of his drink.

The transformation of Hires Root Beer from homespun local beverage into a national brand would have been impossible without the power of advertising. We look at Hires' unprecedented advertising campaign more closely next.

5

NEVER WINK IN THE DARK

IRES ENTERED THE MARKETPLACE in the era when advertising in America was beginning to flex its muscles as a potent tool for selling all kinds of products. Patent medicine makers, who flourished during the nineteenth century, led the way in demonstrating the effectiveness of self-promotion. These drummers of dubious remedies recognized that advertising could be more effective than medicine shows for pitching their products to a wide audience. Producers of Swaim's Panacea, Dr. Kilmer's Swamp Root, Lydia Pinkham's Vegetable Compound, Pink Pills for Pale People, Galvanic Love Powder, Dr. Wolcott's Pain Paint, and other quack nostrums—many high in alcohol and spiked with morphine or cocaine—employed newspaper advertising to foist their "cures" on a credulous public.[1] The yachts, mansions, and ostentatious lifestyles enjoyed by the more successful of these charlatans offered extravagant testimony to advertising's potential to hype sales. A major beneficiary of the medicine makers' promotional largess was the press, which carried their ads. The growth of newspapers in numbers and circulation during the Civil War era paralleled the proliferation of patent medicine advertising.

Makers and sellers of other consumer products took notice. Toward the end of the nineteenth century, new production methods enabled manufacturers to churn out standardized products ranging from canned goods to cigarettes to soap in massive quantities. They turned to advertising to create markets for these products. Similarly, large department stores including Wanamaker's in Philadelphia and New York, Macy's in New York, and Marshall Field's in Chicago found advertising an effective vehicle for moving merchandise as did such mail-order counterparts as Sears Roebuck and Montgomery Ward. Between 1880 and 1920, advertising expenditures in the United States grew from $200 million to nearly $3 billion.[2]

Early ads were product-centered even while using illustrations of children, animals, and trade characters. Over time, however, the utilitarian value of a product became insufficient to move merchandise at the rate required by mass production. The creation of a fancied need was crucial.[3] Advertisers began to appreciate the advantage of selling the benefit rather than the product—illumination instead of lighting fixtures, prestige instead of automobiles, sex appeal instead of mere soap. Woodbury's "The Skin You Love to Touch" campaign was a pathbreaker.[4]

Instrumental in the growth of mass market selling were advertising agencies. These erstwhile purveyors of newspaper and magazine space morphed into essential professionals, designing ads and advising clients on their placement. N. W. Ayer and Son of Philadelphia, one of the nation's earliest and most successful advertising agencies, would become the engine of Hires' magazine advertising campaigns.

Hires recounted his incremental steps and stumbles on the sometimes rocky road to advertising success in trade journal articles. As noted in Chapter 4, his first ad had been a one-column, one-inch insertion in *The Public Ledger* in 1877. The newspaper's publisher, George W. Childs, expressed confidence in Hires by extending him credit until sales increased enough to permit payment for the ads. Hires' early ads consisted solely of simple text. A one- or two-inch single column insertion offered space for little else. As Hires worked down his outstanding debt to the *Ledger*, Childs permitted him to increase his initial one-inch insertion to two- and then three-column inches. Larger ads allowed Hires to use bolder headlines and display woodcuts of the root beer extract box and images of rapturous imbibers, often children.

Breaking the Rules

Before long Hires began to press Childs for still larger ads. "My space continued to increase until finally Mr. Childs broke the rule about the integrity of the columns and allowed me to use all the space I wanted—up to full pages," Hires said.[5] Thus Hires became an early purchaser of multicolumn display ads familiar to modern readers. Until the mid-nineteenth century, newspaper copy and advertisements were usually confined to a single column width. Publishers were reluctant to break the metal rules between columns to allow either ads or newsprint to extend across multiple columns. This dictum reflected aesthetic sensitivity to the traditional newspaper format and a more practical concern: a multicolumn spread required the printer to saw by hand the metal rules separating columns of type.[6] The effect of early display advertising on a public accustomed to viewing ads in the form of small printed notices was electric.[7]

"My experiment with the *Ledger* was so successful that I began to wonder if the same thing could be done in a national way," Hires recalled. "In the late 1870s N. W. Ayer and Son placed a half-inch ad in the standard magazines."[8] Hires did not have to travel far to place the ad; the agency was located just a few blocks away in central Philadelphia. N. W. Ayer would remain Hires' principal advertising agency through the years. The two companies' founders had more in common than their hometown address. Both men began their businesses on a shoestring—Hires with a stake of $400 and Francis Wayland Ayer with $250—at the age of twenty-one. Ayer founded his firm in 1869, respectfully using the initials of his father and partner, Nathan Wheeler Ayer, in its name. He had less than a year's business experience.[9] Hires opened his first drugstore three years later.

Both men would be hailed as entrepreneurial geniuses. Ayer became a leading innovator in his field. While building an industry powerhouse, he helped transform the often unsavory occupation of advertising into a respected profession. Hires would break ground for an emerging American soft drink industry while demonstrating with Ayer's capable assistance the ability of advertising to build a national brand. Another quality the two shared in an era rife with robber barons, confidence men, and assorted charlatans was their basic morality. Both men were deeply religious and subscribed to strict codes of business ethics.

A few years earlier, Ayer had pioneered the "open contract," a concept that would revolutionize advertising. Open contracts allowed an advertiser to pay the agent a fixed percentage commission on the cost of advertising space purchased. Up to then advertising agents had operated as brokers, purchasing space in newspapers and journals and reselling it to advertisers at a profit. This arrangement kept advertisers in the dark about actual space costs and encouraged agents to act in their own self-interest rather than that of their clients. Agents who negotiated favorable rates or discounts from publishers were free to charge advertisers all the traffic would bear. Agents also were tempted to steer ads to publications where they got the best deals rather than those likely to best serve the needs of the advertiser.

The open contract placed ad agencies on the road to becoming advertising experts working to advance the interests of their clients. Advertisers would have access to publishers' actual rates. They would pay their agency a fixed commission, typically 15 percent of the space cost, for its services. No longer were agents middlemen dealing in a commodity. Moreover, as Ayer pointed out, the scheme put an end to ready-made advertising and enabled customized campaigns designed for a particular customer's needs.[10]

N. W. Ayer and Son continued to be an advertising leader and innovator. The firm pioneered the use of fine art in advertising and established the industry's first art department. It was the first agency to hire a full-time copywriter and to establish a copy department.[11] Ayer was responsible for some of advertising's most effective campaigns and enduring slogans: "When it rains, it pours" (Morton Salt), "I'd walk a mile for a Camel" (R. J. Reynolds), "A diamond is forever" (DeBeers), "Reach out and touch someone" (AT&T), "Be all that you can be" (U.S. Army), and "Snap! Crackle! Pop!" (Kellogg's Cereals). Its publication the *American Newspaper Annual and Directory* became a standard reference work.[12]

Ayer confidently advised prospective clients to "choose your (advertising) agent as you would your lawyer or your doctor and to leave the rest of the work to him."[13] The company cemented its allegiance to Philadelphia in 1929 by erecting a fourteen-story art deco landmark headquarters in Washington Square. The building was converted into luxury condominiums in 2006.

A SYMBIOTIC RELATIONSHIP

Napoleon's assertion that "geography is destiny" may be debated, but it seems clear that Hires' proximity to an ad agency of the caliber of N. W. Ayer proved fortuitous for both men. Ayer's innovative ideas and creative genius were instrumental in building mass markets for Hires and myriad other consumer brands. At the same time, Hires' robust advertising buys spurred Ayer's growth. The agency's early clients consisted mainly of dozens of small customers and hundreds of separate ad orders from retail stores, merchants of seeds and nursery stock, schools and colleges, and the like. By 1876 Ayer could offer to place an ad in any paper in the United States or Canada. But the development of larger accounts from advertisers such as Hires, Montgomery Ward, J. I. Case, and Procter and Gamble assured Ayer's success.[14]

Hires grew to rely on N. W. Ayer's advertising expertise as the two companies forged a symbiotic relationship. He recalled with regret once straying from Ayer to place an account for newspaper ads with a Midwestern agency based on its low competitive bid. He later discovered that the agency was placing two lines of copy per issue less than its contract required and pocketing the savings of $1,100 a year. "It's no wonder the bid was low," Hires observed dryly. "Since then I have spent very little time listening to the siren of the cut-rate agent."[15]

Ayer's corporate motto, Keeping Everlastingly at It Brings Success, first appeared in print in 1886. It was intended to persuade businesses to advertise continuously.[16] Hires certainly needed no such encouragement. He recalled that his advertising budget during his first year of Ayer's magazine insertions was about $10,000, while root beer sales yielded only about $2,800.[17] Hires systematically redeployed the profits from his botanical drug and flavorings business into root beer advertising. He would continue to do so for the next ten years. While spending at this rate might seem risky, if not foolhardy, it reflected Hires' abiding confidence in his product and in the power of advertising. Hires' advertising budget continued its ascent. He increased his purchases of magazine ads, and encouraged by his experience with the *Public Ledger*, he began advertising in other metropolitan newspapers. "My newspaper space continued to increase until I was using full pages in the large city dailies," he recalled. "The magazine space increased in proportion."[18]

By 1884 Hires advertised regularly in newspapers and magazines throughout the United States and Canada.[19] He began placing ads in *Harper's Weekly* about this time with insertions in *Harper's Magazine* the following year.[20] As early as 1888, regular quarter- and half-page Hires ads began to adorn the pages of *McClure's*, *Harper's*, *Frank Leslie's Illustrated*, and other magazines.[21] By the 1890s Hires was running half-page two-color ads in such publications as the *Ladies' Home Journal*.[22] Hires was said to be the first advertiser to purchase a color ad on the back cover of that magazine.[23] This "monthly Bible of the American home" belonged to the publishing empire established by another of Hires' fellow Philadelphians, Cyrus Curtis.[24] By 1911 the *Ladies' Home Journal* had become the nation's best-selling magazine. The Charles E. Hires Co. was a prolific advertiser in the *Journal*, the *Saturday Evening Post*, and other Curtis publications. "The proprietors of Hires' Root Beer are great believers in and users of printer's ink," Hires assured the public. "Having found what people want, they are progressive and unremitting in letting people know they have it."[25]

Author Richard Ohmann stresses the critical role played by national magazines and their ads for brand-name products in the formation of an American mass culture. He points out that Hires Root Beer was among other new products, such as Diamond Safety Razors, Pears' Soap, Kodak, and Mellin's Baby Food, that debuted in magazine ads in the 1880s.[26]

Hires did not confine his ad campaigns to the printed media. Patent medicine makers had pioneered the use of "outdoor advertising." Hires enthusiastically joined in their desecration of rural vistas. "For a great many years local sales were stimulated by painted signs on barns, fences and the like," Hires recalled.[27] A contemporary critic likened this practice to visual pollution. As though farm buildings and fences were not sufficient canvases, the critic observed "enormous signs are erected in the fields, not a rock is left without disfigurement, and gigantic words glare at as great [a] distance as the eye is able to read them."[28]

Hires also became an early adopter of transit advertising. He plastered growing fleets of urban streetcars with paeans to the pleasures of his root beer. Lithographed trade cards were added to the campaign as revenue allowed. Point-of-sale ads also contributed to the mix. Retailers who purchased Hires Root Beer concentrate were supplied with hanging ads, along with suggestions for deployment in their stores. Novelties such as whistles and pencils also were distributed widely.[29]

Hires' sales growth bore testament to the efficacy of advertising. In 1878, the year following Hires' first ad, 876 packages of root beer extract were sold. Hires had ordered a thousand boxes. But although his expenses exceeded sales, Hires persevered. His commitment to advertising would pay off handsomely by building future momentum. The next year sales exceeded 3,000 units. Five years later, sales had grown more than fifteenfold to 45,000 units. Approximately 395,000 packages were sold in 1888. By 1890 sales had increased to an astonishing total of 1.3 million units.[30]

TRADE CARDS PITCH THE PRODUCT

Trade cards were an early mainstay of Hires' advertising arsenal. Such cards originated in eighteenth-century England, where tradesmen used them to advertise their services. Advancements in color lithography brought trade cards to the fore in nineteenth-century America. The cards featured the work of the era's leading artists and lithographers. Innovators in chromolithography, a method developed to make multicolor prints, included the firms of Mayer, Merkel and Ottmann, New York; Donaldson Brothers, New York; Bufford and Sons, Boston and New York; and Louis Prang, Boston.[31] Trade cards offered advertisers the opportunity to present their messages in color, a technology not generally available in newspapers and magazines of the day. As sales builders, the cards also provided an incentive for merchants to stock a manufacturer's products.

The 1876 Centennial Exhibition provided the first large-scale opportunity for commercial lithographers to display their products as well as for businesses to hand out trade cards promoting their goods and services. The popularity of the colorful cards spread rapidly. By the early 1880s the three-by-five and two-by-four inch chromolithographed cards were being distributed by businesses ranging from small shops to large manufacturers. Beautiful women, adorable children and animals, flowers and fairies, patriotic scenes, and ethnic caricatures were widely depicted in trade card illustrations.[32] The reverse side of the card carried its sponsor's pitch.

Advertisers distributed cards extolling their products' virtues in stores and other public places. Many households collected trade cards as a pastime during the Victorian era, sometimes using them as part of their homes' interior décor. "Amid multiplying commercial images, the boundaries between art and commerce remained difficult to draw," one historian observed. "In many homes, advertisements became the chief means of brightening a dreary visual environment."[33] Thus the advertiser's message lingered as families read, reread, and traded the cards. Hires trade cards remain valued collectibles and are widely sold and archived today.[34]

Hires began his trade card advertising by using a stock comic card produced by the Errickson Card Works of New York City. He added his message in the blank space provided at the bottom of the preprinted card and on its back as well.[35] He may have also used "Novel Trade Cards" printed by Craig, Finley and Co., at 1029 Arch Street, Philadelphia. That company enlisted a stable of artists to create colorful stock cards with cartoon-like designs and a blank space for the sponsor's sales pitch.[36] Hires accelerated his ad campaign by printing his own trade cards. He installed an in-house printing plant on the second floor of his new Arch Street manufacturing facility in 1891. The plant's steam-powered presses produced full-color trade cards, circulars, posters, signs, and brochures by the millions.[37]

Hires described trade card collecting as a craze that originated among "young folks." He observed that the cards also encouraged the use of sex appeal to sell products. "I think this fad for cards was the real genesis of the pretty girl in advertising," he said. "There was a great rivalry among advertisers to secure attractive pictures, and pretty girls began to be in evidence recommending everything from patent medicines to stove polish."[38]

Hires trade cards featured their share of attractive women. More often, however, they depicted rosy-cheeked children, colorfully clad and holding a glass of root beer, a package of Hires' Extract, or both. These images reinforced the product's pretentions as a veritable fountain of youthful vitality and well-being. The "Hires Root Beer Boy," frequently portrayed on trade cards, stood in contrast to such preternaturally adorable youngsters. This strangely Rabelaisian tot sported a crooked grin. With a near empty glass before him, the boy raised his left hand to demand another helping of Hires Root Beer while gripping an amorphous pastry in his right. Some dubbed the image the "Ugly Kid"—one author unkindly described him as a "strange dwarf-like child."[39] Hires viewed the lad more benignly. He recalled that the likeness was drawn from a photograph of a German boy taken by one of his friends. "The little fellow had a piece of cake in one hand and was trying to attract the attention of some member of his party," Hires said. "He proved so attractive that he has run continuously."[40] The Hires Boy was depicted by various artists over the years in costumes that progressed from a dress and bib in his early incarnations to a bathrobe in 1907 and a dinner jacket in 1915.[41] The lad apparently consumed his pastry somewhere along the way. In later versions he raises an empty hand to demand a refill.

The popularity of trade cards for promotional purposes peaked during the 1890s when color magazine advertisements began to supplant them as a national advertising medium.

JUNK MAIL IS NOTHING NEW

With an in-house printing press at his disposal, Hires also needed a distribution plan. He deployed more than seventy drummers to distribute promotional handbills across the country.[42] They delivered Hires advertising booklets, hangers, and picture cards to pharmacists and grocers in towns large and small. In their remaining time, they appealed directly to potential purchasers by deluging local households with the nineteenth-century equivalent of junk mail. Hires promotional materials, however, were not distributed promiscuously. Sales reps were instructed to ensure that each home received only *one* brochure and that it be placed *inside* the door.[43] This form of advertising was constrained after towns began to adopt ordinances prohibiting the direct distribution of handbills.

Maintaining direct communication with its merchant community was a point of pride for the company. While in the early years his products were typically distributed through grocery wholesalers, Hires bombarded retail merchants with product information and point-of-sale advertising materials throughout the year. The value of such advertising is "incalculable," the company reminded its sales force, because it "suggests Hires to the consumer just at the time he is making up his mind."[44] One five-by-seven-inch cardboard cutout dating to 1897 featured a young child leaning on an oversized box of Hires' Extract. Another depicted the Hires Boy holding his ubiquitous mug. The company boasted that in 1898 it had mailed every grocer and druggist in the United States a copy of *Hires' Business Bringer* circular.[45]

During his company's formative years, Hires advertised on a scale unheard of for a soft drink. "I think we have used every form of advertising which can possibly be applied to our products— magazines, newspapers, trade papers, street cars, billboards, dealer literature, house-to-house distribution—and we are still using them all," Hires explained to an interviewer in 1913.[46] Hires clearly recognized the power of advertising to introduce his root beer and ramp up initial sales. He also understood that quality was the key to assuring continued sales. A company sales manual underscored its founder's philosophy:

> When he [Charles Hires] decided to make a beverage he went to pains to make sure that it should be the purest and most wholesome product possible. This required expensive material but he did not stop at expense because he was sure that

eventually the best would win recognition. . . . When you sell Hires you are not just selling a well-advertised and pleasant tasting soft drink: you are selling an article of clean merit, and you can feel clean and proud of your work and proud of the house you work for. We want men with ideals to sell our product because it is a product built with ideals.[47]

"Business success is built upon two foundation rocks," Hires told an interviewer. "One is to make your product as nearly perfect as possible. The second is to be energetic and tireless in selling it."[48] This theme was echoed by Hires' advertising manager: "You cannot advertise a good article, sell a poor one, and expect to succeed. Your goods will find you out just as sure as your sins will."[49]

Hires' massive ad campaigns established a pattern that would be emulated successfully by the soft drink industry and other advertisers of consumer products. Hires ads relied heavily on the persuasive power of pictures. Copywriters were instructed to use as few words as possible while selecting images that would graphically convey the ad's intended message.[50] Hires advertisements varied widely in form and format but stuck repetitiously to a few basic themes: Hires root beer was a pure and refreshing temperance drink made with the finest ingredients and an elixir of health to boot. "The Hires ads, which featured the brand name, had a clean, crisp appearance; they used strategically planned open spaces and cautioned customers to insist on Hires Root Beer. At a cost of only 25 cents for enough flavoring for five gallons, Hires was the purest, most delicious, health giving beverage possible to produce."[51]

Advertising buys were strategically timed, reaching a crescendo in the peak warmer months. Hires ads obsessively reminded the public of the company's rising sales volume. The latest totals and year-to-year comparisons, trending ever upward, were proudly presented. An 1895 ad of this genre seemed intended to evoke guilt as well as envy. After boldly asking, "Did You Get Yours?" the ad reported that "3,134,393 packages of Hires Rootbeer were sold in 1894, which made 15,675,735 gallons, or 313,494,700 glasses, sufficient to give every man, woman and child in the United States five glasses."[52]

UNPRECEDENTED PROMOTIONAL PUSH

Hires' unprecedented promotional campaign was worthy of the biggest-spending patent medicine makers, who had set the pace for advertising ambition for most of the 1800s with their brazen claims, spectacular medicine shows, and giant billboards.[53] Hires demonstrated that a soft drink could capture a national following, according to one contemporary advertising historian.[54] The lesson was not lost on the creators of Coca-Cola—first advertised in 1886—and other soft drinks that followed Hires into the marketplace. Coca-Cola, for example, initially had little money to spare for advertising. It could afford only $150 the first year, considerably less than the $700 that Hires had spent on his first newspaper ads. But Coca-Cola made the most of its meager ad budget. Large oilcloth banners cost a dollar apiece, streetcar signs a little over a penny, and posters even less. A thousand coupons for free sample drinks could be printed for a dollar.[55] As sales volume grew, however, Frank Robinson, the brand's promotional genius, embarked on an advertising campaign reminiscent of the blitz unleashed ten years earlier by Hires.[56]

Early Hires ads are notable for their arresting art, adorable children, terse captions, and clever wordplay and testimonials. Here are some examples: "Children love it and thrive on it." "The last drop is as good as the first." "Good for all—good all the time." "It cools Sol's rays on the hottest days." "Take it for a tonic in the spring—drink it all summer to keep cool." "A fountain of health in every bottle." One ad bridged the generational divide, promising "health for the baby, pleasure for the parents and new life for the old folks."[57]

At times Hires' ad writers employed gentle humor to appeal to readers who might prove unreceptive to a hard sell. Some of the best examples of such soft-sell ads appear on trade cards picturing children and animals. One such card featured a wide-eyed, brightly clad lass of about eight pouring a dose of Hires' Cough Cure into a spoon. At her feet three small green frogs croak expectantly. "They must be very hoarse," the caption reads. Nearby boxes labeled "Hires' Cough Cure" and "Hires' Cough Candy" complete the tableau. Another trade card depicts a toddler who had been set to savor a glass of Hires. However, to his quite visible distress, the family's pet shepherd has inserted itself between tot and table and is eagerly lapping the child's root beer. The caption simply reads, "An Uninvited Guest."

Hires also recognized the motivational impact of testimonials from satisfied customers. He sprinkled them liberally throughout his advertising. For example, an 1881 newspaper ad featured thirty-two different Hires drinkers from far-flung locales—including Deadwood, Dakota Territory; Sulphur Station, Texas; Montreal, Canada; and Pensacola, Florida—extolling Hires Root Beer under a headline modestly proclaiming: "EVERYBODY LIKES IT!" Other ads brazenly touted Hires Root Beer as a healthy drink for infants. In an 1892 ad captioned "The Baby Knows a Good Thing," a father declares, "Your root beer is so delicious that our baby, nine-months-old, cries for it." Other advertisements equated sipping Hires with marital bliss. A radiant couple attests, "Homes are happy where there's always plenty of Hires Root beer on hand." Hires took pains to assure readers that all testimonials were given voluntarily—and cheerfully.

Hires was among the earliest advertisers to understand that pitching his product directly to children might appeal to their parents while nurturing a future generation of root beer drinkers. As Hires advertising manager W. W Williamson put it, "by pleasing the child, you interest the parent."[58]

The company developed a series of pamphlets aimed at kids with titles like *An Uninvited Guest, Hires' Rootbeer, Little Mabel, Jingle Jokes for Little Folks,* and *The Legend of the Golden Chair.* These colorful offerings conveyed their messages in handscripted letters and verse. *Hires Puzzle Book of Unnatural History,* published in 1890, promised prizes for children who sent in the most names of creatures, natural or unnatural, that could be formed by pairing drawings of the front and back halves of various animals. Each page contained a rhyming reminder of the delights of drinking Hires Root Beer. Contestants were required to submit the signature label from a Hires Root Beer box with their entries.[59]

The devout Hires was not above exploiting religious themes to sell root beer and burnish his brand's credibility among members of the Christian temperance movement. Trade cards and other promotional materials at times featured biblical scenes and scripture.[60] One widely circulated lithograph portrayed "Ruth and Naomi," biblical exemplars of eternal loyalty. Copy on the back of the illustration noted "the pathos of this touching episode of scripture . . . the tenderness of expression and the womanly warmth." After viewing the painting at the Louvre, Hires said he had been moved to commission a $5,000 lithographic reproduction.[61] Fellow admirers could receive a free fifteen-by-twenty-inch color copy suitable for framing in exchange for five labels cut from packages of Hires Improved Root Beer in Liquid. The company ordered more than one million reproductions for distribution.[62]

ADS IN DISGUISE

Hires did not hesitate to pitch his beverage through "advertorials," as they were later labeled. These hybrid insertions disguised advertising copy to appear as editorial content. This subterfuge was commonly permitted by publications throughout the nineteenth century, at times as part of their contracts with advertising agencies. Although the practice continues to this day, modern advertorials are more likely to be discreetly labeled as paid advertisements. An Internet search for news items about the company frequently yields advertorials under the headings of news or editorial. At first glance these appear to be news items, but their cadence, hyperbole, and grammatical gaffes are redolent of the adman's pen.

An example printed by the *Philadelphia Inquirer* in 1890 reads, "Delicious Summer Beverages. There Are Many, But the Best is Hires' Root Beer. The various dealers in soft drinks are unanimous in pronouncing this the banner season for this line of business since the Centennial year. To no one man has this been applied [*sic*] than to Mr. Charles E. Hires, and the extraordinary efforts put forth by Hires' laboratory to meet the summer demand for root beer." The blurb concludes, "Nothing refreshes one more than a glass of Hires' root beer in these warm days, and every man, woman and child would be more healthy, cooler and have a better appetite if they used his delicious drink daily and eschewed many other drinks, including Schuylkill water."[63] The Schuylkill River was the source of Philadelphia's drinking water.

Hires and fellow beverage makers frequently touted their drinks as healthy alternatives to tap water. Their arguments may seem outlandish today but were more credible in an era when the purity of public water supplies was far from a certainty.

Another Hires advertorial, "What Shall We Drink," explored possible alternatives "when the rays of Old Sol are boiling down at a ninety degree rate, the air like the breath of a furnace and everything hot, dry and dusty." The answer, of course, was Hires Root Beer. But the facile ad writer first dispatched other possibilities: "The serious effect of an over indulgence in ice water is well known. The thousand and one cheap gassy beverages are known to be more or less injurious to the health, while mineral waters of known purity and healthfulness are a luxury beyond the reach of but few."[64]

A recurring theme in early Hires advertising was the drink's reputed health benefits. In an era before the federal Pure Food and Drug Act and other bothersome government regulations, no health claim however preposterous was off limits. Patent medicine purveyors were the most egregious hustlers, but Hires was far from reticent in this regard.

"Hires" to Your Health

For example, an 1892 Hires newspaper ad boasted: "Health is Improved by Hires Root Beer. It is beyond all dispute a wonderful health-giving drink and it is very easy for anyone to understand why this is so."[65]

The profusion of Hires ads trumpeting the drink's alleged therapeutic qualities conjured the image of a wonder drug. They portrayed Hires Root Beer as far more than a simple tonic compounded from herbs, roots, barks, and berries. "It is beyond all dispute the Greatest Health Giving Beverage in the Whole World," an 1895 Australian newspaper ad diffidently proclaims.[66] Hires advertisements are rife with dubious health claims, but unlike the promises of patent medicine purveyors, they tend to emphasize the drink's health-enhancing properties rather than claiming to address specific maladies. Here are some examples:

> Every bottle of Hires Rootbeer is a fountain of health.
>
> It keeps your blood cool and your temper even.
>
> It renews the power of assimilation, revives the dormant forces, prevents exhaustion.
>
> It makes the weak strong and gives the feeble nerve.
>
> A drink of the highest medicinal value.
>
> Improves the appetite, purifies the blood and tones the whole system.
>
> Keeps the system in a healthy condition during the warm weather.
>
> Largely used in hospitals, sanitariums and sick rooms.
>
> The blood is improved, the nerves soothed, the stomach benefitted.
>
> For Weakly and Sickly Children. It will make them healthy, strong, rosy and happy.
>
> It is recommended and prescribed by some of our best physicians.

Glowing testimonials from satisfied users documented these debatable declarations.

"Doctors Commend It"

Hires ads frequently boasted that Hires Root Beer was recommended by physicians, whom the company also took great pains to indoctrinate by purchasing ads in their professional journals. These often bore laudatory endorsements from other doctors who seemed to prefer anonymity. For example, this advertisement, perhaps penned by a physician, appeared in *The Cincinnati Lancet-Clinic: A Weekly Journal of Medicine and Surgery* in 1897:

> Admittedly the most wholesome, refreshing beverage that can be prescribed for convalescents. It contains nothing that is not readily and perfectly assimilated. Composed of fresh,

pure natural roots, berries and barks, it contains two most
valuable diuretics—triticum repens (dog grass) and juniper
berries—in addition to sarsaparilla, pipsisewa [sic], hops,
birch bark, etc. These are scientifically combined, prepared
with sterilized distilled water and carbonated. The tannin of
the barks is converted by the action of peptone, in the process of fermentation, into gallic acid—producing a healthy
action of the kidneys. Any reputable physician is free to inspect the manufacture and formula of HIRES Rootbeer. Doctors commend it.[67]

Physicians' families were fair game as well: "Doctor, May I Send
Your Wife a Free Bottle of Hires Extract?" asked an ad in the *American Journal of Public Health* accompanied by a mail-in coupon.[68]

Hires promoted his cough remedy with similarly far-fetched
promises. "Hires Cough Cure will be found to be the best, sur-
est and safest remedy for Coughs, Colds, Croup and Whooping
Cough ever discovered," an 1891 trading card suggested.[69] Hires
stretched his advertising dollar by touting the cough suppres-
sant at the bottom of Hires Root Beer ads.

In Hires' defense, it is only fair to note that his health claims
were not wholly specious, especially considering the prevailing
medical knowledge of his era. Several of his root beer ingredients enjoyed histories of use in folk or standard medicine. Hires
shrewdly pointed this out in an 1892 *Philadelphia Inquirer* advertisement: "The roots, herbs, barks and berries from which
Hires' Root Beer is skillfully made, are the identical things from
which physicians get their most helpful remedies."[70] Another
1892 insertion shows a bottle of Hires root beer being poured
into a glass bearing an Rx symbol followed by a partial list of
its ingredients: ginger, sarsaparilla, juniper berries, spikenard,
birch bark, and dog grass. "Here is your prescription for the best
of good health," the ad proclaims.[71]

Sarsaparilla, for example, a standard remedy of the day, had
appeared in the first *Pharmacopoeia of the United States* in 1820.[72]
Doctors prescribed it for conditions believed to result from "blood
impurities." These included digestive problems, skin diseases, "fe-
male problems," and syphilis.

Native Americans used the leaves of wintergreen, a key component of Hires Root Beer, to treat rheumatism, headaches, and sore throats. Modern medicine has determined that the wintergreen leaf contains an aspirin-like chemical that might reduce pain, swelling, and fever.[73] Sassafras, another major root beer ingredient, boasts a long folk medicine history. The root, indigenous to the Appalachian region, was widely sought by Europeans as a cure for venereal disease. Sassafras was in fact a profitable export for early English settlers in the New World.[74] Tea brewed from sassafras root or bark was widely used as a household cure for gastrointestinal complaints, colds, kidney ailments, rheumatism, and skin eruptions. Conversely, safrole, a principal component of sassafras, was determined to be carcinogenic and banned in the United States in 1960. This finding produced a short-term crisis for the root beer industry until a safrole-free substitute was developed. Dog grass or couch grass (*triticum repens*), another Hires ingredient, is a diuretic that has been used in herbal medicine since classical times to promote healthy kidney function.[75]

But just how healthful was sugar, the second largest component of Hires Root Beer after water? Hires ads alluded to the sweetener's possible beneficial effects while avoiding specific mention of its presence as an ingredient. However, sugar's short-term benefits—raising energy levels and banishing fatigue, for example—were probably offset by its long-term risks that are now understood to include obesity and diabetes.

UNTESTED HEALTH CLAIMS ENDORSED

Whether the concentration of herbs, roots, and barks in Hires Root Beer was sufficient to affect a soda drinker's well-being one way or the other is problematical. No evidence exists of empirical studies to determine the validity of Hires' claims of health benefits. Nonetheless, the placebo effect of Hires' pervasive advertising campaigns should not be discounted. Many imbibers professed to feeling healthier after simply drinking Hires Root Beer.

The company supported its health claims with a fanfare of testimonials from the rejuvenated and restored. In an effort to authenticate such assertions, these ads identified the endorsers by name and locale. "There is no medicine like it to keep the system in tone," enthused Mrs. A. Toomis of King City, Kansas in 1881. "I used it last season and can't do without it." After drinking Hires for two months, a Cape May, New Jersey user declared, "It has quite cured my back and kidneys." A Delaware drinker affirmed that Hires Root Beer had relieved his long-standing dyspepsia, while an Arkansan found that swigging Hires restored his appetite following a mining injury and provided "a pleasant and positive cure." An 1889 *Philadelphia Inquirer* advertisement presented glowing testimonials from across America. "An Excellent Tonic," proclaimed a New Englander, "I have used your root beer for a year and have become healthy by its use." An Iowa resident, after having drunk Hires Root Beer for two years, simply declared it to be "all the medicine we need."[76] Private citizens were not the only ones to endorse Hires. Following the passage of the Pure Food and Drug Act of 1906, Hires won a seal of acceptance from the American Medical Association Committee of Foods.[77]

Overcoming Hurdles

The cause of temperance in America was gathering momentum during the latter half of the nineteenth century. Maine and other states had begun to prohibit the manufacture and sale of alcoholic beverages. The WCTU took up the cause in 1874. For Hires, who had actually set out to brew an alternative to demon rum, the groundswell of temperance fervor proved opportune. He skillfully surfed the swelling teetotaler tide by proclaiming his drink's purity and noninebriant nature. His advertising boldly anointed Hires Root Beer the "Temperance Drink" while emphasizing its universal appeal: "A temperance drink for temperance people—a health-giving drink for the masses."[78] Hires chronicled the comments of fellow abstainers who seemed eager to endorse his beverage. "Ice water will make a person sick, strong beer will make him drunk, but Hires' Root Beer just hits the spot," attested a user in Troy, New York, perhaps coining a commercial phrase that would later be adopted by Hires rival Pepsi-Cola.[79] Ironically, Hires, a committed temperance advocate, would later come under attack by an increasingly militant

WCTU when it mounted a boycott of his beverage (see Chapter 6). Hires was compelled to defend his drink against zealots who believed any "beer" must be alcoholic.

In marketing a do-it-yourself home brew, Hires faced an advertising hurdle not shared with most of his competitors. Theirs were primarily soda fountain drinks that a consumer might pop into the corner drugstore and enjoy; no messy home preparation required. In contrast, Hires drinkers were called on to meticulously mix the root beer extract with sugar, water, and yeast; bottle and cork the resulting mixture; and delay gratification while the beverage aged. Hires ads needed to educate consumers to prepare the drink while also persuading them that the finished product would justify their efforts.

Hires confronted this challenge by tweaking the maternal instincts of home brewers, understanding that the majority of them were probably mothers. In illustrations and text, his ads portrayed root beer making as a wholesome and fulfilling family ritual. "Home is made happier by Hires . . . a home-made and home-making beverage," read an 1892 newspaper ad. "It is very easily prepared, and if the plain directions are followed, it will always be good. . . . In thousands of homes, 'the Hires Root Beer that mother made' will be among the happiest recollections of childhood."[80] Advertisements also noted that those who took the time to prepare Hires at home would be rewarded for their labors with a drink less expensive than any soda fountain draft.

Those needing further encouragement could find a recipe and directions for making root beer in other Hires ads. These instructions were detailed, cautioning on the type of yeast required, the need for warmth to assure proper fermentation, and to avoid substituting baking powder for yeast. One deviation from the standard formula was permitted. Granulated sugar might be replaced by molasses or common sugar "to make the beer more cheaply."[81]

McKINLEY VICTORY BUOYS HIRES

Republican William McKinley's victory over populist Democrat William Jennings Bryant in the 1896 presidential election found Hires in a jubilant frame of mind. He announced plans to boost advertising expenditures in 1897 to new heights, a business journal reported. "He intends to do it not only through the daily newspapers, but the trade journals as well, and expects to reap considerable benefit from it."[82]

By 1904 Hires' advertisements had adopted a more moderate tone, shifting away from newspapers, the driver of his early advertising success, toward magazines and direct marketing to consumers and retailers. However, the company continued to raise its annual ad budget aggressively. This strategy appears to have paid off. Sales increased at an average yearly rate of 29 percent from 1904 to 1909.[83]

Although acknowledged as a trendsetter, Hires prudently sought and heeded the advice of specialists in developing advertising strategies. Once his resources permitted, he recruited experienced ad managers and solicited expert advice from his advertising agencies, principally N. W. Ayer and Son. Hires recalled agonizing over the wording of a circular designed to convince dealers of the advantages of selling an advertised root beer extract rather than an unknown brand. "Almost any good advertising agency nowadays could instantly recommend better dealer promotion literature than that," Hires observed. "I was required to purchase my experience first-hand, while the modern advertiser, in return for a commission of 15 percent, can get the experience of a lot of other people."[84]

Hires' groundbreaking advertising campaign catapulted his humble root beer extract from relative obscurity to national prominence. His ad budgets reflected his belief in the power of the medium, rising from an initial $700 outlay in 1877 to $500,000 by 1900.[85] In succeeding years he effectively adapted his ad campaigns to meet the demands of a dynamic marketplace. The impact of Hires' marketing and promotional skills has been widely recognized.

"He was the right man with the right product, and he promoted it in a way no one else had done," according to food historian Andrew Smith. "At that point there wasn't much advertising of food and beverages. He created a lot of excitement and made it possible to expand his business very quickly and nationalized it in ways most companies weren't able to do prior to that time."[86]

Historian Frank Presbrey paid tribute to Hires' pioneering role in the evolution of soft drink advertising: "Hires Root Beer blazed the path since followed by a long line of soft-drink advertisers, including Coca-Cola and the ginger ales," he observed. "The Hires contribution to the development [of advertising] was a demonstration that through advertising the soft drink could be made a national product."[87]

Hires expressed a more modest view of his advertising achievements in an article he wrote for the trade journal *Printers' Ink* in 1913:

> In the course of forty-odd years I have tried many experiments, some of which have failed and many of which have succeeded. . . . Sometimes I like to think that my experiments have made the advertising business plainer to a good many other people, and since in the meantime I have been moderately successful, I suppose I have not advertised altogether in vain.[88]

Hires' confidence in the power of advertising remained unshakable throughout his lifetime. Looking back over his career since placing that first five-line insertion in 1877, Hires summarized his advertising philosophy metaphorically: "Doing business without advertising is like winking at a girl in the dark," he observed. "You know what you are doing, but nobody else does."[89]

Until now Hires' biggest challenge had been one most businesses would welcome—expanding capacity rapidly enough to keep pace with demand. But dark clouds were approaching from an unexpected direction. The success of Hires Root Beer would be sternly tested by a presumed ally suddenly turned adversary, the temperance movement.

"Newspaper Hat" trade card. The hat is fashioned from a copy of Philadelphia's *Public Ledger*, which carried the first advertisement for Hires Root Beer in 1877. Printed by Donaldson Brothers, New York, c. 1890. (Boston Public Library, American Broadsides and Ephemera)

"An Uninvited Guest," Hires Root Beer trade card. Printed by J. Ottmann Lithographing Co., New York, c. 1890. (Boston Public Library, American Broadsides and Ephemera)

"Very Hoarse," trade card advertising Hires' Cough Candy and Hires' Cough Cure. Printed by Donaldson Brothers, New York, c. 1890. (Boston Public Library, American Broadsides and Ephemera)

THEY MUST BE VERY HOARSE.

ALWAYS BRINGS HEALTH.

This 1894 trade card suggests Hires Root Beer is a wholesome beverage for babies. The message on the reverse reads: "The health and happiness of childhood. The joy and comfort of old age." (Boston Public Library, American Broadsides and Ephemera)

"Jingle Jokes for Little Folks," a twelve-page booklet of wit and humor for young readers promoting Hires Root Beer. Published by Charles E. Hires Co., c. 1901. (The Alan and Shirley Brocker Sliker Culinary Collection, MSS 314, Special Collections, Michigan State University Libraries. Available at: http://www.lib.msu.edu /exhibits/sliker/detail .jsp?id=3533)

"Say, Mama. I want another glass of Hires Root Beer." This trade card featured the notorious Hires Boy. Although some considered him ugly, the child was a favorite of Hires. The Hires Boy appeared frequently in Hires ads in varied garb and became an unofficial company trademark. Printed by Knapp Lithography, New York, c. 1890. (Hagley Museum and Library, Wilmington, DE, Box 3, Advertising Cards Collection [Accession 1992.229])

"All gone, could I have another glass of that Hires' Rootbeer?" Reverse side of this 1895 trade card declares other brands are "destitute of roots and detrimental to health." Printed by Donaldson Brothers, New York, 1895. (Boston Public Library, American Broadsides and Ephemera)

BELOW: Portrait of "Hires Girl of 1917" painted by Haskell Coffin. (The Alan and Shirley Brocker Sliker Culinary Collection, MSS 314, Special Collections, Michigan State University Libraries. Available at: http://www.lib .msu.edu/exhibits/sliker/detail .jsp?id=3538)

FACING PAGE, TOP: Dr. Swett's Root Beer, an early Hires competitor, was concocted by George W. Swett, a Boston pharmacist. It was first sold as an extract for home brewing and then as a bottled drink. As clever label imagery suggests, it could be enjoyed from childhood to old age. (Ephemera Collection, EP001, Historic New England, Haverhill, MA)

FACING PAGE, BOTTOM: "Uncle Sam Drinks Hires," 1902 national newspaper advertisement. (N. W. Ayer Advertising Agency Records, Archives Center, National Museum of American History, Smithsonian Institution)

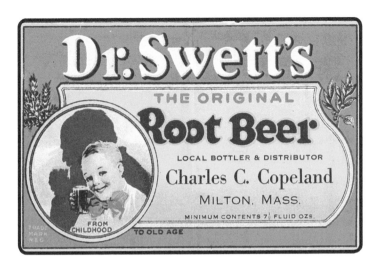

The Milk Test That Proves

Try a can of Gold Milk alongside any other kind — compare it even with the liquid usually bought as dairy milk. Then, and not till then, will you fully appreciate the full significance of what absolutely pure, wholesome and whole milk means.

Even though dairyman's milk may be pure and clean you have no assurance of it. With Gold Milk, on the contrary, there is no chance for it to be anything else. It starts pure, is sterilized, then sealed into tins and reaches the home pure, sweet and fresh.

A 10 cent can will make 3 pints of heavy milk by the addition of 2 pints of water.

Write a postal *to-day* for our new recipe book.

10c. a Can

Ask Your Grocer For It.

HIRES CONDENSED MILK CO.
Philadelphia
Makers of Silver Brand Milk
The Best Condensed Milk

The Modern Cow

It is no longer necessary to depend upon the milkman for your milk. In fact, you will be on the safer side if you will use Gold Milk instead of dairy milk.

Gold Milk is just pure milk concentrated and sterilized, then sealed in air-tight tins. For table use add two pints of water to a 10 cent can. This will give you three pints of milk far superior to dairy milk. It is pure, clean and germless.

Try a can of Gold Milk for drinking, cooking and all other purposes where milk is necessary. A single can will prove to you, as it has to thousands of others, that once and for all — the *Pure Milk Problem* is settled by using

GOLD MILK

Write a postal *to-day* for our new recipe book.

10c. a Can

Ask Your Grocer For It.

HIRES CONDENSED MILK CO.
Philadelphia
Makers of Silver Brand Milk
The Best Condensed Milk

Newspaper ads for Hires Gold brand evaporated milk, c. 1908. (N. W. Ayer Advertising Agency Records, Archives Center, National Museum of American History, Smithsonian Institution)

FACING PAGE, LEFT: This 1902 newspaper ad stresses Hires Root Beer's natural ingredients and promises health benefits to those who drink it. (N. W. Ayer Advertising Agency Records, Archives Center, National Museum of American History, Smithsonian Institution)

From Mother Nature for Human Nature

HIRES
Rootbeer

Hires Rootbeer brings to the home, in the most delightful form, a preparation of herbs, roots, barks and berries—Mother Nature's most helpful gift to Human Nature. A temperance beverage that satisfies the thirst and pleases the palate.

The more the children drink of it the stronger they grow; the more grown folks drink of it the better they feel. Hires Rootbeer purifies the blood, tones the nerves and aids digestion. You make it right at home.

25c package makes 5 gallons. Send 2c stamp for booklet of "Unnatural History." Cash prizes for solving combinations.

Charles E. Hires Company, Malvern, Pa.

Make Rootbeer at Home

IT IS really very easy. One bottle of Hires Household Extract will make five gallons of rootbeer. The cost — *including sugar and yeast*—is less than a cent a glass.

And what wonderful rootbeer it is! How sparkling — how effervescent—how delicious!

Hires
HOUSEHOLD EXTRACT

is the original — the genuine — the kind you have known all your life.

Hires Extract is made direct from the pure juices of Nature's roots, barks, herbs and berries.

Make Rootbeer at home again this summer — even as your mother used to make it when you were a child.

If you cannot get Hires Extract from your dealer, order direct from us.
Send 25c in stamps.

Hires Expansion Bottle Stoppers
No strings or wire to cut the hand. Easy to use and keep clean. Fit almost any bottle. Can be used again and again. Will hold great pressure. If your grocer cannot supply you, order direct from us.
50c a dozen

HOUSEHOLD EXTRACT

Be sure you get this package. It brings you the genuine Hires Household Extract.

THE CHARLES E. HIRES CO.
Philadelphia, Pa.

ABOVE, RIGHT: Hires newspaper ad directed to do-it-yourself root beer fanciers. (N. W. Ayer Advertising Agency Records, Archives Center, National Museum of American History, Smithsonian Institution)

Advertisement for Hires's patented dispensing keg,
which combined soda water with Hires syrup to produce
a mug of root beer with a single pull of the handle.
(*Pharmaceutical Era*, December 1919, 12)

Charles E. Hires at age twenty-three. (Hires Family Papers, Historical Society of Pennsylvania)

Hires' beloved first wife, Clara Kate (née Smith), who died in 1910. They were wed in 1875 and had six children. (Courtesy of Jeff Groff)

Portrait of Hires that appeared in self-authored article, "Seeing Opportunities" in the *American Druggist and Pharmaceutical Record*, October 1913 (University of Wisconsin Libraries, Ebling Library)

The family relaxes at the home of Hires' son Harrison, c. 1925. Hires Sr. (seated right of center) holds grandson William, age five. Emma Waln Hires, in floral hat, is to the right. (Courtesy of Jeff Groff)

A good day's catch! Hires and his youngest daughter, Clara, show off their haul of marlins, c. 1920. (Courtesy of Jeff Groff)

Hires purchased a modest yacht to pursue his passion for deep-sea fishing. He named it *Emwal*, a contraction of his second wife's name, Emma Waln. (Courtesy of Jeff Groff)

In 1894 the Hires family moved to Rose Hill, situated on twenty park-like acres in Merion on Philadelphia's Main Line. This photograph appeared in *King's Views of Philadelphia. Part I* (New York: Moses King, 1900). (Special Collections, Bryn Mawr College Library)

In 1906 the Hires family sold its Merion estate and moved to a new home on Buck Lane in Haverford, another Philadelphia Main Line community. Although more modest than the Merion estate, the Colonial Revival–style house had fourteen rooms, four baths, and a large garden and conservatory. This image appeared in *Country Homes*, January 1920. (Courtesy of Jeff Groff)

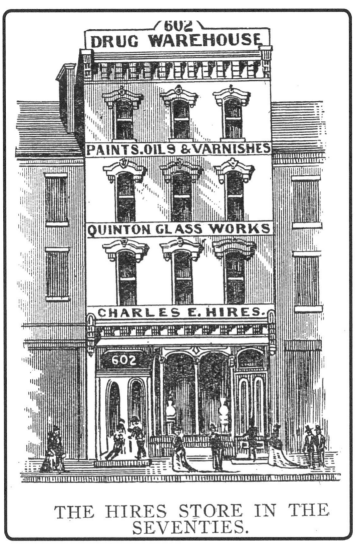

THE HIRES STORE IN THE
SEVENTIES.

Hires opened his first drugstore at 602 Spruce Street in Philadelphia in 1872. ("Seeing Opportunities," *American Druggist and Pharmaceutical Record*, October 1913, 27, University of Wisconsin Libraries, Ebling Library)

In 1890 Hires moved his "laboratory" into this four-story commercial building at 117–119 Arch Street in Philadelphia. (*Philadelphia Daily News*, February 14, 1891; Courtesy of Jeff Groff)

In 1896 the Charles E. Hires Co. relocated its Philadelphia plant from Arch Street to this sprawling property on the Delaware River at Delaware and Fairmount Avenues. [J. P. Lippincott Co., *Philadelphia and Its Environs: A Guide to the City and Surroundings (1896)* (Philadelphia: Lippincott, 1896)]

Hires's close friend, Reverend Russell H. Conwell, was a spellbinding orator and founder of Temple University. This photo was taken in 1884 when Conwell was forty-one. (Special Collections Research Center, Temple University Libraries)

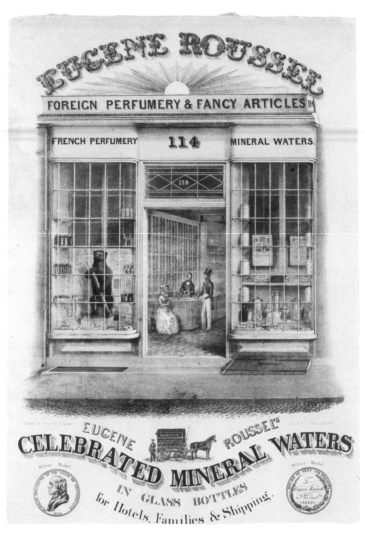

Eugene Roussel, a French perfumer, sold flavored mineral water in glass bottles at his shop at 114 Chestnut Street in Philadelphia from 1843 to 1849. [Nicholas B. Wainwright, *Philadelphia in the Romantic Age of Lithography* (Philadelphia: Historical Society of Pennsylvania, 1970)]

6

TEMPERANCE TRAUMA

HIRES ROOT BEER advertisements amplified Hires' heartfelt commitment to the temperance cause. They consistently positioned the drink as an alternative to alcoholic beverages. "A Temperance Drink for Temperance People," was an oft-repeated theme in Hires' early newspaper advertisements and trade cards. Rising root beer sales confirmed Hires' wisdom in melding credo with commerce during an era when public antipathy toward alcoholic drinks was on the rise. The temperance movement had been gaining strength during the nineteenth century in reaction to a culture where heavy drinking had become for many a social norm.

Abstinence was a virtue conspicuous by its absence among early European settlers in the New World. The consumption of strong drink is a tradition as American as Plymouth Rock. The ship that carried Puritan John Winthrop to Massachusetts in 1630 was stocked with ten thousand gallons of wine and three times as much beer as water. Imbibing alcoholic beverages was "as intimately woven into the fabric of early American life as family or church," author and editor Daniel Okrent points out.[1] Their drinking habits were part of the culture that the colonists brought with them. Beer and ale often accompanied family meals in England, where they were viewed as socially and religiously accepted elements of the daily diet.

The hardships of survival on the new continent encouraged heavy drinking. Alcohol supplied that burst of energy demanded by hard physical labor and served as a relaxant and social lubricant. It was also an analgesic. Furthermore, alcoholic beverages were safer than water of uncertain purity. At first settlers relied on European imports, but they soon discovered that the New World offered a bounty of raw materials for making alcoholic beverages. Almost anything that grew—including pumpkins, parsnips, and pine boughs—could be fermented or distilled to produce an intoxicant of some sort. Settlers mastered the preparation of whisky and beer from wheat, rye, corn, and barley. As apple orchards flourished, the production of hard cider, popular in England, became a household industry in America. Other fruits, flowers, and berries were inventively transformed into wine and brandy. As if these native resources were not enough to quench their collective thirst, the colonists imported shiploads of rum and its components, molasses and sugar, from the West Indies after about 1650.[2]

Community and religious leaders condemned excessive drinking. Then as now, they were inclined to accept moderate alcohol consumption as a useful, even pleasurable, accompaniment to everyday life. However, their commitment to moderation was not widely shared among their fellow citizens. By the American Revolution, heavy alcohol consumption pervaded colonial society. This drinking "crossed regional, sexual, racial, and class lines," one historian noted. "Americans drank at home and abroad, alone and together, at work and at play, in fun and in earnest. They drank from the crack of dawn to the crack of dawn."[3]

The devastation wrought by this unrelenting binge on health, productivity, and domestic tranquility did not escape notice by thoughtful observers. One of the earliest to call attention to alcohol abuse was Philadelphia physician Benjamin Rush, hailed today as the "Father of American Psychiatry." In 1805 he declared excessive drinking detrimental to physical and psychological health and estimated that as many as four thousand deaths a year were caused by hard liquor.[4] Rush viewed alcoholism as a disease rather than a moral failing. He urged the establishment of "sober houses" specifically designed to treat alcoholics.

By 1810 more than fourteen thousand distilleries slaked the national thirst for booze, a fivefold increase in two decades. Western farmers shipped their grain crop in the form of whiskey to eastern markets, competing with cheap rum imported from the West Indies. The price of hard liquor declined to a level competitive with beer or milk. By 1830 American adults were guzzling the equivalent of seven gallons of pure alcohol a year, about three times the present rate.[5]

MAVENS OF MODERATION PERSIST

Early temperance associations established in Connecticut and other states failed to achieve popular support, but as excessive drinking continued apace, the champions of moderation persevered. Benefiting from a renewed popular interest in religion and morality, the American Temperance Society was organized in 1826. Within ten years it enrolled more than eight thousand local chapters with one and a half million members. At the same time, a number of Protestant churches took up the temperance cause. Many Methodists, Baptists, and Quakers opposed the consumption of distilled spirits. Temperance organizations initially called for moderation or voluntary abstinence from strong drink. But over time many began to campaign for laws to prohibit any consumption of alcohol whatsoever.[6]

The push for temperance slowed during the Civil War era but gained traction when the conflict ended. The Woman's Christian Temperance Union (WCTU) was founded in Cleveland, Ohio, in 1874 following a series of "Woman's Crusades" against the saloon and the liquor traffic across the United States. Members pledged:

> I hereby solemnly promise, God helping me, to abstain from all distilled, fermented and malt liquors, including wine, beer and hard cider, and to employ all proper means to discourage the use of and traffic in the same.[7]

Under its second president, Frances Willard, the WCTU became a formidable advocate of abstinence, women's suffrage, and other popular causes. During its first five years, the organization established a network of more than a thousand local affiliates.

The Anti-Saloon League (ASL), organized in 1893 by an Ohio minister, abjured Willard's "do everything" approach to reform. The ASL would focus with laser intensity on a single issue: the prohibition of alcoholic beverages. Combining political savvy with raw electoral power, the organization was instrumental in securing adoption of the Eighteenth Amendment establishing national prohibition in 1919.[8] Prohibition was the high-water mark for the forces of abstinence, but it did not happen overnight.

Temperance advocates had long displayed their determination to reshape the nation's public attitudes and revamp its drinking laws. In 1851 Maine became the first state to prohibit the manufacture and sale of liquor, though the law was repealed five years later. By 1855 a dozen other states had enacted similar prohibition laws. When Atlanta and the rest of Fulton County, Georgia, went dry in 1885, local druggist John Pemberton bowed to temperance pressure and removed the alcohol from his popular drink, French Wine Coca. He called the reformulated beverage Coca-Cola.

Hires Root Beer appeared well positioned to benefit from the trend toward moderation. It was perhaps the best known— certainly the most publicized—of a multitude of self-styled temperance drinks. Charles Hires was no latecomer to the temperance crusade. From its introduction in 1876, Hires Root Beer had been unequivocally portrayed as a "temperance beverage." Although the word "beer" suggested otherwise, the brand's name had been coined to lure tipplers to the temperance cause. The young druggist had intended to call his newly perfected beverage "root tea" until he was dissuaded by the Rev. Russell H. Conwell, a prominent temperance advocate. Conwell, envisioning a beverage that might appeal to habitual drinkers, advised Hires to name it root beer.

The selection of "root beer" over "root tea" would prove to be a shrewd marketing decision that would enhance the drink's popularity in the long run. In the near term, however, the brand's name was destined to provoke unintended consequences that threatened its commercial success.

A "Temperance Beverage"

An 1883 trade card identified Hires Root Beer as a "delicious, sparkling and wholesome temperance drink." "All the comforts of home includes (sic) the great temperance drink, Hires Root Beer," another declared. "Temperance is promoted by Hires Root Beer," asserted an 1892 ad. "It is doing more to advance practical temperance than many people realize."[9]

Advocates of practical temperance held that alcohol use was controllable if not eradicable. They sought to curb problem drinking rather than to flatly prohibit the consumption of alcohol. Hires described himself as a proponent of this view. Of course, the term "practical temperance" was itself a fuzzy descriptor embraced by such diverse activists as moral reformers, drinking fountain manufacturers, and proponents of higher liquor taxes. Even the brewers of real beer, who supported laws to outlaw hard liquor, marched proudly under the "practical temperance" banner.

Hires' promotion of his root beer as an aid to practical temperance suggests he was aware that it contained some amount of alcohol however slight, but his coyly evocative advertising copy offered few specifics. What exactly was a "temperance drink," and what, if any, beverages was Hires Root Beer intended to supplant? The ads, of course, neglected to disclose that alcohol was a natural product of the fermentation process integral to brewing Hires at home. Curious consumers were left to interpret the meaning of "practical" and ponder how Hires Root Beer might promote temperance, practical or otherwise. In fact, Hires' product was one of the genres of so-called small beers. Long before it was scientifically understood, fermentation had been used to create these drinks of low alcohol content often brewed for home consumption. George Washington famously left to posterity his recipe for small beer. These brews were characterized by short fermentation periods that resulted in an alcoholic content far lower than that of higher octane beers consumed in taverns.

Conceivably, Hires' loudly trumpeted temperance protestations were a calculated strategy intended to boost sales among members of the burgeoning antiliquor movement. Other manufacturers, including Coca-Cola, Dr. Pepper, and Welch's Grape Juice, would follow his example by anointing their drinks as temperance beverages. Yet there seems little reason to doubt Hires' sincerity.

Like many abstainers, Hires' temperance position had religious roots. Hires grew up in a devout Baptist family. He was baptized in the Cohansey Baptist Church of Roadstown, where his father served as a deacon, and maintained his affiliation with the church as an adult. Baptists tended to be outspoken temperance advocates. Later, Hires would be drawn to another faith where many members took a similar stance, the Religious Society of Friends, known as Quakers.

Pennsylvania had been founded as a Quaker colony by William Penn. Throughout the nineteenth century, Quakers continued to occupy prominent positions in Philadelphia's business, professional, and institutional spheres. Quakerism grew out of the teachings of George Fox, a shoemaker's apprentice who believed that divine revelation was accessible to anyone. He rejected the authority of an organized clergy. By gathering in silent meeting with other believers, Fox taught, individuals could be directly influenced by God to offer vocal ministry. After suffering religious persecution in England, many Quakers immigrated to the New World. Quakers generally advocated religious freedom, nonviolence, and the abolition of slavery.[10]

A traumatic schism earlier in the century had split the Philadelphia Yearly [Quaker] Meeting. It was provoked by reformer Elias Hicks, who preached the absolute authority of the Inner Light as opposed to that of Scripture.[11] In 1827 Hicks' followers stormed out of the Arch Street Meeting House in Philadelphia. The "Hicksites" would later establish their own meeting house at Fifteenth and Race Streets, while the faction that remained at Arch Street would be labeled "Orthodox." Sociologist E. Digby Baltzell observes that wealthy and urbanite leaders and members tended to adhere to the Orthodox branch. Two-thirds of the area's Quakers would eventually join the Hicksites.[12] The schism was not fully healed until 1955.[13]

Hires felt a strong attraction toward the Quaker faith, and while living in Philadelphia, he began to attend the Race Street Meeting. Why Hires chose to associate with the Hicksite branch rather than participate in the Orthodox Arch Street Meeting is not apparent. After moving to Merion in 1894, Hires faithfully attended the Hicksite Radnor Monthly Meeting.

Quakers have no ordained clergy. As they note with pride, theirs is a religion of strong beliefs but no formal creed. Rather than taking doctrinaire positions on strong drink or other controversial issues, Quakers are encouraged to discover their own truths and act upon them.[14] Nonetheless, by the mid-nineteenth century abstinence was increasingly gaining favor among members of the Society of Friends. Both branches of Quakerism established committees in support of temperance in Philadelphia. The Hicksite Quakers appointed a Yearly Meeting Temperance Committee in 1881. The Friends' Orthodox branch worked to spread knowledge about the dangers of alcoholic stimulants through the Friends' Temperance Association, founded at about the same time.[15]

Hires frequently advocated in support of the temperance cause. In 1883 he received a note of thanks from the board of trustees of the Reformers' Gospel Temperance Union of Camden for his "elegant and instructive" lecture in behalf of temperance.[16] But as the forces of abstinence gathered strength toward the end of the century, Charles Hires, disciple of practical temperance, was confronted with the charge that his root beer was actually a "Devil's brew" in disguise.

In the early 1890s, a self-styled chemist one F. G. Minshall analyzed Hires Root Beer and determined that it contained a "high percentage" of alcohol. His findings were published in *The Voice*, a New York City publication associated with the temperance cause.[17] Although blindsided by the report, Hires wasted little time in refuting Minshall's findings and impugning his competence. After somehow determining the culprit's address, Hires boarded a train to New York City, where he personally confronted his drink's accuser. Following their meeting, Hires intemperately branded Minshall "a second-hand junk dealer with about as much knowledge of chemistry as a dog. He was totally unable to give an intelligent explanation of how he analyzed our root beer or how to discover alcohol in liquids."[18]

SCIENCE COMES TO THE RESCUE

Next Hires commissioned a scientific analysis of his root beer by a reputable chemist of his own choosing. Dr. Henry Leffman, M.D. and Ph.D., was professor of chemistry and toxicology at the Women's Medical College of Pennsylvania and chemist to the Dairy and Food Commission of Pennsylvania. After several analyses, the learned academic determined that Hires' brew contained just a trace of alcohol—half the amount present in a loaf of homemade bread.[19] "I am forced to the conclusion," he reported, "that the results published by Mr. Minshall are grossly erroneous and . . . that the fermentation in Hires Rootbeer does not develop in it any of the qualities of an intoxicating beverage."[20] Hires called the public's attention to Leffman's analysis by presenting his findings verbatim in a series of newspaper ads. These ads may have represented the earliest use of scientific test results by an advertiser.[21]

Armed with the professor's analysis, Hires demanded that *The Voice* and other publications that had reported Minshall's claims print retractions and apologize for their error. Those who refused were threatened with libel suits. Familiar with Hires' reputation for dogged pursuit of root beer imitators in the courts, several publishers agreed to rescind their reports. After all, a company press release righteously concluded, "Mr. Hires and the Company are all practical temperance men and would not manufacture anything that would promote intemperance."[22] Hires' generous advertising expenditures in newspapers across the nation may also have encouraged the publishers' *mea culpas*.

The company took pains to assuage the concerns of temperance advocates as part of a verbose four-page insert in *Harper's Weekly* explaining and defending its product. "Hires has nothing whatever in common with the beer that is drunk over sloppy bars and behind slatted doors," readers were reassured. "Hires' Rootbeer has been analyzed time and again by the best chemists in the country and under all conditions has always been pronounced a strictly temperance and nonalcoholic drink."[23]

Another ad adroitly spun the drink's defense as a moral allegory with errant accuser recanting in the face of indisputable evidence:

> Some years ago an expert shoemaker thought he discovered a good deal of alcohol in Hires Root Beer and rose up to tell the public of his find. When called upon to prove it, he found he was mistaken, and took his "discovery" back. The most expert chemists in the country have repeatedly analyzed Hires Root Beer, and the largest quantity of alcohol found was one-fifth of one percent. This is about one-half as much as contained in bread; so the most scrupulous abstainer can enjoy Hires Root Beer himself and recommend it to others as an agreeable and healthful substitute for the strong drink which he opposes.[24]

Hires might have heaved a hard-earned sigh of relief. His timely response to Minshall's meretricious attack seemed to have blunted any lasting damage to root beer sales. Hires could ill afford complacency, however. Although Minshall's allegations had been quashed, they refused to die. A short time later his charges would be resurrected by a more formidable opponent, Hires' erstwhile ally in the war against demon rum, the WCTU.

In 1895 the WCTU proclaimed that root beer was an alcoholic drink and called for a nationwide boycott of Hires Root Beer. The ladies explained their reasoning in the organization's newspaper, *The Union Signal*. Without referring to Hires by name, the article described his root beer's ingredients—sugar, warm water, yeast, and bottled extract—and quoted directions for its preparation almost identical to those included with Hires' distinctive yellow extract box. After repeating its mantra opposing "the use of and traffic in all distilled, fermented and malt liquors," the WCTU pointed out that the fermentation process used to brew root beer inevitably resulted in the production of alcohol:

> The chemist has taught us that the fermentation of sugar, yeast and water produces alcohol. In the manufacture of root beer there is the fermentation of these substances, flavored with herb extracts; there must, therefore, be alcohol

in it, varying in quantity according to the time it stands before using.

This is simply a recipe for making alcohol and all temperance people ought to recognize it as such. Analyses of the drink by unprejudiced and well-qualified and equipped analysts have shown that the proportion is often larger than in malt beers, which no religious or literary periodical would in these days of temperance enlightenment think of advertising.[25]

Inexplicably, the WCTU had endorsed Hires Root Beer two years earlier as a "temperance product" during a Women's Congress held in connection with Chicago's 1893 World's Columbian Exposition.[26]

"Beer" Raises Red Flag

Fervent temperance advocates reasoned that any drink labeled "beer" must be dangerously alcoholic. The WCTU's condemnation of root beer may have been overwrought, but its contention that the drink contained alcohol was not baseless. Fermentation generated the carbon dioxide bubbles that imparted the fizz in home-brewed Hires. As the ladies understood, however, carbon dioxide is but one of the products created when sugar is metabolized by yeast. The other is alcohol. French chemist Antoine Lavoisier had diagramed the process in the eighteenth century: $C_6H_{12}O_6$ [glucose (sugar)] $\rightarrow$ 2 C_2H_5OH [ethanol (alcohol)] + 2 CO_2 [carbon dioxide].[27]

Many Americans viewed alcohol more pragmatically before it was demonized by temperance advocates. Farmers, for example, knew they could produce drinks with alcohol percentages ranging from low (root beer and other so-called small beers) to moderate (table beers) to high (tavern-style beers). Rather than being an all-or-nothing property, a drink's alcohol content fell along a spectrum and was controlled by its brewer.[28]

As a chemist Hires was doubtless aware that his root beer contained some amount of alcohol. His recipe for its preparation was calculated to minimize this amount. He advised home brewers to bottle the drink "at once" after mixing the ingredients. This precaution helped control the formation of alcohol. After corking the bottles, preparers were instructed to set them in a "warm place" for several hours until they became effervescent, then to store them in a "cool place."

In his guide to preparing homemade beverages, history professor and passionate home brewer Stephen Cresswell notes that bottling root beer within an hour of mixing yeast with sugar yields a "virtually nonalcoholic drink."[29] However, it is likely that some home brewers, either by accident or intent, may have increased the alcohol level by allowing their batches of root beer to ferment longer. A degree of vagueness in Hires' directions also may also have resulted in batches with a higher alcohol content. For example, the terms "warm" and "cool" were subject to interpretation. Chilling the brew would have stopped fermentation, but storing it just slightly below room temperature may have slowed but failed to fully stop the process. This might have increased the drink's alcohol content while also overcarbonating it and creating a geyser when the cork was removed.[30]

David B. Fankhauser, chemistry professor and root beer aficionado, measured the alcohol in a batch of root beer he prepared by using extract and a brewing method quite similar to that recommended by Hires. He reported an average alcohol content of about 0.4 percent.[31] One would have to drink a dozen twelve-ounce bottles of this brew to imbibe an amount of alcohol equal to that of a similar-sized container of 5 percent beer.

The WCTU's call for a national root beer boycott was greeted wryly by a skeptical press. "Many newspapers have treated the matter as a joke, but the WCTU is entirely serious," observed the *Boston Globe* in reporting on a boycott motion at the Massachusetts chapter's convention.[32] As an article in the *Denver Evening Post*, "Against Root Beer, Temperance Women Place the Ban on It," put it: "The much-advertised and heretofore thought-to-be harmless root beer has been declared an instrument of the devil by the Women's Christian Temperance Union and hereafter it will be classed by that organization in the same category with hofbrau, dogshead, whiskey sours, Manhattan cocktails and other unmentionable concoctions."[33]

"Is Root Beer 'Insidious'?" asked an editorial in the *New York Times.* The tone of the piece betrayed a degree of impatience with strident advocates of temperance. The newspaper quoted a delegate to a Brooklyn WCTU convention bemoaning "the insidious inroads of root beer into Christian families." The delegate had excoriated root beer as part of "the devil's plan to induce people to drink alcoholic drinks without knowing it," declaring that "liquor men could not themselves devise a better plan for propagating the insidious liquor habit." She cited the redoubtable F. G. Minshall as her source for this information.[34]

The *Times* responded in mock dismay: "The chief manufacturer and advertiser of root beer sets forth pictorially that it is fit for babes and depicts a mother in the act of commending a poisoned chalice of it to the lips of a child. If it be indeed 'insidious,' what a horrible malefactor the man must be!"[35]

TIMES DISCOVERS "MISSING LINKS"

However, the same *Times* editorial continued, "there seem to be some missing links in the chain of evidence that leads to this frightful conclusion. We have never read a harrowing account of the interior of a root-beer drinker's home. We have never even seen a colored plate representing the awful ravages wrought by root beer on the coats of the human stomach. We have never heard of a man, woman or child who had succeeded in getting tipsy on root beer, although tramps have been driven for stimulation to *eau de cologne* and Worcestershire sauce. The Legislature ought really to have some evidence before basing enactments on the unsupported Minshall and the delegate to the WCTU."[36]

Life Magazine, a weekly humor publication, published a verse titled "A Limit" by a wag named Tom Masson:

> *O Ladies fair, desist, I pray! You know not what you do. You must have viewed a mouse the day root beer you did taboo.*
> *Of rum I could not touch a drop and champagne was as bad. To gin I had to put a stop—root beer was all I had.*
> *I've felt its subtle poison steal up to my eager brain. And now to know I cannot feel its deadly power again!*

To know each morn as I awake with systems out of gear that
I may no more hope to take my cocktail of root beer!
   This is too much! If I must drag myself intemperate down, O
ladies on a root beer jag pray let me paint the town.[37]

Hires was stunned and angered by the WCTU's call for a boycott. But he stubbornly refused to reformulate or rename his product in the face of the organization's assault. Some have speculated
that he considered forsaking his signature drink altogether at this
time to concentrate on the production of condensed milk.[38] It is
true that he had been planning to enter the condensed milk business in a major way (see Chapter 8), But it was not in his nature
to retreat or shrink from what he considered an unjust attack.
What's more, the future of his lucrative soft drink business was
at stake.

Mounting a defense, however, presented a tactical challenge.
Hires did not attempt to directly confront his accusers, as he had
the hapless Minshall, or to strong-arm the press into recanting
its reports. He could ill afford to directly dispute or denounce an
organization as large and powerful as the WCTU without risk
of alienating its members or their sympathizers. And, after all,
he shared the organization's basic aspirations when it came to
curbing strong drink.

Instead, Hires counterattacked with a renewed advertising
blitz stressing the nonalcoholic nature of his root beer. Neither
the WCTU nor its boycott campaign was mentioned. He blan-
keted the media with ads in which Professor Leffman reiterated
his findings: "I have no hesitation saying that Hires Rootbeer
does not belong to the class of Intoxicating beverages. It be-
longs rather in the class of soda water, or aerated waters, in all
of which the active ingredient is dissolved carbonic acid."[39]

Hires beseeched the public to "note carefully the moderate
language of the man of science who knows exactly what he is
about, and so wastes no time or words in scolding those who
through mistaken methods have said otherwise. The refreshing taste of Hires Root Beer comes from carbonic acid gas—not
alcohol—and when that escapes, there is nothing left to be de-
sired. This is not the case with alcoholic beverages."[40]

An advertisement in *The Interior*, a Presbyterian journal, assured the faithful that "a multitude" of temperance advocates regarded Hires Root Beer as a temperance drink: "Anyone who states that Hires Rootbeer is not a temperance drink either willfully misrepresents the fact or has not investigated the subject in an impartial fashion. The leading chemists say so without qualification and stand ready to prove their assertion."[41] The company displayed measured patience toward benighted souls who continued to harbor doubts in the face of such irrefutable evidence. The ad concluded with an appeal to their conscience: "Hires Rootbeer is a strictly temperance drink. Its manufacturers are strictly temperance people. They ask in the name of the 'golden rule' for fair treatment from people of the same kind."[42]

Hires was not the only beverage maker whose branding decision would later prove troubling. Just as "beer" suggested inebriation to some skeptics, the first word in Coca-Cola's hyphenated moniker evoked visions of drug addiction. "Coca" did indeed refer to the cocaine-bearing coca leaf, one of the drink's early ingredients. When Coca-Cola was introduced in 1886, cocaine enjoyed a reputation as a beneficial drug. Sigmund Freud termed it a "magical" substance in an 1884 paper.[43] He promoted cocaine as a tonic to cure depression and sexual impotence.

Advertisements for Coca-Cola touted the "invigorating properties of the coca leaf" and promised that the drink would relieve "fatigue that comes from over-working or over-thinking" and put "vim and 'go' into tired brains and weary bodies."[44] Coca-Cola's cocaine content stimulated its early sales as well; some patrons even began to request "a dope" when ordering the drink.[45]

However, as cocaine's less beneficial effects began to be recognized, Coca-Cola was hard-pressed to defend the presence of even a trace of the drug in its drink. Following the turn of the century, the federal government was reporting yearly cocaine-related deaths in the thousands. By 1914 the drug's nonmedical use was effectively banned. Coca-Cola Co. removed the cocaine from its coca leaves in 1903, but the company was loath to jettison half of its popular brand name.[46] The term "coca" would continue to feed the suspicions of regulatory agencies and other skeptics over the years.

HIRES EXPANDS BUSINESS DESPITE BOYCOTT

Despite the WCTU boycott, Hires remained optimistic about the future of his root beer business. In 1896 he announced plans to relocate his manufacturing facility to a sprawling industrial building along the Delaware River waterfront.[47] The plant had ready access to both a railroad line and a shipping port on the river. The building was also spacious enough to allow Hires to begin experimenting with the manufacture of condensed milk.[48] The company's executive offices in the Philadelphia Bourse would be moved to the factory complex the following year.

To raise the funds necessary to expand his manufacturing capacity, Hires returned to the capital market. Six years earlier he had obtained $300,000 in an initial stock offering while incorporating the Charles E. Hires Co. The company now offered investors additional stock valued at $200,000. The stock prospectus, *A Profitable Investment*, painted a revealing if effusive picture of the company's ambitious growth plans.[49]

"Hires Rootbeer can fairly claim to be an established commercial success," the company declared. "It is the most popular and widely advertised article of its kind in the world. The company has spent in advertising over $2 million. The world-wide reputation which this outlay has secured, together with the improved business conditions now universally indicated, leads it to expect for its product even greater demand and popularity."[50]

The prospectus proudly noted Hires' debt-free balance sheet and its dividend, which had averaged more than 9 percent a year since the company's incorporation. After recounting the growth of root beer sales from a few hundred packages in year one to 400,000 by year ten, it declared: "The last eight years, however, witnessed still greater and more rapid growth, the figure going upward sometimes in jumps of 50 percent, until the sale last year was over 3,500,000 packages, the equivalent of 17,000,000 gallons of Hires rootbeer."[51]

Hires depicted its physical plant as the "most completely equipped for the expeditious and economical transaction of its business." The company noted that over three acres of floor space were supplied with steam power and fitted with every appliance

for the best as well as most rapid work. At the height of the season, three to four hundred "hands" were employed in the works
and seventy-five in the office and on the road. An additional
twenty-five to thirty staff were said to be deployed in a "thoroughly equipped printing and advertising department."[52]

Amid its welter of facts and hyperbole, the prospectus boasted of the company's new carbonated beverage bottling plant. Its
"patent[ed] automatic bottling machinery" was capable of filling 3,500 dozen bottles of root beer a day, according to the prospectus.[53] The state-of-the-art device was manufactured by the
American Soda Water Co., a trust formed by the nation's largest
makers of soda apparatus in 1891. Reputed to be the world's largest for the production of soda water, the machinery boasted three
carbonators mounted in battery with two huge soda generators.[54]

The company was clearly impressed with this new equipment. "This production capacity will allow Hires to reduce prices
enough to make Hires' Root Beer Carbonated competitive with
'bottled lager,'" the prospectus confidently predicted.[55] It is unlikely these corporate aspirations caused concern among the
brewers of lager beer.

However, the company's tenure on the Philadelphia waterfront would be short-lived. The city was also growing and Hires'
root beer plant stood in the path of progress. Between 1897
and 1900 the city would widen Delaware Avenue, its port-side
thoroughfare, from 50 to 150 feet.[56] Stephen Girard, a wealthy
merchant and philanthropist who died in 1831, had willed the
original funds for the roadway's improvement to the city.

Rather than relocating to another site in Philadelphia, Hires
decided to pack up his plant and move to the country. In 1899
he began construction of a new root beer factory adjacent to the
condensed milk plant he was constructing in a former flour mill
in rural Malvern. The root beer factory would open the following
year, consolidating Hires' enterprises on a single site. The plant's
relocation from Philadelphia does not rank among Hires' more
astute business decisions, however. Within five years he would
move the root beer factory back to Philadelphia after the city's
advantages as a shipping point for its products became evident.

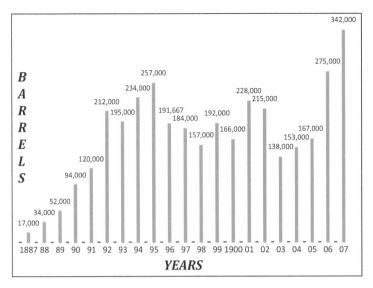

Figure 6.1 Hires Root Beer Sales, 1887–1907

Note: Root beer extract and fountain syrup represented a significant portion of Hires sales from 1887 to 1907. Thus barrels as tallied in the graph represent barrel equivalents—that is, the liquid volume resulting when extract and syrup were converted into root beer. No information is available on the volume of the barrels represented, however, the graph provides a rough proxy for year-to-year changes in company sales.

Source: Graph derived from sales data in Hires Family Papers, Historical Society of Pennsylvania.

Expanding manufacturing capacity in 1896 just as the WCTU's boycott was beginning to exact a toll on his business was a gutsy move for Hires. As Figure 6.1 indicates, Hires Root Beer sales plunged 25 percent that year. The slide appears to have been arrested the following year when it was limited to 4 percent, but the downward trend accelerated in 1898 with a 15 percent drop. To be fair, factors unrelated to the boycott probably contributed to the sales slippage. These include the public's growing infatuation with soda fountain soft drinks as opposed to home-brewed root beer.

Hires' counterattack against the WCTU's boycott eventually paid off. In 1898 that organization decided it had had enough and called off its campaign against Hires Root Beer. In the end the ladies came to accept Hires' protestations. An item captioned "There's Alcohol, But Not Much" in the *Pharmaceutical Era* reported: "The WCTU says we may drink root beer. It has found by chemical analysis and announces that although this beverage contains alcohol, it is in such small proportions that even the most immoderate indulgence would not result in intoxication."[57] The WCTU, however, did not concede graciously. At its 1899 annual meeting in Philadelphia, the ladies declared the very term "beer" to be highly objectionable. The convention reportedly adopted a resolution that urged Hires to change the name of his root beer to "root beverage." This claim could not be verified by a search of WCTU annual meeting minutes.

Despite such continued sniping, the company's sales resumed a positive trend, with annual increases offsetting periodic declines over the next several years. Hires' swift and determined response to the boycott accompanied by widespread press and public skepticism regarding the WCTU's assertions seemed to limit any long-term harm. The evolving market for Hires' products tended as well to protect the company from future damage by zealots who deemed even a trace of alcohol in root beer intolerable. In the mid-1890s, Hires' household extract, which produced a carbonated beverage through fermentation, remained the company's major line. But in succeeding years a growing portion of Hires' production consisted of ready-to-drink Hires Carbonated in bottles and syrup for soda fountain use. Neither form of Hires Root Beer relied on fermentation to produce its bubbles.

In the long run, Hires' decision to call his drink "root beer" proved a mixed blessing. The name probably incited radical temperance advocates to mount their boycott, but Hires' choice seemed shrewd in the wake of national prohibition, which began in 1919. The word "beer" enhanced the drink's appeal among those who enjoyed real beer prior to Prohibition. And Hires' persistent claim to the title of "Great Health Drink" seemed to protect it from further damage by temperance advocates.[58]

In 1915 the growing likelihood of national prohibition emboldened the prescient entrepreneur to market a new alcohol alternative. To complement what some had characterized as its faux beer, the Charles E. Hires Co. introduced a brand of mock champagne. This so-called discovery was christened "Champanale." It was described as a combination of the "rich, unfermented juice of full ripe Niagara white grapes and grape fruit, infused with a trace of pure ginger." The company declared its new drink was stimulating, highly carbonated, and just plain "wonderful."[59] The drink's champagne pretentions were enhanced by the bottle's foil-wrapped neck and two ornate labels. The Bellevue Stratford, Waldorf-Astoria, and other fancy hotels were said to be thrilled to serve the exciting new beverage to their guests. Prestigious organizations including the Manufacturers Club and Union League drank to the excellence of Champanale and stocked it for their members. Consumers were urged to secure their supply of the bubbly in splits, pints, or quarts from their grocers and advised to serve it in champagne glasses. Curiously, the beverage was advertised as a product of Hires' subsidiary Purock Water Co., perhaps to insulate it from temperance suspicions about root beer. Whether temperance leaders hoisted flutes of Champanale to toast the enactment of Prohibition four years hence will never be known.

Throughout his battles with the forces of radical temperance, Hires' business as importer and dealer in vanilla beans, flavoring extracts, and botanicals continued to flourish. To expand this enterprise, Hires would open a branch office in the Woodbridge Building at 100 William Street, New York City, in 1907.[60] Meanwhile, another threat to the continued success of Hires Root Beer loomed. This one was self-induced.

7

Twenty Years Too Late?

B Y THE MID-1890s soda fountain sales in the United States
were bubbling to new heights. In 1895 more than fifty
thousand fountains were in service across the country.
Their mushrooming growth was transforming the soft drink
marketplace in a manner that Charles Hires had failed to fully
anticipate. Innovations including iceless fountains and automatic carbonators spurred this growth.

The American Soda Fountain Company offered the first modern counter-service fountain in 1903. These customer-friendly
units began to supplant wall fountains, which had gradually
become the industry standard after their introduction in the
1870s.[1] The soda jerk could now face the purchaser across the
counter while preparing his or her drink rather than turning his
back to draw it from a wall-mounted dispenser. The newfangled
fountain, dubbed the "Innovation," caught on quickly with retailers. They found it more efficient than the old wall units. It also
allowed faster service and increased eye contact with customers.[2]

The temperance movement also contributed to the soda
fountain surge. For example, as more men decided to switch to
soft drinks, soda fountains started to displace saloons in the
business districts of New York, Chicago, and other big cities. "Industry efforts to promote the soda fountain as an alternative to

the saloon were paying off," Anne Cooper Funderburg, author of *Sundae Best: A History of Soda Fountains*, writes.[3]

Beverage makers adapted their products to the latest fountain technology. A growing number of heavily promoted soft drink syrups drove customer demand. Coca-Cola, introduced in 1886 by Atlanta druggist John Pemberton, sold its product almost entirely in this form. Asa Candler, an astute businessman, gained control of the company after the death of its founder in 1888. He wasted little time in following Hires' example by aggressively promoting Coca-Cola through heavy advertising and coupons good for a free glass of the drink. Coca-Cola's marketing thrust not only boosted its own sales, it expanded the market for other fountain syrup producers such as Dr. Pepper and Moxie.

Thus the core soft drink market began to shift away from beverages like Hires Root Beer, mainly brewed and consumed at home, to those sipped at the drugstore soda fountain. A trade journal described the industry's metamorphosis:

> Twenty-five years ago the family gathered around and imbibed home-brewed root beer which was made with "household extract" and yeast purchased at the grocery store. Five gallons of the product were prepared at a time to be used as wanted. Today the family foregathers at the nearest drugstore and chooses from a large assortment the drinks which are prepared on the spot in exactly the quantity desired for immediate consumption. They pay more per drink, it is true, but there are no bottles to open or to rinse afterwards, no thoughts of the glassware that must be washed up and no danger of a discovery the supply is exhausted.[4]

The public's growing infatuation with Coca-Cola and other branded fountain drinks posed a threat that Charles Hires was slow to recognize. Although his root beer concentrate was by then a widely known brand, the drink had not become a significant player in the growing soda fountain trade. A number of druggists had been preparing Hires Root Beer, using the company's bottled extract, to dispense at their soda fountains. In 1884

Hires had encouraged this practice by offering pharmacies his extract in more convenient pint-size bottles.

Yet soda fountain sales remained a small part of Hires' soft drink business. Although he had also begun to sell Hires Carbonated in bottles in 1893, most of his production was still sold by grocers and pharmacists as a concentrate for home brewing. The era was marked by the growing popularity of all soft drinks as the public discovered tempting alternatives to such standards as coffee, beer, and milk. The rising tide lifted Hires' Household Extract sales as well, perhaps masking any immediate adverse impact from fountain beverages. But it seemed inevitable that surging fountain traffic would make inroads into the home-brewed beverage market. Ironically, the beverage perfected by a pharmacist laboring at his modest soda fountain was being challenged by the increasing popularity of these same devices.

"The tremendous advertising campaigns for Coca-Cola and other ready-prepared syrups began to bring the soda fountain into its own," Hires observed. "From a negligible factor, the fountain became a very serious competitor. The home brewing of root beer was driven farther and farther back into the strictly rural districts, more people lined up in front of the marble and onyx counters to drink something else."[5]

Printers' Ink agreed that while Hires' attention wandered, branded drinks had captured a significant share of the soda fountain market: "Coca-Cola, Moxie, Grape Juice, etc.—came in with the force of consumer advertising behind them, and took a large share of the soda fountain trade. The consumer stopped even calling for 'root beer' and began to demand drinks by their trade names. And all the while there was less and less demand for home-brewed refreshments."[6]

A Costly Hesitation?

Hires conceded he had been slow to change with the times. Perhaps the still healthy sales of his household extract had lulled the usually forward-thinking entrepreneur into complacency. Like Coca-Cola's Candler, whose dedication to fountain sales led him to give away the bottling rights to his drink in much of the country just as bottled beverages were gaining popularity, Hires seemed reluctant to adapt his tried-and-true home-brewed formula to the soda fountain. Hires could hardly be faulted if he had become preoccupied with another recent enterprise. Root beer was no longer the prime focus of his attention. In 1900 Hires had launched an entirely new venture, transforming an abandoned flour mill in Malvern into a condensed milk plant. Hires would rapidly expand this operation to become a major producer of canned milk (see Chapter 8).

Even after the gravity of the soda fountain challenge claimed his attention, Hires was loath to alter his manufacturing and distribution strategy. One reason was the specter of "substitution," which, as noted in Chapter 4, would plague Hires throughout his business career. Proud of his drink's pure natural ingredients, Hires was scornful of knockoffs using cheaper substitutes or coal tar–derived flavorings. At the same time, he was jealously protective of the "Hires" brand, which he had spent tens of thousands of advertising dollars to promote.

"There was a good deal of substitution going on all the time," Hires recalled. "The customer who asked for root beer at a soda fountain might get 'Hires,' but was likely to get some concoction put up by the druggist himself or by some wholesale drug house. That was not very serious (at first) because (our) soda fountain trade did not amount to much anyway."[7]

Hires feared that his increased participation in the soda fountain marketplace would give rise to even greater substitution. "How was the consumer going to know whether he was served with Hires at the fountain or with something else?" he argued. "When he bought a package of the household extract to take home, he could read the proprietor's name on the label, but there is no label on a glass of root beer at a soda fountain. Labeling glasses won't stop it. The clerk can put anything he pleases into a Hires glass. And service from a bottle is just about as bad because an unscrupulous clerk will keep the bottle under the counter where the customer can't see it."[8]

The prospect of being ripped off by duplicitous druggists and shady soda jerks was not all that gave Hires pause about plunging into the soda fountain market. He also feared that soda fountain mixtures might fail to live up to the rigorous standards of quality and consistency he had established for his root beer extract. "Indeed, I hesitated about putting a fountain syrup on the market because I felt it was necessary to the success of the drink that the syrup and soda water be mixed more accurately than the average soda clerk is accustomed to handle them," he explained.[9]

As Hires pondered whether to redirect his company's thrust from home brewers to fountain frequenters, he encountered resistance from within his company to abandoning the status quo. "When I suggested putting out a fountain syrup, I came into conflict with my own sales force," Hires acknowledged. "Their customers were the wholesale grocers and to put out a fountain syrup would be competing with our own trade. On this account I hesitated, much longer than I should have done perhaps. It was not until the season of 1905 that we put out any syrup at all."[10]

DOUBTERS PREDICT THE WORST

Doubters scoffed that Hires' delayed entry into the soda fountain market was twenty years too late and that his company's growth prospects had been irreparably damaged. "It looked as to a good many observers that the market had gotten away from us indeed," Hires recalled. "I was told more than once that it was a hopeless job to get distribution in a new field which already was plentifully supplied with 'root beers' of one kind or another. Advertising could not help me, some people said, because while it might be possible to persuade people to ask for 'Hires Root Beer' at the fountain, there was no possible way to prevent them from accepting any substitute root beer that came handy."[11]

However, Hires refused to let the skeptics discourage him. In 1905 he finally began to distribute a prepared syrup that soda fountain proprietors could combine with carbonated water to produce root beer by the glass. Hires was convinced he would not succeed by merely plunging into the crowded pool of fountain drinks with a copycat offering. He paused to analyze the soda fountain delivery system with the same concentration that he had displayed in formulating his root beer recipe. The weakest link in the vending process, Hires determined, was a lack of uniformity in the finished beverage served up by the soda jerk. Could he market a proprietary dispenser that would combine precisely measured amounts of syrup and soda water to produce a uniform mug of root beer every time? Such a device might appeal to fountain operators while allaying his own concerns over inaccurate mixing and substitution. After carefully reviewing the marketplace and the latest soda fountain technology, he concluded the answer was "yes."

Over the preceding decades, American inventors had been filing hundreds of patents to improve the soda delivery process. In fact, as early as 1864 A. D. Puffer had introduced a "magic draft" tube that allowed syrup and soda to be drawn in sequence through the same nozzle.[12] In 1904 two St. Louis inventors applied for a patent on a sophisticated soda vending device that they prosaically described as an "improved faucet for carbonated beverages." In their patent application, John J. Fitzgibbon and John M. Travis claimed their design would "effect a thorough mixture of water and syrup within the faucet without the necessity of mixing the two in the glass from which they are served, as is now generally the case." Their invention may well have inspired Hires' full-scale entry into the soda fountain market. This innovative vending system was later augmented by the addition of a nozzle that would deliver a fine stream of carbonated water independent of the premixed stream. Frank W. Calvert of Malvern, PA. applied for a patent on this improvement in 1909 and assigned the rights to his device to Charles E. Hires Co. in 1912.[13]

With his accustomed panache, Hires commissioned the manufacture of an innovative countertop dispenser. He described it as a "miniature soda fountain." A single pull of its handle would mix one part fountain syrup with exactly seven parts of carbonated water to produce a foaming mug of root beer. The beauty of the new device, in Hires' view, was its ability to draw a "perfect" glass of his root beer time after time. Precision and speed of operation would be the dispenser's biggest selling points. By exactly measuring the ingredients for each glass of root beer, it eliminated guesswork at the fountain. No longer would the operator lose money when the soda jerk used too much syrup, as was often the case. In fact, Hires' research showed that his new dispenser would produce up to forty more five-cent drinks per gallon of fountain syrup than the standard method of apportioning syrup and soda water by eye.[14]

The new dispenser also streamlined the vending process. By premixing syrup and soda water, it eliminated the normal two-step method of drawing these ingredients in sequence. It was claimed that three steins of Hires could be drawn in the time required to produce one under the traditional system. Fountain operators quickly grasped the value of providing speedier service. "Because time is money, it is just as important to get customers away from the counter as it is to get them up to it," *The Soda Fountain* pointed out.[15] Patrons were pleased as well to get their drinks more rapidly.

True to form, Hires launched a persuasive advertising campaign to broadcast the dispenser's virtues to druggists and other soda fountain operators. Orders poured in at a rate that surprised him. His initial order for the production of fifty dispensers was increased to two hundred then five hundred. Then an entire factory was engaged to keep up with the demand.[16] Hires sold the first dispensers in 1905 below his cost at $25, accompanied by twelve boldly captioned "Hires" steins. He would later raise the dispenser's price to $50 and then $75.[17]

Feedback Spurs Improvements

Hires did not take the initial success of his new dispenser for granted. He solicited feedback from fountain operators and worked to correct any reported flaws or problems. The following year he responded to complaints of excess foam by adding a settling chamber and automatic float that produced a "semi-creamy" drink.[18]

But the best was yet to come. Hires followed up with a deluxe model featuring a marble box, silvered faucet, and onyx handle. A turn of the handle to the right drew a perfect stein of root beer. A turn to the left yielded a glass of plain soda water. This was a significant innovation. It allowed purchasers of the new Hires dispenser to also serve other drinks by mixing flavoring syrups of their choice with the dispenser's stream of unflavored carbonated water. "The machine plus a few bottles of flavoring syrups was a full-fledged soda fountain in itself," it was observed.[19]

The company christened its new dispenser the "Hires Automatic Munimaker" and copyrighted the name. Some five thousand of the devices were purchased at $150 apiece.[20] Hires earned a few dollars on each unit, but his real payoff resulted from increased fountain syrup sales. Dealers who purchased a machine were obliged to sign a contract requiring the exclusive use of genuine Hires fountain syrup. The company fulsomely described the device as "a mechanism that will work and materials that will last; an apparatus wholly in harmony with the finest store fixtures. Its simplicity of operation cannot fail to appeal to everyone. It will find its place on every soda fountain."[21]

The stand-alone dispenser enabled Hires' salesmen to pitch their wares in unconventional venues, many of which lacked the capacity to prepare soft drinks in the traditional manner, such as cigar stores, poolrooms, five-and-dime stores, and recreational areas.[22] A department store reported that a single Hires Munimaker dispensed more than a thousand drinks in one day. Young Men's Christian Associations (YMCAs) proved another fertile field for placement of the device. Local branches could earn a little income by selling root beer while advancing their campaign against the liquor traffic.

Remarkably, liquor traffickers were themselves fascinated by the dispenser. One barkeep was so pleased with the Munimaker that he asked the company for an exclusive agency to sell it among saloons. He liked the machine because it earned a profit, saved the opening of bottles, and reduced the frequency of drunks.[23]

Hires continued to improve and embellish his patented dispenser. The ungainly original Munimaker evolved into a rotund countertop keg bearing a bright Hires logo. The Hires Root Beer Keg would become a familiar fixture at soda fountains throughout the country. Hires promoted the Munimaker, as he continued to call the new keg, relentlessly. "Little Leaks and Little Wastes are the Foxes that Eat into Your Profit," warned an ad to the trade adorned with images of the sly thieves. "One leak is the loss of syrup due to your not being able to accurately measure how much should be drawn into each glass. . . . The Munimaker makes such loss impossible . . . it accurately measures the syrup and soda water—does it mechanically and automatically. You simply press the lever one time in one direction and in a jiffy the stein is full of sparkling Hires." The ad maintained that such accidental leaks might reduce a fountain operator's profits by as much as $80 per barrel of syrup.[24]

The *National Druggist* hailed the success of the new dispenser: "The marvelous growth of Hires Root Beer at the soda fountain has exceeded the most sanguine expectations of even the manufacturers themselves. They attribute this rapid growth largely to the use of their patent[ed] dispensing keg, of which idea they are the originators. The two great features which have made this Keg so successful are that it dispenses Hires' Root Beer in its most delicious form and pays the dispenser a remarkably good profit. The Keg must have made a hit because nearly 2,000 of them were placed last year and the company has ordered double that quantity for 1907. . . . This Keg has ceased to be an experiment."[25]

Another virtue of the Munimaker was that it used less ice than traditional soda fountains. Before the widespread adoption of mechanical refrigeration, fountains required ice for cooling. Natural ice harvested from frozen lakes had to be carefully preserved, transported, and broken into chunks for chilling a fountain's soda pipes. Cooling was costly and labor-intensive and consigned fountain operators to the mercy of the "Ice Trust." The trust controlled prices, which soared when a mild winter reduced the supply of ice.[26] "Shut up your soda fountain during the cold weather and draw your soda thru the MUNIMAKER at a saving of many dollars for ice," Hires counseled pharmacists. "We are making HIRES' a WINTER DRINK. . . . Winter buyers get special terms."[27]

In 1907 the Charles E. Hires Co. contracted with the German firm of Villeroy and Boch/Mettlach for fine ceramic mugs in three sizes featuring an image of the well-known Hires Boy holding aloft an identical mug of root beer. These mugs were used as part of an incentive program to reward retailers based on the amount of fountain syrup they ordered.[28] Hires did not

neglect vendors who preferred to mix root beer in the traditional way. He commissioned Villeroy and Boch/Mettlach to also
produce an hourglass-shaped porcelain jar that dispensed Hires
syrup through a silver-plated plunger pump. These mugs and
dispensers, along with decorative trays and other memorabilia,
are prized by modern collectors.

Although the company's "perpetual license" required the sole
use of genuine Hires fountain syrup in its patented dispensers,
the keg proved irresistible to fraudsters. They produced beverages using spurious fountain syrups and dispensed them from
prominently labeled Hires Kegs. In 1908 Hires obtained a permanent injunction with damages against one such Massachusetts fountain operator who misused the keg.[29]

FARTHER OUT ON THE MAIN LINE

In 1908 Charles and Clara Kate sold their estate in suburban
Merion and moved their family into a large house on Buck Lane
in Haverford, another well-heeled community on Philadelphia's
Main Line.[30] Their new home, built in 1903 in the Colonial Revival style, was a bit less imposing than Melrose but still boasted sixteen rooms and four baths. Other amenities on the 1.3
acre property included a large garden and conservatory. Visitors
could reach the house via a poplar-lined driveway. The family
would manage its new $20,000 home (about $500,000 today)
with the assistance of three servants.[31]

Their planned move to a somewhat smaller house necessitated significant downsizing. The couple commissioned an auction-
eer to sell off a plethora of no longer needed household furnishings, carriages, toys, agricultural implements, décor items, and
assorted bric-a-brac. The fourteen-page sale catalog offers a
snapshot of the possessions an upper-middle-class family of the
era might accumulate.[32]

Dining room furniture included a twelve-foot-long quartered oak dining table with carved legs, a set of maroon leather-
upholstered chairs, a decorated china service for twelve, a superior
oak sideboard, an oak china cabinet with beveled French plate-
glass mirrors and doors, and a butler's tray and stand. Breakfast

room furnishings offered for sale included an extension table and upholstered chairs, walnut sideboard, child's table and chair, and a china closet complete with contents. The Kioto tête-à-tête tea set, Tokio fruit plates, Kaga teapot, and Kutani vase suggested the family's preference for oriental ceramics.

The furnishings of several upper-floor bedrooms and bathrooms were also declared surplus. Bedroom sale items consisted of various bedsteads and mattresses, marble-topped bureaus, wardrobes, chiffoniers, a walnut rolltop secretary desk, rocking chairs, reading lamps, and a Turkish prayer rug. Bathroom elements included towel racks, French plate-glass mirrors, and rugs. Fashionable décor items included paintings, an engraving (*Calling the Ferryman*), vases, rugs, clocks, and candelabra. Contents of a third-floor billiard room—a Manhattan pool table, bowling game, Crokinole table, two pillow armchairs, and a walnut bookcase full of magazines and books—were also consigned to the auction block.

The time seemed right to dispense with a variety of children's playthings. Clara, age eleven, was the youngest of the five Hires children. The brood had grown up amid an array of stimulating toys, games, and books. More than fifty were listed for sale. These included a rosewood piano and stool, a furnished "baby house," gramophone, magic lantern, violin, several cameras, rocking horses, toy trains, and an assortment of balls, bats, and tennis racquets.

Conveniently shelved in a walnut cabinet bookcase were a thirteen-volume set of Charles Dickens' works; five volumes by G. A. Henty, a prolific writer of historical fiction for children; six volumes by "Oliver Optic," a pseudonym for William Taylor Williams, author of action yarns for girls and boys; and six volumes by Edward L. Stratemeyer, whose works included *The Rover Boys*, *Bobbsey Twins*, and *Nancy Drew* series. Not unexpectedly perhaps, the children's library included an eight-volume collection of Horatio Alger's novels. The popular author of such inspirational fare as *Ragged Dick*, *Strive and Succeed*, and *The Telegraph Boy* might well have used their father as a model for one of his rags-to-riches yarns.

Perhaps the lack of space for a stable at its new abode forced the Hires family to forgo the luxury of farm-fresh milk. Its two young thoroughbred Jersey cows were offered at auction. No horses were included in the sale, though, perhaps reflecting Hires' passion for swift trotters and pacers. Whether these essential steeds would be quartered on the grounds of the family's new home or stabled nearby is unknown. However, an assortment of riding tack and equestrian equipment was open to bids, including a farm wagon, covered wagon, single and double sleighs, and various harnesses, bridles, saddles, and horse collars. A variety of farming and gardening equipment also was offered.

A FIGHT FOR MARKET SHARE

Competition intensified for the Charles E. Hires Co. as soft drink makers battled for a share of the booming market for trademarked fountain drinks. Industry attrition increased apace. "The temperance drink graveyard is quite as crowded a locality as the breakfast food graveyard," *Printers' Ink* observed. "The number of those brands which have fallen by the wayside is legion . . . The chief causes of failure have been inefficient or spasmodic advertising or lack of knowledge of trade conditions."[33]

Despite his belated decision to distribute a fountain syrup, Hires managed to escape a similar fate. His newfangled dispenser launched root beer sales on an upward trajectory reminiscent of the company's early years. The Munimaker lived up to its name for both the company and soda fountain operators. Sales volume for 1906, the first full year following the dispenser's introduction, jumped by 65 percent. The following year saw an additional increase of nearly 25 percent.[34]

Between 1904 and 1909, Hires' revenues rose by an average of 29 percent a year. And the company reported that sales were poised to "bust the traces in 1910."[35] In that year the company estimated that soda fountains dispensed 65 million servings of Hires Root Beer. This figure was fewer than 90 million claimed by Moxie and a mere fraction of Coca-Cola's 600 million, but at a nickel a mug, fountain operators would have grossed $3,250,000 from the sale of Hires Root Beer, not an insignificant amount.[36]

With the reinvigorated root beer business hitting its stride and sales from the condensed milk subsidiary breaking annual records, 1910 was indeed shaping up as a banner year for the Hires

companies. However, it would become a year of deep personal trag-
edy for Charles. Clara Kate, his devoted wife of thirty-five years,
mother of his five children, and accomplice in the discovery of his
signature drink, died. She was fifty-eight. The cause of death was
determined to be meningomyelitis, an inflammation of the spinal
cord. Mrs. Hires had suffered from the affliction for about eight
months, according to her death certificate.[37] After a funeral at the
Hires' residence, she was buried in the family plot in Westminster
Cemetery in nearby Bala Cynwyd.

Two of their children were still in their teens: Clara, thirteen,
and Charles Jr., nineteen. Hires was devastated and reportedly
spent weeks grieving while taking meals in his room.[38] Their
union had been marked by mutual admiration and affection.
Their love was expressed poetically in notes the couple ex-
changed like the following, which Charles had mailed to Clara
while he was away on business:

> *My Valentine,*
> *In absence dearest, thou art dearer still*
> *Thy voice, thy smile, thy form, thine eyes' sweet light*
> *I only know I miss you every hour*
> *Morning and noon, at evening and at night*
> *Like a ship-wrecked mariner, my days are spent*
> *Seeking a sail, a shore, a light, a sign to tell me of thy coming*
> *My heart burns to embrace thee, press my lips to thine*
> *Bathe in thy eyes glad light, hear thy sweet voice*
> *Clasp thy dear hands and bid thee welcome home*
> *Then hasten to me, make no long delay*
> *My heart of hearts cries out and bids thee "Come."*[39]

No less ardent was an affectionate "apology" that Clara composed to Charles one Christmas Eve:

> *My Dear Husband,*
> *Accept these little gifts as a small token of love. I wish it*
> *were possible to give you something more suited to the day and*
> *something to show my appreciation for all your kindness and*
> *forbearance for my many faults.*

*It seems as though your share of presents is always the least,
but I hope the share of love which I bestow with them will atone
for their lack of number.*
Faithfully yours,
Clara[40]

Hires began to lean on Emma Waln, a family friend and long-time acquaintance, for support through the difficult period following his wife's death. They shared a staunch commitment to principles of the Quaker faith. Emma belonged to a prominent Quaker family that had arrived in America with William Penn on the good ship *Welcome*. She was a teacher at Friends' Central School in Philadelphia, where some years earlier she had taught the Hires' eldest daughter, Linda.

HIRES WEDS "MISS E"

Charles and Emma's friendship blossomed. They married in 1911 at the home of the bride's aunt at 1202 Spruce Street in Philadelphia. The simple Quaker-style ceremony, attended only by a few friends and close members of the two families, was solemnized by the Society of Friends, although Charles would not become a formal member of the society until later. Following a wedding trip the couple would live at Hires' home in Haverford. He was sixty and she was forty-two. She brought social prestige to the union; he brought a substantial fortune.[41] Hires would later name the family's yacht as well as their Haverford estate *Emwal*, a contraction of Emma's first and maiden names.

Although devoted to her husband, Emma was less comfortable with his German ancestry, perhaps more of an issue in the lead-up to World War I. "She was very bitter against Germans and didn't want any German connection," Hires' grandson William recalled. "She fabricated various stories of who the Hires were. One was that they were Welsh, and another one that they were French."[42]

His marriage to "Miss E," as she was affectionately known, reinforced Hires' growing attraction to Quakerism. Although born and raised a Baptist, Hires began attending the Fifteenth

Street Friends Meeting while living in Philadelphia. After moving to Merion in 1894, Hires attended services at the Radnor Monthly Meeting, which he joined in 1915.[43] Hires also funded and participated in the restoration of the historic Merion Meeting House, where William Penn had once worshipped. The stone structure had been built in 1695 by Friends from the county of Merionethshire in northern Wales. It replaced a log cabin where the group worshipped following its migration in 1682 to join Penn in the New World.

While overseeing the restoration of the structure, Hires helped to keep the meeting alive for several years. At times he was reportedly its sole attendee.[44] In 1914 the old meeting house was reopened. Three years later Hires published a slim book about the venerable structure titled *A Short Historical Sketch of the Old Merion Meeting House*. In an endnote Hires suggested his restoration efforts had not been in vain. "The Meeting House is open Friday mornings at 11," he wrote. "For the past two years, a greatly increased interest has been taken by its members and friends. Generally, a goodly number meet to worship."[45]

Looking back several years later on the predictions of his company's impending demise, Hires expressed satisfaction that his belated move into soda fountain sales had been vindicated. "That these prognostications were unfounded is fairly evident, I think," he said, "from the fact that sales of Hires Root Beer for 1920 exceeded $5 million and by far the greater part of it consisted of fountain syrup."[46]

Like other self-made captains of industry of his era, Hires sincerely believed that anyone endowed with a strong work ethic and a will to succeed could likewise reach the winner's circle. "I have often thought when I have heard of the difficulties of a young man in getting along," he told a reporter, "that surely the reason . . . is their lack of initiative or the lack of making or seizing opportunities when they come. I think a business life is continually full of opportunities if one can grasp and utilize them."[47]

Hires Root Beer had indeed emerged as a formidable soda fountain contender. But its "reimaging," to borrow a later term, was incomplete. Hires relied on the power of ads to build the beverage into a national brand, not to mention to gain a foothold at the soda fountain. But thanks to Hires' success, root beers of various brands and recipes seemed to pop up everywhere. Some brands, such as Dr. Swett's and Barqs, could be considered legitimate competitors. Others, often of dubious ingredients and questionable quality, capitalized on Hires' advertising while tarnishing his drink's hard-won reputation. Hires vigilantly pursued imitators and substitutors in the courts (see Chapter 4). However, since 1879 generic terms such as "root beer" had been excluded from trademark protection. Root beer had become a commodity with a name that could not be defended.

Hires proposed a starkly simple solution to this predicament. He decided to stop selling root beer and reposition his soft drink as a "specialty product." The company that had spent the modern equivalent of millions of dollars to make "root beer" a household term banished it from advertising copy in 1909. Henceforth, the bottled and soda fountain versions of his signature drink would be referred to simply as "Hires." The generic term "root beer" was abruptly relegated to competing brands and the dozens of imitators and knockoff artists who had reaped unmerited benefits from Hires ads. The goal was to convince consumers to ask for "Hires," rather than accepting lesser root beers or inferior imitations.

This bold move would test whether Hires' ceaseless promotion over the years had conditioned consumers to readily connect the brand name to the generic product. There would be no identity crisis for "Hires Root Beer Extract," which the company continued to market under its historic name.

"ROOT BEER" DEEMED PASSÉ

Fountain operators as well as consumers would be required to make an adjustment. The following insertion in the *Druggists Circular* explained "What Hires Means" to the unenlightened:

> Hires' is much easier to say than "root beer" and means more to the one saying it—as well as to the white coated attendant behind the marble counter. "Root beer" may mean almost anything and sometimes means almost nothing, whereas

"Hires" means a root beer that has been made, advertised, sold, liked, come back for, and been paying a dealer profit for so many years that nobody seems to know or be able to remember when it wasn't.[48]

Whether Hires' rebranding exercise had an appreciable effect on his business is difficult to determine. There is no evidence that it hurt sales, which continued to rise. However, in 1931 the company concluded that the rebranding strategy had not worked as planned. It conceded that, irrespective of its efforts to create a specialty drink, "the majority of consumers as well as dealers still looked upon the product and spoke of it as root beer." Meanwhile, sales of competitive root beer brands had grown substantially. "Hires Root Beer" would reemerge as an advertised national brand.[49]

Hires' success at the soda fountain was accompanied by a push to increase sales of bottled root beer which he had begun producing in 1893. Soft drink makers could ill afford to ignore the steady rise in bottle sales. Between 1889 and 1909, consumption measured in twelve-ounce bottles had increased from 6.6 to 10.8 per capita, a 64 percent jump.[50]

While responding effectively to these changing consumer preferences, Hires also hedged his corporate bets. As explained in the next chapter, he had embarked on a new venture that would offer his company a degree of protection from the vagaries of the soft drink market place.

8

MILK AND SUGAR

THE CHARLES E. HIRES CO. approached the twentieth century
on sound financial footing. However, annual sales remained
volatile due to soda fountain competition and spurious at-
tacks that branded Hires Root Beer an alcoholic beverage. Hires'
spirited defense of his product had largely refuted charges of the
temperance zealots and led the WCTU to call off its ill-advised
boycott in 1898. Yet root beer sales would not exceed their 1895
high of 257,000 barrels for ten years.[1] Hires confidently issued
new company shares in 1896 to fund the expansion of his root
beer business. But the recent temperance trauma may well have
led him to prudently consider the future risks that might befall a
company that depended on a single product for most of its sales.

In any event, Hires decided to diversify his business by in-
vesting in one of his era's burgeoning growth industries—the
manufacture of condensed milk. Although it lacked the zest and
sparkle of root beer, canned condensed milk filled an important
nutritional need in this period before the home refrigerator.

The new venture would bring challenges that Hires may have
failed to fully anticipate. The condensed milk business was highly competitive, dependent on a perishable raw material supplied
by hundreds of independent producers and subject to rigorous
purity standards. The learning curve for the new enterprise
proved steeper than Hires expected. He initially lost a bundle

in its pursuit. In the long run, however, abetted by his flair for promotion and the desperate demands of a war-ravaged Europe, he managed to milk a profit from this most recent sideline.[2]

Drinking fresh milk could be risky during the nineteenth century. Cows' milk was laden with bacteria and liable to spoil within hours in summer heat. Ills contracted from contaminated milk were popularly referred to as the "milk sick," "milk poison," and "the slows." Those who avoided food poisoning still had to worry about unscrupulous suppliers who watered their milk, whitened it with chalk, or added molasses to simulate creaminess. Few options existed for storing, transporting, or preserving even the purest milk. By midcentury, inventors on both sides of the Atlantic had milk on their minds.

The most creative American was Gail Borden, a native New Yorker who, after living in Texas for a number of years, resettled in New York City. An inveterate tinkerer, Borden was celebrated for inventing a concentrated nugget of nourishment he called the "meat biscuit." One ounce of this indestructible dehydrated meat-and-flour concentrate could be brewed into a pint of nourishing soup. Borden patented his creation and set out to convince the world of its merit. A state-of-the-art model of food preservation, it won a gold medal at the Great Council exhibition in London in 1851. But Borden struggled to make a commercial success of the meat biscuit, ultimately failing when an expected government contract did not materialize.[3]

Borden's voyage to England to pick up his prize, however, had not been for naught. His attention turned to milk preservation after he witnessed infants going hungry when shipboard cows became too seasick to be milked.[4] In 1856 Borden received a patent for a vacuum condenser that removed as much as 75 percent of the water from fresh milk.[5] He sweetened the concentrated milk with sugar to reduce the growth of bacteria and preserved it in metal cans. The result was a sanitary product that could be safely stored for extended periods without refrigeration. Borden opened a factory in 1856 in Wolcottville, Connecticut, to produce condensed milk, which he later dubbed "Eagle Brand."[6] Borden set a high bar for the nascent industry, insisting that his raw milk suppliers observe strict purity standards.

Borden's condensed milk was credited with reducing infant mortality in the United States. Additional markets soon emerged. The federal government ordered large shipments of condensed milk as a field ration for Union troops during the Civil War.[7] A ten-ounce can fueled a soldier with 1,300 calories of protein, fat, and carbohydrates. With returning veterans helping to spread the word, postwar demand for the product grew.

Condensed milk signaled opportunity for Reconstruction-era businessmen. Borden's invention had turned an agricultural commodity into the raw material for a new manufacturing industry. Technology continued to improve the product and expand its scope. In 1884 Swiss-born John B. Meyenberg received a U.S. patent for preserving milk without the use of sugar.[8] His process for creating "evaporated milk" used high-pressure steam for sterilization. The dependability of evaporated milk as a safe, sterile, transportable whole-milk substitute was demonstrated by its use as a troop ration during the Spanish-American War in 1898.[9] Hires' companies would produce both varieties of canned milk—condensed and evaporated.

CONDENSED MILK PRODUCTION SOARS

A raft of competitors entered the canned milk business. U.S. production of canned milk increased nearly 400 percent between 1870 and 1880 and over 300 percent in the following decade. By 1900 production soared to 207 million pounds, a fiftyfold increase over the 4 million produced in 1870.[10] Between 1899 and 1909 more than two hundred condenseries were established, contributing to a 260 percent increase in condensed milk production according to census data. Inevitably, this lactic boom presaged a later glut of canned milk that would lead to industry consolidation.

Growth prospects for canned milk must have looked promising to Hires. He began to invest in the condensed milk business in the late 1890s. Hires produced his first batches of condensed milk at his Delaware Avenue root beer plant in Philadelphia.[11] But his ambitious plans required a more spacious facility. In 1899 he purchased a property at the corner of King and Bridge

Streets in Malvern, a borough of about a thousand residents twenty-five miles west of Philadelphia. Hires would rapidly transform the former William Penn Evans flour mill on the site into a condensed milk plant.

The production of condensed milk consumed huge quantities of fresh milk and required a convenient supply of this raw material. Hires selected Malvern as the site of his condensery after inspecting various locations in the countryside around Philadelphia. Based on his research, he declared that the finest dairies and most wholesome surroundings in the Philadelphia area existed in Malvern's Chester County and neighboring Lancaster County. The town's location on the main line of the Pennsylvania Railroad attracted him as well. The renovated mill became the first of twenty-two condenseries that Hires would establish or acquire across several states and in Canada.

The citizens of Malvern welcomed Hires warmly. "The little borough of Malvern has captured a large flourishing industry— one which will enhance not only the prosperity of the people of that municipality, but that of the farmers of the surrounding county as well," the *Daily Local News* effused.[12] "The wheels of prosperity will soon turn in our town," another journal predicted.[13] Hires had still grander plans for the sleepy village. Even before his condensed milk plant had been completed, he announced plans to construct a three-story brick building at a cost of $250,000 adjacent to the condensery.[14] The structure would house Hires' root beer factory, which he intended to relocate from Philadelphia.[15] That plant faced imminent demolition due to the city's planned widening of Delaware Avenue where it was located.[16] Hires also announced plans to purchase ten additional acres in Malvern to build housing for relocated workers.

Enticed by the prospect of hundreds of new jobs and other expected economic spinoffs, the borough contributed $1,500 of the site's $6,500 purchase price.[17] Residents objected, however, when Hires further requested the abatement of the property's real estate taxes.

The economic impact of the company's arrival reverberated throughout the town and surrounding countryside. Dozens of construction workers were hired to erect the factories and ancillary facilities that Hires would need for water treatment, shipping, and the manufacture of tin cans. Contractors geared up to build as many as seventy new houses, some commissioned by Hires for transferred employees.

The condensed milk plant itself was expected to provide up to two hundred new jobs at full capacity. To be sure, many of these would be low-wage positions filled by young women on a seasonal basis. The company used a novel approach to recruit such workers: It backhandedly promised jobs to their fathers. "We will give permanent employment in our factory to a number of able-bodied men with family of grown daughters; girls wanted at once; can make from $4 to $7 per week," a Hires classified ad read.[18]

Farmers in the vicinity increased their dairy herds to meet the plant's anticipated demand for fresh milk and received an initial bump up in price per gallon as well. "The borough of Malvern is enjoying a genuine, healthy boom and residents of this peaceful habitation are consequently contented and happy," the local newspaper opined. "The Hires Root Beer and milk condensing plants are of a much greater magnitude than any one contemplated and have already created increased business in all lines of trade."[19] The Pennsylvania Railroad announced the construction of a new freight depot at Malvern to meet increased shipping demand.[20]

What was good for Hires was hailed as good for Malvern. Boosters predicted the boom would double the town's population. Their cheers drowned out the reservations expressed by a handful of dissenters. Three residents questioned whether a producer of root beer, a beverage containing alcohol, should be so warmly welcomed. They were branded as "unpatriotic to the interests of the town."[21]

Malvern Condensery Opens

The condensed milk plant opened in July 1899 to the delight of townsfolk and the small army of farmers who had signed contracts to supply Hires with raw milk. The contracts required the dairymen to deliver sweet, pure, unadulterated milk with no preservatives to the condensery. Hires reserved the right to inspect their herds and barns for sanitary conditions. Prices would be based on the butterfat content of the milk and the time of year.[22]

Company officials optimistically predicted that the plant would process forty thousand or more quarts of fresh milk per day at full capacity.[23] However, start-up glitches dogged the operation. Initial production was low because of delays installing the necessary machinery. Residents who queued at the factory seeking work were told to return in a few weeks; milk that could not be processed was shipped to Philadelphia. The plant's initial workforce numbered about thirty, many fewer than anticipated. This included a number of young women who were assigned to solder the sixteen-ounce cans in which the factory's production would be shipped.[24]

Once the start-up snafus were resolved, however, production revved up rapidly. The month the plant opened, Hires received sizable government contracts for condensed milk for shipment to armed forces in the Philippines and Cuba.[25] American troops continued to occupy these former Spanish possessions following the Spanish-American War. Within six months, the plant reported it was processing twenty thousand quarts of raw milk a day and projected an increase to fifty thousand quarts.[26] Enterprising farmers established daily routes to collect milk from their neighbors for delivery to the Hires condensery, but a number of suppliers preferred to deliver milk using their own wagons.[27] At times King Street was all but jammed with horse-drawn wagons and, in the winter, sleighs. More distant dairymen shipped their milk by rail.[28]

The Hires Condensed Milk Company was incorporated in February 1900 with a capital of $500,000.[29] A month later the first whistle sounded at the new Hires Root Beer factory, which was expected to employ an additional two hundred workers. Hires assigned his brother William to manage the plant.

But as all honeymoons must end, relations between Hires and the area's farm community began to sour. The main issue of contention was the price that Hires offered the dairy farmers who supplied raw milk to his condensery. Indeed, the dairymen were grateful to Hires for providing a new market for their milk. His initial price—nearly 4 cents per quart—had exceeded that offered by Philadelphia creameries. But once the plant's supply seemed secure, the company proposed to reduce the price it paid for raw milk and to impose stricter sanitary rules on the dairymen.

"Very much dissatisfaction is reported . . . among the farmers supplying the Hires plant at Malvern with milk," the local press reported. The company's proposed contract fixed the price of milk for the summer at 1 cent per pound, the equivalent of 2.5 cents per quart, and provided that all dairies be inspected by a vet-erinarian once a month. It also specified that milk tainted with garlic would be rejected, and that the company would not be lia-ble for milk shipments that did not meet the plant's standards.[30]

Farmers complained that the proposed price reduction, com-bined with the cost of implementing new sanitary requirements, would wipe out their profits. Some declined to ship their milk to Hires; others hinted at a strike. Dairymen dissatisfied with Hires' proposed changes met to rally support. Letters to the editor re-flected a spirited debate between the company and dairymen, spiked with such terms as "agitators" and "greedy corporation."

Charles and William Hires agreed to meet with a committee of the dissidents. But the proprietor was unyielding. He told the farmers that the price reduction was necessary to keep the Mal-vern plant competitive with Borden's and other New York con-denseries. He refused the farmers' request to increase his fresh milk price or to change any other provision of the proposed contract.[31] Hires described some of the committee members as "agitators of business" akin to labor organizers. He declared that the dissident dairymen did not represent the broader supplier community.[32] Whether the protesters were agitators or merely financially pinched farmers seeking a better deal was a matter of perspective. But Hires was right about one thing: His vocal opponents lacked broad support among their fellow dairymen.

The protesters retreated, grumbling about a possible strike and threatening to seek new markets for their milk. However, the group's leaders failed to persuade enough of their fellow farmers to withhold their milk from the Hires condensery. An account of their efforts was headlined "The Farmers as Strikers

Are Not a Success."[33] Ultimately, a few of Hires' suppliers managed to find other markets for their milk. Many more, it seemed, grimaced while signing the new contract and continued to deliver their milk to the Hires plant.

Neighbors Charge Hires with Pollution

The condensery's environmental impact raised other concerns in the surrounding rural community. A West Whiteland Township woman asked a court to enjoin Hires from polluting a stream that ran through her property. Several others threatened similar actions to stop the firm from fouling creeks and groundwater with the plant's "milk refuse." Hires heeded their complaints. The condensery installed a new filtering plant to fully clean its waste water before discharging it.[34]

The company proved less understanding when a dozen "bright girls" took a Saturday holiday without permission during the condensery's busy season. The circus was in town. Their unsympathetic manager fired the lot of them when the women reported for work on Monday.[35]

In August 1900 the company began work on a separate factory to manufacture the tin cans essential for the shipment of condensed milk. Across the industry, machine-made cans were beginning to replace those laboriously fabricated by hand. The early machines produced about sixty cans per minute.[36] The company alerted dairymen that it would need even more raw milk once the can factory came online.[37]

Although by now something of a hard-nosed businessman, Hires recognized the need to assuage lingering resentment stemming from his confrontation with the farmers. He proceeded to awe the community with a lavish reception aimed at mending relations with his suppliers. On a Saturday in late September, farm wagons carrying more than a thousand dairymen and their families clogged the roads leading to Hires' Malvern condensery. Four large hacks waited at the depot to transport those who arrived by train. The guests were invited to tour the plant before assembling on the third floor, where pretty young women in "Sunday gowns" guided them to tables set with "the daintiest linen, glistening china and a glittering silver service." After their fill of oysters, raw or broiled, guests feasted on chicken salad and croquettes, salmon, lobster, rolls, coffee, ices, and mixed cakes. An orchestra from Philadelphia offered classical selections interspersed with ragtime airs. The affair set the root beer magnate back around $2,000, according to press estimates.[38]

Hires' welcoming remarks may have struck some guests as disingenuous, considering their recent altercation over milk pricing. He thanked them warmly for attending and demonstrating their faith in his company. "For if I cannot have the confidence of a man, I would rather not do business with him," he observed. Hires conceded that "the brotherhood of man and the duty we owe to one another" is frequently overlooked in the hurly-burly of life and the pursuit of the almighty dollar. The honorable Thomas S. Butler, the district's congressman, praised the company for locating its plant in Malvern. He was followed at the podium by Hires' longtime friend Reverend Russell H. Conwell, who spoke for twenty minutes in his familiar "electrifying style," and a local farmer who rambled on about the superior quality of the county's milk. The event appeared to achieve its sponsor's purpose. "The farmers went and saw and were satisfied," the *Daily Local News* reported. "They ate and drank and listened to music and speeches, thus delighting in all that was pleasant."[39]

With the dairy community more or less placated, a steady supply of raw milk seemed assured. By November 1900 the plant was again processing twenty thousand quarts of milk per day. But difficulties involving another vital liquid would soon bedevil condensed milk operations. Dairymen were shocked by a letter from the company in January 1901. Due to a lack of sufficient water to process their milk, Hires was halting purchases until further notice. The condensing process required twenty-five gallons of water to produce one gallon of condensed milk. But the wells and springs that supplied the Hires plant had run low due to a drought. The Borough of Malvern initially supplied Hires with enough water to take up the slack, but later turned off the tap to maintain its own reserves for fighting fires.[40]

In his letter to farmers, Hires invoked a clause in the standard supplier contract that allowed the company to cease purchases if manufacturing was hindered or delayed by "an accident of any kind." The company said it was digging a new deep well, and purchases would resume once water was found.[41] Dairy farmers, required to rapidly find new buyers or dump their milk, were understandably unsympathetic to the company's plight. They questioned whether the failure to plan for an adequate water supply could be construed as an accident.

Spoiled Milk and Spring Water

Suppliers who ignored Hires' warning and shipped their milk by rail to the plant saw much of it unceremoniously left to spoil on the station platform.[42] To absorb some of the excess milk supply, the company installed separators and began producing butter at a rate of three hundred pounds a day.

Hires assured farmers that the condensery would soon have enough water to resume regular operations: "Two gangs of men are at work on our well, boring night and day, at an expense of $5 to $6 a foot."[43] However, finding a reserve water supply proved challenging. After seven weeks the drillers had bored an eight-hundred-foot dry hole. Five months later, after failing to find water at a thousand feet, the company decided to drill in another place.[44]

The drought eventually eased, and the plant was able to begin condensing milk again. However, turning the fresh milk spigot back on required some convincing. Dairymen who "were dumped last spring" when Hires stopped accepting their deliveries declared themselves "chary of starting again."[45]

The restoration of the condensery's water supply inspired Hires to plunge into another enterprise. In 1902 the company began to market a line of bottled spring and distilled water. As noted in Chapter 3, the distribution of bottled water had predated the nation's independence. Naturally carbonated spring water was bottled by the Saratoga Mineral Water Company of Saratoga Springs, New York, as early as 1772. The Rickers of Poland Springs, Maine, introduced another popular brand. That family began to commercially market the bottled water enjoyed by guests at its fashionable Gilded Age resort. Improvements in glass technology and bottling techniques coupled with concerns about the safety of municipal water supplies fostered the bottled water industry's growth during the nineteenth century.

A natural spring on the company's Malvern property was the first source of its branded commercial water, a former employee recalled.[46] It was aptly named "Malvern Spring Water." Later Hires would purchase a bottling plant at Colonial Springs in nearby Valley Forge and adopt the brand name "Purock" for his water. The springs had been supplying pure water to area residents since Revolutionary War soldiers had filled their canteens there. The sale of bottled Purock water for home and office consumption became another profitable Hires sideline business. The venture led synergistically to a line of branded water coolers, later manufactured for Hires by the Frigidaire Division of General Motors. No fewer than 521 prominent Philadelphia physicians endorsed the use of water cooled to an even temperature through the Purock-Frigidaire Sanitary Cooler, according to Hires ads. One of the doctors purportedly termed Hires' "even temperatured drinking water" a refreshing form of "preventive medicine."[47]

Purock helped the company's cash flow by evening out the seasonality of root beer sales. An earlier attempt to promote year-round root beer consumption by suggesting that Hires was delicious "served hot" had met with a decidedly cool consumer response.[48]

With water again flowing freely, condensed milk output at the Malvern plant accelerated. In March 1903 a record thirty-four thousand quarts of raw milk were processed in a single day.[49] Production schedules of the milk and root beer plants were complementary. Condensed milk volume tended to peak in the cooler months and drop off during the summer. Summer was the busiest season for root beer, when hourly workers could count on overtime to keep up with demand through July. Root beer production all but ceased during the fall.

A disquieting rumor began to circulate in Malvern in the summer of 1904. After making root beer there for four years, the Charles E. Hires Co. had decided to pull up stakes again and move that operation back to Philadelphia. By the end of August, local reports indicated workers at the plant had begun preparations to relocate.

"It is said the reason for making the change is that Philadelphia is more convenient as a shipping point and that after trying the experiment in Malvern for some years, the managers have found they can work more satisfactorily in the city," the local newspaper explained.[50] In this rail-dependent era it seemed evident that doing business in the big city was in many respects more convenient. Hires had sited his condensery in rural Malvern to reduce shipping costs due to the proximity of dairy farms, its major suppliers. This made economic sense. But the relatively remote location was not as advantageous for the manufacture of root beer. Raw materials such as sugar and flavorings had to be shipped twenty-five miles from Philadelphia. Much of the factory's finished production, which by then included bottled root beer, would make the return trip to Philadelphia for transshipment throughout the country. The move was also motivated by the city's more abundant labor pool. Hires relocated his root beer factory to a plant on North Broad Street in Philadelphia.

Hires' condensed milk operations continued to thrive in Malvern. Fortunately for the town, the growing volume of condensed milk cushioned the economic impact of losing the root beer factory. Strong demand in domestic and overseas markets was requiring the company to hire extra workers, raise the price it paid for raw milk, and canvass area farmers to increase supply. Hires recycled the idle root beer factory as part of the condensery.[51]

"MILK FAMINE" FEARS ALLAYED

Hires introduced his condensed milk to the public with a series of clever ads. Although reminiscent of his historic root beer launching blitz, the milk campaign was more laid back. Unlike root beer, a discretionary purchase that required a vigorous sales pitch to entice consumers, condensed milk fulfilled a basic dietary need. This was especially true for mothers of young children, who were becoming increasingly enamored with the product's advantages. A less hard-edged and repetitive sales campaign was in order. Some Hires ads even injected a touch of humor.

One ad, for example, assured consumers that, regardless of winter blizzards, they need not fear a "Milk Famine." "Dairymen may not get to the railroads; trains may fail to reach the city; milkmen may not come to your house. But you can get Hires Condensed Milk at your grocer's." Another ad enumerated the virtues of the best milk money can buy: "Richest in butterfat and nutritive properties. A 12-cent can diluted makes two quarts of rich, sweet wholesome milk—for the baby, for the table, for cooking."[52] The curious were whimsically invited to write for an illustrated booklet explaining *How the Cow Became Sacred in India*. Hyperbole, while less frequent, was not abandoned. "Better Than Cream," declared a series of ads that maintained the Hires product as far superior to cream and "city milk with its frequent impurities and adulteration."[53]

Hires milk brands included Silver Spoon, Square, Gold, and Blue Ribbon as well as Hires Condensed Milk. Condensed milk ads synergistically reminded consumers that it was produced by the maker of the "celebrated Hires Root Beer."

Hires dusted off a once-failed promotional gimmick to boost sales. Buyers were offered a variety of gifts in return for condensed milk labels. The company had earlier offered premiums for trademarks cut from root beer extract boxes, but the promotion had fallen flat. "I found that on a seasonable product the premium interest did not carry over from one season to the next," Hires explained. "So I switched the premium offer to the condensed milk business, where it works splendidly."[54] Ads urged milk buyers to save the labels for free premiums. To promote this scheme, the company introduced "Premium" brand condensed milk. A premium redemption store was opened in Philadelphia.

Despite extensive advertising, Hires' strategy for increasing his share of the condensed milk market differed from the model used to expand his root beer business. Instead of plowing all his profits back into advertising, Hires expanded the milk business through acquisition and consolidation. He purchased several companies that operated a total of twenty-two canned milk plants in the dairy regions of New York, New England, Michigan, and Canada.[55] They included the Ithaca, Hudson, and Clover Farm Condensed Milk Companies of New York, the Federal Packing Co. of Vermont, the Lake Odessa and Page Milk Companies of Michigan, and the Maple Leaf Condensed Milk Co. of Canada.[56]

Hires is credited with pioneering contributions to the science of condensing milk. Drawing on his knowledge of chemistry and pharmacy, he was able to reduce the risks of contamination during the canning process and extend the shelf life of the finished product. Consumers were thus assured of healthier and longer-lasting canned milk.[57]

DOMESTIC PRODUCTION DOUBLES

Domestic consumption of condensed milk more than doubled during the first decade of the twentieth century.[58] World War I, which began in Europe in 1914, provided an even bigger bonanza for Hires and other domestic producers. European milk supplies were seriously disrupted by the conflict. Huge amounts of condensed milk were exported by U.S. companies as field rations for the Allied armies. Fifty new American condenseries were built to meet wartime needs.

Philadelphians' initial reaction to the war in Europe, like President Wilson's, was marked by neutrality in thought and action. Sentiment for the Allies grew after Germany invaded Belgium. But even after a German U-boat sank the British liner *Lusitania* in 1915 with twenty-seven Philadelphians aboard, few cries for war were heard.[59] This detached view of the conflict would not last; the United States entered the fray in 1917. As thousands of their sons boarded Europe-bound troop ships, some civilians conjured images of German spies and enemy schemes on the home front. The city school system elected to stop teaching German, and sauerkraut was renamed "liberty cabbage." One far-fetched rumor depicted a condensed milk famine, with enemy agents buying up all available supplies in a plot to starve American babies.[60] Whether this canard increased sales of Hires milk is unknown.

The city's industries shifted into high gear to meet military needs. A rapidly constructed shipyard at Hog Island employed thirty thousand workers and by the armistice was launching a new ship every four working days. The Baldwin Locomotive Works at Broad and Spring Garden Streets rolled out more than five thousand locomotives as well as producing artillery shells and gun mounts. Ford Motor Co. fabricated steel helmets in its ten-story plant at Broad Street and Lehigh Avenue.

In addition to accelerating canned milk production, Hires began to manufacture instant coffee and cocoa to supply the armed services.[61] Instant coffee gained attention after David Strang, a New Zealander, patented a process for dehydrating brewed coffee in 1889.[62] The Hires company's wartime coffee production effort was recognized in a citation issued by the War Department in 1920. It congratulated Hires for rapidly developing a new method of producing soluble coffee and for furnishing its entire output to the army.[63]

The European-based Nestlé and Anglo-Swiss Condensed Milk Co. became a major buyer of the output of Hires and other American firms. The company had a contract to supply the British government with condensed milk as part of the war effort. Its U.S. subsidiary, Nestlé Food Co., purchased three million cases of canned milk in 1916 and five million the following year for export to Europe.[64] To help Hires and other American companies increase production, Nestlé advanced funding for the purchase of raw milk, for additional equipment and supplies, and, in some cases, for the opening of new plants.

Despite his German roots, Hires staunchly backed the nation's war effort. Neither did he find any conflict between his support for the war and his growing attraction to Quakerism. Sentiment among members of the historically pacifist faith was divided over the war.

Shortly before the United States entered the conflict in 1917, a national Quaker peace conference upheld the faith's traditional opposition to war. "The causes for which men fight—liberty, justice and peace—are noble and Christian causes," the conference noted, "but the method of war is unchristian and immoral. War itself violates law, justice, liberty and peace, the very ends for which alone its tragic cost might be justified."[65] The Philadelphia Yearly Meeting, a group of local Quaker congregations, echoed this view the following year without a dissenting voice.[66]

But a reasoned dissent to this position was voiced by Charles Hires and other prominent Philadelphia Quakers who took issue with the advocates of pacifism. "There are certain fundamental principles of right and humanity which every man must feel called upon to defend, even to the extent of forcible resistance, if long continued intolerable conditions caused by morally defunct people are to be ended before the world is enslaved," their public statement declared. "Many distinguished Friends in the past have realized that in cases of great collective oppression mere submission only renders the objects of the oppressor more easily attained."[67] Hires and his cosigners urged individual Quakers to heed the dictates of their own consciences, irrespective of official statements or the utterances of public speakers.

Meeting the wartime demand for condensed milk was a challenge. Hires overtly appealed to dairy farmers' sense of patriotism as he struggled to increase his supply of raw milk. "If you are not going to the trenches yourself, do your bit over here; send us your milk," a company ad implored. "By helping us, you will be doing your bit for Uncle Sam and his fighting boys. We are doing our bit, are you doing yours?"[68]

Hires continued to acquire smaller competitors in an effort to increase production. In 1917 he consolidated his condensed milk operations with those of another conglomerate producer, John Wildi Evaporated Milk Co. of Columbus, Ohio.[69] The firms would retain their separate corporate identities, but their plants reportedly would function as a single unit. Exactly how the two companies would accomplish this feat was not explained. Hires operated twenty-two condenseries and thirty receiving stations at the time, while Wildi operated nineteen and forty-four, respectively. Their combined annual production of canned milk was estimated to exceed that of any manufacturer in the United States or elsewhere.[70]

Armistice Deflates Milk Bubble

The armistice ending World War I also deflated the canned milk bubble. Demand shrank precipitously, threatening dire consequences for American manufacturers. For example, Hires' annual production, swelled by Nestlé's purchases, increased from 500,000 to 2 million cases over the course of the war, an amount the domestic market could not have absorbed.[71]

Fortunately for Hires and other domestic producers, Nestlé made a strategic decision to expand its American canned milk business. With limited condensing capacity of its own on this side of the Atlantic, the international food giant elected to purchase its U.S. suppliers rather than build new factories. It set aside $15 million to purchase American canned milk companies.[72] Responding to an offer presumably too lucrative to refuse, Hires sold all of his condensed milk operations to Nestlé in 1918.

The terms of the sale, including the precise purchase price, are not available. One account places the figure at "more than $1 million."[73] Given Nestlé's $15 million allocation and the extensive scope of Hires' condensed milk operations, however, it seems likely that the company received substantially more than $1 million.

Other factors as well may have influenced Hires' exit from the condensed milk business. A letter in the Hires Family Papers written by his grandson William Hires suggests that skullduggery may have played a role. "The milk business was the victim of industrial sabotage," William wrote. "An employee was paid by [a rival condensed milk company] to ruin batch upon batch of canned milk and the milk business quickly became unprofitable."[74]

Hires timed the sale well, exiting the condensed milk business near its peak. American production of canned milk declined nearly 25 percent between 1919 and 1921, when the accumulated war surplus flooded the market and depressed prices.[75]

While World War I produced handsome returns for Hires' Condensed Milk Company, its effect on the soft drink side of his business proved less sanguine. The conflict severely disrupted Europe's sugar beet industry, which had provided more than 40 percent of the world's sugar supply before the war.[76] Resultant price increases and shortages of sugar, the principal component of soft drink syrup in this era before high fructose corn syrup and artificial sweeteners, whipsawed Hires and other manufacturers during the war and its aftermath.

When the federal government lifted its wartime restrictions in December 1919, the price of sugar soared. Alarmed soft drink makers went into hock to protect themselves from further increases by stockpiling the vital ingredient. Coca-Cola, for example, handed over the sole copy of its secret formula to a New York bank as collateral for a loan.[77]

A prominent U.S. senator, who proposed curtailing sugar use by soft drink and candy makers as a means to relieve the shortage, was chastised by *The American Bottler*: "Securing sugar is the most aggravating problem facing the carbonated beverage manufacturer today. The situation is identical the nation over. Our members, located in every state in the union, all are very much harassed. Nearly every bottler has been forced to curtail production and many have been forced to close temporarily." Instead of imposing sugar quotas on the soft drink and candy industries, the journal advised politicians to deal with hoarders and speculators, whom it blamed for the shortages.[78]

However, inflated sugar prices began to collapse in August 1920 as European beet growers returned to the market. Some soft drink makers were stuck with huge debts and tons of devalued sugar. Two of Hires' strongest competitors, Moxie and Pepsi-Cola, were forced into bankruptcy. Moxie responded by slashing its advertising budget, a move that would have devastating consequences for its market share.[79]

Hires responded in typically bold fashion to the sweetener crisis. Bolstered by profits from the sale of his condensed milk business, he acted decisively to ensure his company's sugar supply. In 1919 the company announced the purchase of a sugar plantation and mill at Dos Rosas near the port of Cardenas, Cuba. The mill drew its supply of sugar cane from an area of approximately 15,000 acres. Its production capacity was 25 million pounds of sugar a year. Hires' purchase included twenty miles of private railway and private shipping docks. The price was reported at about $2 million.[80] In addition, Hires contracted to buy the sugar cane production of another 7,000 acres and planned extensive improvements to increase the mill's capacity to refine 30 million pounds of sugar a year. The company planted fields of Jamaica ginger, Mexican vanilla beans, and other ingredients used in the company's beverages.[81] It also reported plans to establish a Havana bottling plant to distribute soft drinks to Cuba, Mexico, and South America.

Cuban sugar production had been rising in response to the wartime shortage. Its 1920 crop yielded 23 percent of the world's sugar compared to about 12 percent before the war.[82] Cuba had become increasingly attractive to U.S. investors following the Spanish-American War. Businessmen found it reassuring that the island nation fell under the jurisdiction of the 1901 Platt Amendment, which limited Cuban sovereignty in favor of U.S. control. Under its terms, the United States reserved the right to intervene in Cuban affairs when necessary to protect life, property, and individual liberty; Cuba's authority to negotiate treaties was limited, and the rights to the naval base at Guantánamo Bay were ceded to the United States.

"We found the safest way to assure ourselves of a supply of sugar was to buy a plantation outright," Hires explained to a reporter. "How important sugar is to us is evident from the fact that our production last year was 850,000,000 glasses. If we were unable to get sugar, it would obviously bar us from maintaining this pace and absolutely prevent expansion."[83]

WHERE PIRATES ONCE ROAMED

Hires' purchase was on the north coast of Cuba, about seventy-five miles east of Havana. It was situated on a finger of land, once the site of a number of small sugar mills and rum distilleries. A colorful company brochure titled *From Rum Running to Soft Drinks* described this most recent exploit of "a modern American soft drink having its origin a half century ago in a small dwelling on one of the numerous side streets in the city of Philadelphia."[84] It explained that a quest for the finest raw materials led this proud enterprise to venture into "foreign fields" to ensure its supply. The history of its Cuban acquisition was recounted in florid fashion:

> Today an entire sea-coast and thousands of acres of land are giving their yield to one of the oldest soft drinks, when but a few generations ago slave running flourished along its coast, pirates infested its harbors and the slaves ashore worked under the whiplash of their drivers, making rum, sugar and molasses of trade. Can you imagine the face of the hearty buccaneer and hear the flow of language that would follow

if he were to look down on the Dos Rosas of today, the raw
products center of a soft drink manufacturer?

Who says business today is not laden with adventure and
romance, for the children of the slaves of yesterday still labor at Dos Rosas and the story of the two beautiful Rosas . . .
is rich in love and adventure. What a wealth of material for
the story writer could be gleaned from the lips of a few of the
hombres whose life has been spent among the sugar fields
of Dos Rosas.[85]

The Charles E. Hires Co. was not the only Pennsylvania firm
to appreciate the advantages of sweetener self-sufficiency. Milton Hershey purchased a Cuban plantation and mill in 1916 to
assure an adequate supply of sugar for his candy company.[86] The
chocolate baron built a model industrial town he called Central
Hershey. It was designed to meet all of its workers' residential, social, and recreational needs. Interviewed following the
U.S.-Cuban rapprochement in 2015, longtime residents fondly recalled Hershey's amenities, especially an electric railroad
that continues to operate sporadically today. The former Central
Hershey, now mostly in ruins, was renamed for guerilla fighter
Camilo Cienfuegos after the Cuban Revolution.[87]

Following World War I, Hires added another liquid asset to
his corporate portfolio. He determined that the instant coffee
that he had manufactured for the armed forces during the war
could win a place in the civilian market. Hires promoted his Instant Soluble Coffee to the public as an "instantaneous" brew
created by "a new and exclusive process." To distinguish its coffee
from competing brands, Hires ads pointed out that it could be
dissolved instantly in ice water to create a summer beverage.[88]

As America entered the tumultuous 1920s, the Charles E.
Hires Co. could look forward to a future of growth and profitability, but for Hires himself, it was also a time to begin letting go.

9

LETTING GO

THE ADVENT OF the 1920s found the nation poised to enter an era of unprecedented economic expansion attended by exhilarating, if at times confounding, social change. For Charles Hires, about to celebrate his sixty-ninth birthday in 1920, the decade would mark a period of transition as his sons assumed a growing role in the day-to-day management of the firm he founded. The one-man drugstore Hires opened almost fifty years earlier had grown into a multimillion-dollar corporation. Now the last remnants of the agrarian horse-and-buggy America of his youth were about to be rudely swept away in the rush toward modernity that would characterize the decade ahead.

The Great War had ended in victory for the Allies. But President Wilson's quest to ensure lasting peace by joining a League of Nations came a cropper in the United States Senate. Millions of Americans were "fast becoming sick and tired of the whole European mess. They didn't want to be told of new sacrifices to be made—they had made plenty," wrote one contemporary historian.[1] They yearned to savor the promise of an economy refocused on their needs and wishes rather than on wartime priorities. The Nineteenth Amendment, ratified in 1920, granted the franchise to women across the nation. Voting in their first national election that year, they helped to sweep Republican Warren G. Harding into the White House. He promised a return to "normalcy." Harding easily carried Pennsylvania, where Charles E. Hires served as a member of his campaign's finance committee.[2] The election result was interpreted as a rebuke to Progressive Era reforms and a return to laissez-faire capitalism.

For the first time more Americans lived in cities than on farms. Working-class families had extra income to spend on consumer goods. Low prices and generous credit allowed many to buy their first car. (A Ford Model T could be purchased for $295 in 1924.) Affordable motor vehicles and a growing network of paved roads allowed Americans to travel as never before and relieved the isolation of rural communities. Radio broadcasting blossomed from an esoteric fad into a mass media. The nation's first commercial station, KDKA in Pittsburgh, took to the air in 1920, broadcasting Harding-Cox election returns. Movie attendance set records with the advent of "talkies" such as the *Jazz Singer* starring Al Jolson, produced in 1927. These trends, accompanied by the spread of national magazines and chain stores, helped foster a common culture. People from coast to coast bought the same goods, listened to the same music, danced the same dances, and even used the same slang.[3]

Mass-produced goods, ranging from ready-to-wear clothing to electric appliances, enticed buyers. Ad agencies hired psychologists to better understand and manipulate public taste. Their goal was to persuade consumers they needed and deserved to own the client's products. Nationally advertised brands, including Hires Root Beer, flooded the marketplace.[4]

Rising consumer demand rippled powerfully through the nation's economy. Car sales, for example, spurred the production of gasoline, steel, and rubber as well as supplying the impetus for more paved roads and service stations. The gross national product grew robustly at an average rate of 4.2 percent a year between 1920 and 1929.[5] There seemed little concern that this economic boom might end with an excruciating crash.

Philadelphia, Hires' adopted hometown, celebrated the era with a civic construction spree. Some 1,300 homes and businesses were razed to clear the way for a broad boulevard designed to emulate the Champs-Élysées in Paris. Officially completed in 1926, the Fairmount Parkway carved a broad diagonal across the city's historic street grid. It connected the towering French Second Empire–style city hall with a massive neoclassical-style art museum under construction atop a rise at the edge of Fairmount Park. Notable cultural and educational institutions would join the Academy of Natural Sciences and the Cathedral of Saints Peter and Paul along the grand boulevard. These included the Free Library of Philadelphia and a Rodin Museum embellished with the sculptor's *Thinker* and *Gates of Hell*.[6]

SESQUICENTENNIAL A COSTLY FLOP

A work of arguably lesser artistic merit adorned the portal to the 1926 Sesquicentennial International Exposition—an eighty-foot-high Liberty Bell festooned with twenty-six thousand 15-watt light bulbs. Despite this candlepower, the fair proved to be a dim shadow of the Centennial Exposition, where fifty years earlier Hires had introduced his root beer to the world. Even the company's bid to establish a concession at the Sesquicentennial was derailed by an alleged shakedown scheme.[7] Visitors stayed away in droves, making the event a costly flop for the city.[8]

Before the twenties' roar could reach full pitch, however, a pair of sobering events reminded Americans of their mortality. The worldwide influenza pandemic of 1918–1919 was followed by the recession of 1920–1921.

The flu epidemic exacted a tragic toll on Philadelphia. By October 18, 1918, Pennsylvania reported 6,081 deaths from influenza and 2,651 deaths from pneumonia, with the greatest number occurring in Philadelphia. The disease was most prevalent in the city's industrial districts. Grim as these numbers were, they were probably underreported by overwhelmed health officials. Philadelphia banned public gatherings and ordered places of amusement closed to stem the contagion. The city later estimated the ban resulted in the loss of $2.5 million in potential revenue and that its streetcar company had lost $250,000.[9]

The brief but sharp deflationary recession that gripped the nation was blamed on steep cuts in government spending that followed World War I. The federal budget was slashed from $18.5 billion in 1919 to $6.4 billion in 1920. Rather than encouraging private spending to offset the decrease, Congress hiked taxes on individuals and corporations. The Federal Reserve Bank, opened in 1914, compounded the problem by raising interest rates. Unemployment climbed from 4 percent in 1919 to nearly 12 percent in 1921 but fell back to 3 percent in 1923.[10]

Prosperity would not be long denied. Neither would Charles Hires and his inspired corps of N. W. Ayer advertising copywriters. They portrayed Hires Root Beer as an essential component of the decade's new good life. Smartly suited gentlemen and lithesome ladies graced the pages of the *Saturday Evening Post* and similar popular magazines. These modish men and women insisted on being served only "genuine Hires," which they blissfully quaffed while relaxing at home, reveling in nature, or vacationing.

Indeed, images of the "smart set" had become the common currency of soft drink advertisers. But Hires, ever the iconoclast, decided that more than pretty faces were needed to distinguish his root beer from inferior offerings. His company had banished the term "root beer" from its advertising vocabulary, hoping to distance itself from the dozen or so others that had invaded its market. Thus it became essential to persuade consumers to ask for "Hires" rather than a generic "root beer." One of the firm's marketing strategies was to emphasize its use of only the finest natural ingredients regardless of cost.

Hires wracked his brain for a convincing way to illustrate this claim. Enter the "Hires Wood Gnomes." Hires paid an artist $3,000 to produce a tableau of exuberant elves brewing a cauldron of Hires Root Beer from ingredients freshly harvested near their woodland home. The scene was reproduced on posters and billboards and later in magazine ads. Despite the *American Bottler's* suggestion that such billboard displays might become the "outdoor murals of our time," it remains ungnome whether Hires' inspiration paid off.[11]

PROHIBITION BENEFITS SOFT DRINK INDUSTRY

Fortune had smiled broadly on the soft drink industry in 1919. The Eighteenth Amendment to the Constitution prohibited the manufacture, transportation, and sale of intoxicating liquors. Early the following year, the Volstead Act closed every bar, tavern, and saloon in the country. Historians continue to parse the unintended consequences and distressing impacts of Prohibition on American society, but clearly, soft drink sales boomed. "The men who ran the soda pop business couldn't lose," Okrent points out in *Last Call: The Rise and Fall of Prohibition.* "Americans who violated Prohibition laws required the bottlers' product to make liquor palatable, and those who obeyed the laws needed it to quench their thirst."[12] Soda fountains replaced bars and taverns as Main Street social centers. To please their new patrons, fountain operators spiced up their drinks with salt and chili pepper.[13]

A trade journal article titled "Volstead Act Helps Soda Men" proclaimed that only savings banks had profited more from Prohibition than the soft drink industry. Presumably, dollars once frittered away on booze were now being deposited in banks rather than taverns. Ice cream manufacturers ranked third among purported beneficiaries of the law.[14]

Coca-Cola focused on the law abiders with slogans like "The Drink That Cheers but Does Not Inebriate." Hires, on the other hand, adopted a more subtle approach. For decades he had touted his root beer as the quintessential temperance beverage. But his ads following the advent of Prohibition soft-pedaled such claims, seeking perhaps to enhance root beer's appeal among those who longed for the real thing.

Ginger ale, like Hires Root Beer an early soft drink, became a Jazz Age darling. Mixed in cocktails, it helped disguise the foul flavor of bootleg hooch. Clicquot Club and Canada Dry were popular brands.[15] Early to the party, Hires had been marketing ginger ale since 1901. The company declared its drink to be a formidable competitor for Belfast ginger ale, an Irish import of quality heretofore unequaled.[16]

By 1921 the net worth of the Charles E. Hires Co. was estimated to exceed $2 million ($27 million today).[17] That year jewel thieves decided to help themselves to a share of the senior Hires' personal fortune by staging a daring robbery of his Haverford home. While the family ate dinner on the first floor, the bold burglars ascended to Charles and Emma's upstairs bedroom by means of a makeshift rope ladder. They made off with Emma's jewelry, valued at $4,500, and $150 in cash.[18] Industry prospects became even rosier in 1922 when Congress repealed the federal excise tax on bottled soft drinks and soda fountain sales. Imposed in 1919, the tax had helped to retire the nation's war debt but was considered onerous by manufacturers and retailers.[19]

Soft drink consumption soared during the twenties. Between 1920 and 1929 bottled soda sales in the United States jumped from 175 million to 273 million cases per year, or an average of fifty-three bottles per person. Consumption rose dramatically due not only to Prohibition but to aggressive advertising campaigns and expanding merchandizing venues.[20] Bottled beverage sales overtook soda fountain sales for the first time during the decade.

The widespread use of motor vehicles also spurred the industry's growth, according to one chronicler:

> The automobile made a trip to the corner grocery a more frequent event and also created the "roadside stand" as a place to stop for a cold bottle of soda. Furthermore, the replacement of the delivery wagon by the motor truck . . . and the subsequent building of roads greatly expanded the area in which the bottler was able to deliver his drinks.[21]

The Charles E. Hires Co. had prudently prepared for its anticipated growth. In 1917 Hires had closed its manufacturing facility on North Broad Street in Philadelphia to move into a spacious plant at the corner of South Twenty-Fourth and Locust Streets. The complex of brick buildings had adjacent railroad access and a private dock on the Schuylkill River. Hires purchased the property from A. H. and F. H. Lippincott, Inc., which had manufactured soda fountain apparatus there. Inexplicably, the purchase price was reported to be "a nominal consideration," despite the property's assessed valuation of $150,000.[22] The renovated complex would remain the company's headquarters for many years.

Booming Sales and a Confident Prediction

The prospect of booming sales sparked optimism in the Hires boardroom. In 1920 the company optioned a defunct trade school building in San Francisco, where it planned to establish a manufacturing plant. Earlier that year it had established a Toronto plant to serve an expanding Canadian market.[23] The company had acted the previous year to secure its supply of a crucial raw material by purchasing a 15,000-acre sugar plantation and mill in Dos Rosas, Cuba (see Chapter 8). The acquisition freed Hires from the vagaries of a postwar sugar market that played havoc with some of its competitors.

Hires sales for the fourth quarter of 1921 were triple those of the comparable period the previous year. Charles E. Hires Jr. confidently predicted 1922 would be a record breaker for the soft drink industry. Early results showed bottled root beer orders increasing at a rate double that of the year before. Sales of root beer extract, by now a minor contributor to the company's bottom line, were rising as well.[24] "The 18th amendment has increased consumption of soft drinks and economic changes have brought about more brewing of all beverages at home," Charles Hires Jr. declared.[25] He noted that an exceptionally warm summer the previous year had depleted supplies and forced jobbers to increase their orders.

During the decade Hires bottled several carbonated beverages in addition to root beer. These included its mock champagne, Champanale, as well as its own brands of ginger ale and lemonade, trademarked "Hires Ginger" and "Hires Lemonade." Hires continued to sell bottled spring and distilled water under the brand name "Purock" and distribute its own brand of iceless water coolers. The company also produced birch and ginger beer extracts in addition to its original root beer extract. In 1925 Hires products were sold through 4,000 jobbers and bottlers and approximately 300,000 dealers in the United States and Canada. In addition to its Cuban sugar mill, Hires operated manufacturing plants in Philadelphia, Pittsburgh, Houston, and Toronto.[26]

Despite its respectable growth, Hires was far from the industry leader. Coca-Cola and Pepsi-Cola dominated national soft drink sales during the decade. Coke led the pack with million-dollar promotional campaigns and memorable slogans, including "The Pause That Refreshes." Coca-Cola sales in 1926, for example, topped $30 million, dwarfing Hires' reported gross of $3.5 million.[27] Dozens of other national and regional brands competed with the giants. Nineteenth-century standbys Dr. Pepper and Moxie were joined by 7 Up, Orange Crush, and A and W Root Beer. At least two of Hires' rivals faced severe financial setbacks due to the collapse of sugar prices in 1920. As noted in Chapter 8, both Pepsi-Cola and Moxie were forced to file for bankruptcy.

The Charles E. Hires Co. faced financial difficulties of its own in the mid-1920s. The company's Cuban sugar plantation and mill had assured it a cheap supply of that commodity. But unforeseen expenditures related to the Cuban operations and the seasonality of root beer sales resulted in cash flow problems.[28] The company posted profits from 1920 to 1925, except for the national recession year of 1921.[29] However, it had accrued substantial debt, and its liabilities in some years exceeded assets. The company had reincorporated in Delaware in 1920, but a large share of its stock remained in the hands of founder Charles Hires Sr. A financial reorganization in 1925 broadened the company's shareholder base and shored up its finances. Money raised through the issuance of $2 million in preferred shares also enabled it to reduce indebtedness. Hires shares became listed on the New York Stock Exchange at that time.[30]

A Family Company

Hires would never fully disengage from the company he founded. But as early as 1916 he had begun to gradually reduce his involvement in day-to-day operations as his sons increased their role in the firm's management. Hires could be justly proud of the accomplishments of his three sons and two daughters, all born during his first marriage. His sons participated actively in the family business, with the youngest, Charles E. Hires Jr., succeeding him as president. Charles Jr., born in 1891, joined the company following his graduation from Haverford College in 1913. With his father's encouragement, he gained hands-on experience in areas ranging from the boiler room to the shipping department. It is never smart to "feel above" any job that must be done, he later told an interviewer. To prepare himself for a management position, Charles Jr. also studied chemistry at Temple University and attended night classes in accounting.[31] In 1925 he was named company president. His father assumed the position of chairman of the board.

Charles Jr. treasured a yellowed clipping of his own obituary printed following a life-changing experience.[32] While a student at Haverford College, the star halfback was severely injured by a kick to the abdomen during a football game at Lehigh University.[33] After eight hours in the operating room to repair a ruptured spleen, there appeared to be little hope for his survival. A premature announcement of his death was published in the Philadelphia *Public Ledger* and reprinted in newspapers across the country. Not only did young Charles survive, he was able to graduate on time and with honors. After the ordeal, he became generous to a fault and "a true Quaker," according to a friend.[34] He would retain the post of president at Hires until 1950, guiding the company through some of its most profitable years.

The founder's other sons held executive positions with the company. John Edgar served as vice president for operations and Harrison as vice president for sales. But both men pursued other interests as well.

John Edgar, born in 1885, had an accomplished career as a mechanical engineer. After graduating from Swarthmore College, he worked for a time for the Nestlé Company. In 1926 he organized the firm of Hires, Castner and Harris, consulting engineers, in Philadelphia. Like his father, he displayed an inventive turn of mind, receiving patents for soft drink dispensing and capping devices. He also served as commandant of the Ocean City Yacht Club of New Jersey and was an organizer of the Sea Scouts of America.[35]

Harrison, born in 1887, graduated from Haverford College in 1910. In addition to his business career, he maintained an enthusiastic interest in the arts. An author and poet, he published *Invitation and Other Poems* (1938) and *For My Children* (1943), a book of essays, and corresponded with prominent figures in government, education, the arts, and science.[36] Harrison was active in several educational and cultural organizations, including the Philadelphia Art Alliance, where he served as vice president, and the Philadelphia College of Pharmacy and Science, where he was a trustee.[37]

Although not involved directly in the family business, Hires' two daughters distinguished themselves in other fields. Linda, the eldest of his five surviving children, born in 1878, graduated from Wellesley College in 1903 and trained as an architect.

Hires' youngest child, Clara, born in 1897, also attended Wellesley. She later became a botanist following her graduation from Cornell University with a degree in plant physiology. Her specialty was ferns, spores, and pollen cell structures. In 1929 she founded Mistaire Laboratories, a plant nursery and research facility in Milburn, New Jersey. There she developed and improved techniques for propagating ferns, orchids, and other difficult plants. The nursery supplied seeds and spores to biologic supply houses and educational institutions. In 1965 she authored a work entitled *Spores. Ferns. Microscopic Illusions Analyzed*.[38] She published another book in 1978 at the age of eighty-one. Her obituary six years later described Clara as "an authority on the reproduction of sporophytes."[39]

The senior Hires' interests had always ranged well beyond the confines of his soft drink business. His partial retirement provided the opportunity to explore them more fully. He remained active in the Poor Richard Club, an association of advertising executives, as well as the Philadelphia Board of Trade and the Philadelphia Drug Exchange. But he now had time to satisfy a yen to see the world. He was inclined to travel in rather "grand style," his grandson William recalled.[40] In addition to visiting the company's sugar holdings in Cuba, Hires toured Europe at least twice with his wife, Emma. On one journey, the couple crossed the Atlantic during a storm on a voyage from New York to the Middle East by way of Madeira and Greece. Hires wrote detailed accounts of their sojourn to his daughters and sons. He cautioned them about the dangers of beggars in Madeira and commented on such wonders as Constantinople's Blue Mosque and underground cisterns and the teeming street life and striking Arabian horses of Cairo.[41] In a passport application Hires listed his occupation as "manufacturing chemist."[42]

Hires' active involvement with the Society of Friends continued undiminished. Supporting the historic Merion Friends meeting house, which he had helped restore, remained a pet project. He maintained an active interest in church affairs, together with Emma, whose family had deep Quaker roots. For example, the couple wrote an impassioned letter to their friend Hugh McIlvaine warning of "threatened decadence in the Society of Friends." They named certain church members who they intimated might lead the society toward "anarchy and Bolshevism" by substituting "some ethical idea for the teaching of Jesus Christ."[43] In 1924 Hires read a paper to a Quaker assembly that he had written commemorating the three hundredth anniversary of the birth of George Fox, a founder of the Religious Society of Friends.

"The birth of George Fox brought into life a new factor, a new human element in the psychology of religious life that was destined to astound the religious thought of the world," Hires reminded an audience assembled in the Merion meeting house. "The proclaiming of the thought that God speaks directly to every human soul put the responsibility upon each one to recognize a divine sense of his obligation to our Heavenly Father to live a pure and correct life for the upbuilding of his kingdom here on earth with the children of men."[44]

QUAKER CAUSES AND OTHER RETIREMENT PASSIONS

Hires drew liberally on his fortune to support Quaker programs and causes. In 1917 he contributed to the purchase of three Ford ambulances by the Friends' Central School of Philadelphia for use by the Allied forces in France.[45] A few years later the team of Charles and Emma was instrumental in relocating that school from Philadelphia's Center City to the Main Line suburbs.

The school had been founded in Philadelphia in 1845 by the Hicksite Friends who separated from the more traditional orthodox Quakers in 1827. By the 1920s the school's enrollment, which included boys and girls, exceeded two hundred and was straining the capacity of its building at Fifteenth and Race Streets. Several factors influenced the school's decision to relocate. Hemmed in by the city, the school could not provide the open space for athletics and recreation that were considered vital to a proper Quaker education. Also, many Quaker families that once lived near the school had moved away from central Philadelphia. At the same time, the "country day school" model had come into vogue among educators. Supporters believed a pastoral setting would foster learning amid the "freedom and joy of the out-of-doors, not subject to the restraints and fears of the city streets."[46]

In 1925 the Friends' Central School purchased the fifteen-acre Wistar Morris estate in suburban Overbrook complete with its Scottish castle–style mansion, which would be converted into classrooms. Emma Waln Hires, who had been a teacher at the school, served on the committee that oversaw the purchase and arranged for its payment. The committee's financing scheme included a guarantee fund of $25,000 a year for five years. Charles was enlisted as a major backer. He pledged to contribute precisely $7,437 annually over the life of the fund. Emma pledged a more modest $200 a year.[47]

Hires remained an ardent sportsman during his retirement. He belonged to exclusive sporting organizations, including the Merion Cricket Club and Philadelphia's Penn Athletic Club, as well as various yachting associations. In his younger years, Hires' eye for fine horses and skill as a carriage driver had been well regarded. He had competed enthusiastically behind his swift pacing mare in races with fellow gentlemen drivers. In his retirement years, deep-sea fishing became his special passion. Hires fished for the sport of it; he preferred to use a light line and play his catch until it tired. One of his prizes, an eighty-five-pound sailfish, hung among member trophies at the Penn Athletic Club.[48] Although the deep seas were his fishing grounds of choice, Hires also enjoyed surf casting and angling for trout in mountain streams.

He purchased an unpretentious motor yacht for ocean fishing, naming it *Emwal* in honor of Emma. Hires docked the craft south of Atlantic City in Ventnor, New Jersey, where the couple had a summer home. A 1920 photograph in Atlantic City depicts Hires in white commodore's garb.[49] When not fishing, the couple passed their time among friends in Atlantic and Ocean Cities, communities patronized by leading Quaker families. Hires served as a director of Atlantic City's Chalfonte and Haddon Hall Hotels.[50] The Quaker-owned properties forbade consumption of alcoholic beverages on their premises.[51] Ironically, the structures were transformed in 1978 into Resorts Casino Hotel, Atlantic City's first legalized gambling mecca.

In the winter Hires based the *Emwal* in Florida. After retiring, he spent winters pursuing tarpon, marlin, and other large species off that state's Atlantic and Gulf coasts. In 1933 Hires was honored by the Isaak Walton Club of Useppa Island for landing a fifty-six-pound kingfish, reported to be the second largest ever taken in Florida waters.[52] An undated newspaper clipping from Key West, Florida, credited Hires with landing three of the largest amberjacks caught in local waters during the season.[53] Hires also fished the Caribbean during visits to his company's Cuban sugar plantation.[54]

While on vacation, Charles and Emma socialized with other members of their well-heeled set. For example, the *Philadelphia Inquirer*'s society page reported that Mr. and Mrs. C. E. Hires had entertained H. J. Heinz, the Pittsburgh processed food magnate, aboard their yacht during a fishing excursion from Miami.[55] During the winter of 1929, the couple spent several weeks trolling the waters off Key West for marlin. When Emma requested a change of scenery, they traveled to St. Petersburg, Florida, where they lodged for several weeks at the toney Vinoy Park Hotel.[56] On their arrival, Hires told a newspaper reporter that he was eager to stalk kingfish and tarpon in the Gulf of Mexico. At the interviewer's request, he took time to recount the highlights of his life story and reflect modestly on the basis of his achievements. "My success is by no means due to any extraordinary ability or mentality, but merely the result of a little practical vision, a great deal of ambition, and absolute honesty," he remarked. "To be able to establish trust with one's creditors is, I firmly believe, the first essential for the young man who would succeed in the business world and in life."[57]

During Hires' retirement travels, company business did not stray far from his thoughts. While vacationing in Miami, for example, he wrote to sons Charles Jr. and Harrison about his visits to local soda fountains, including one in an F. W. Woolworth five-and-dime store. Although all displayed the Hires keg, none were actually dispensing Hires Root Beer in the manner that their contracts required. "It is a pity that after getting started here in such a nice way," Hires chided his sons, "we should neglect to take care of the business."[58]

AN ECONOMIC ROLLER COASTER RIDE

The Charles E. Hires Co. enjoyed a banner year in 1929. Its sales exceeded $4 million—more than $56 million in today's dollars. Since 1923 net earnings had increased 64 percent, rising to over $1 million ($14 million today). The company's profit margin in 1929 topped 19 percent.[59]

But unbeknownst to its blissful riders, the economic roller coaster of the Roaring Twenties was nearing the apex of its ascent. It would descend with frightful speed after October's stock market crash. The Great Depression of 1929 walloped the soft drink industry. Its products were, after all, an indulgence that consumers, hard-pressed to pay their rent, could readily forgo. Soon the soda fountains and retailers who distributed the industry's products were going under by the thousands. Coca-Cola bottlers reported that many small outlets could afford to purchase only a single case of Coke at a time.[60] By 1933 per capita soft drink consumption had plummeted nearly 50 percent, from fifty-three to twenty-seven bottles a year.

Hires sales dropped precipitously between 1931 and 1935, falling from approximately $4.5 million to $1.8 million, or 60 percent.[61] Ratification of the Twenty-First Amendment in 1933 ending Prohibition only served to exacerbate the decline. The company did not regain sales traction until 1936 along with the rest of the soft drink industry. Oddly enough, the transition to a bigger bottle fueled the resurgence as Hires followed a trend established by rival Pepsi-Cola. In late 1933, desperate to gain an edge in its battle with Coca-Cola, Pepsi doubled the size of its bottle to twelve ounces. Its new motto, "Twice as much for a nickel too," was clearly aimed at Coke's six-and-a-half-ounce bottle.

Soda drinkers agreed that this was a bargain. Hires and other soft drink manufacturers also got the message: "Bigger Is Better."[62] In 1936 Hires began distributing its root beer in a twelve-ounce bottle.[63] Sales that year recovered to $2.6 million with net profits of almost $400,000. By 1939 almost 25 percent of the industry's production was being sold in twelve-ounce containers.[64]

Three years earlier the Charles E. Hires Co. had retired the signature yellow box that made "root beer" a household term. It had enjoyed a fifty-seven year run and millions of sales. But the company concluded that its future lay in bottled root beer and soda fountain beverages.[65]

LEGACY OF THE "ROOT BEER KING"

Charles E. Hires died unexpectedly on July 31, 1937. He suffered a stroke while preparing to leave his Haverford home for his summer house at the New Jersey shore. He was eighty-five. His wife, Emma, had died the previous year at sixty-seven, also following a stroke.[66] The local and national press eulogized the "Root Beer King" by recounting his accomplishments as entrepreneur and businessman. A tribute in the advertising journal *Printers' Ink*, however, paused to examine Hires' character. After describing him as an industry trailblazer whose daring use of advertising set localized manufacturers thinking about national markets, writer Mark O'Dea wryly observed:

> "Many considered Mr. Hires' chief deficiency to be stubbornness. For years he defied his friends, his sales organization and his dealers regarding the Hires formula.
>
> "'Put caffeine in it,' they urged, 'or something to make it habit-forming. Otherwise you'll fail.'
>
> "'Never!' Mr. Hires would shout.
>
> "Purity and healthfulness were qualities that appealed to him as a chemist and as a Quaker. Much of the appeal of Hires Root Beer has always been among young people—this held Mr. Hires back. 'I couldn't give them anything habit-forming,' he said. 'I'd rather fail. Hires Root Beer must be, as always, a natural drink, never an imitation.'"[67]

Although he slipped several times, Hires "was not an obsessionist [sic] like [Henry] Ford," O'Dea remarked. "He often strayed from the promotion of Hires Root Beer," wrote O'Dea, alluding to Hires' hegiras into the intriguing worlds of perfumes, cough remedies, and condensed milk, "yet it withstood his neglect. His weakness was in adjusting himself to routine business. At heart an experimental chemist, his laboratory lured him away."[68]

O'Dea summarized Hires' mortal journey succinctly:

Charles E. Hires lived a long life—from candle to tungsten, from ocean clippers to air clippers—he saw the coming of the telephone, the automobile, the radio—he lived through several depressions, world wars—he saw the country progress from slavery to the New Deal—in his own world he saw chemistry march ahead triumphantly, he saw advertising become a part of American life—born in 1851, he not only viewed a great pageant but was a distinctive personage in it.[69]

Hires was buried in Westminster Cemetery near Cynwyd, Pennsylvania, where his first wife had also been laid to rest. His estate was estimated to exceed $200,000 (approximately $3.5 million today) with additional real estate valued at $106,450, according to probate records. His bequests included a $25,000 trust fund for a sister, Sarah Kirkley of Pitman, New Jersey, and a gift of $2,500 for his personal secretary, Josephine Lucas. Of the remainder, Hires willed one-third to his wife, Emma—he had neglected to change his will when she predeceased him. The remaining two-thirds of his estate were deposited in a trust with the income to be paid to his two daughters, Linda and Clara.[70]

THE FATE OF CHARLES E. HIRES CO.

For its remaining twenty-three years of independence, the company Hires founded would achieve modest growth in the face of heightened competition and changing public preferences. By 1948 Hires earned $457,135 on sales of $8,576,090.[71] It reported that it operated twenty-two plants in major cities and had three hundred franchised bottlers. The following year Hires raised cash by selling its sugar plantation and mill near Cardenas, Cuba. It received $1,250,000 on the sale from "Cuban sugar interests," $221,000 less than the amount carried on its books for the property.[72] Nevertheless, the sale was timely. Fidel Castro would take over the Caribbean island in 1959 and nationalize U.S.-owned businesses there the following year.

By the 1950s the company was still managing to boost annual sales but profits lagged. In 1953, for example, sales were on target to set a record of more than $10 million. But Hires was forced to cut its quarterly dividend from twenty to fifteen cents. With sales increases below their historic pace, Hires was able to raise its prices only marginally. Intense competition precluded increases sufficient to cover rising expenses. Among these were the cost of labor and a 40 percent increase in its advertising budget.[73]

Hires had built his business by selling a high-quality product at a competitive price. A twenty-five-cent bottle of Hires extract would yield five gallons of root beer. The drink's appealing flavor and Hires' reputation for using only the finest natural ingredients allowed it to command a price slightly higher than its direct competitors. But such pricing power was no longer an option. A modestly sized company in a market dominated by giants, Hires could not achieve the same economies of scale—critical to reducing unit costs and spreading expenses over a larger sales base—as its bigger rivals. Moreover, the company adamantly refused to cut costs by using cheaper artificial ingredients such as synthetic vanilla. These challenges would loom larger as industry consolidation mounted.

Advertising had ceased to work its old magic. Hikes in the ad budget failed to generate commensurate sales increases. It is not clear whether the ads had become less effective or were simply drowned out by the huge and ceaseless campaigns of the cola goliaths. In 1955, for example, Coca-Cola spent $15 million on advertising, half again as much as Hires' entire sales for the year.[74]

Peter Hires, son of Charles E. Hires Jr. and grandson of the founder, took over as company president in 1955. He replaced Edward W. David, a nonfamily member, who had succeeded Peter's father as president in 1950. David had reached retirement age.

Peter was only thirty-two, but he knew the soft drink business from the ground up. He had left Haverford College before graduation to drive a Hires truck at a salary of $40 a week. He later rose to the positions of salesman and general merchandizing manager. Peter promised to boost sales 20 percent by being "a lot more aggressive."[75] "The days of 'cracker barrel' selling are over," he declared. "In this business, as in every competitive consumer business, the product must be kept in the public eye. It's part of the formula for staying alive and going forward."[76] Hires announced plans to expand the company's network of franchised bottlers in the United States and to add bottlers in Canada, Alaska, Hawaii, and Puerto Rico as well. He also planned to replace the company's Houston, Texas, plant with a larger facility.[77]

BUSINESS DOCTOR SUMMONED

A modern manager, Hires called upon a business doctor to diagnose his company's marketing ills. He commissioned the Institute for Motivational Research to conduct a pilot study. The consultants assembled a consumer focus group to help them understand Hires' public persona and submitted their findings in a report, *A Psychological Research Pilot Study on the Sales and Advertising Problems of Hires Root Beer.*

The institute's initial finding failed to astonish. As had been abundantly clear to Charles Hires some eighty years earlier, the study determined that "nearly everybody likes root beer." This discovery led the consultants to conclude the potential for increasing Hires' sales indeed existed. But they were quick to caution that Hires was "not anywhere near realizing" that potential. Despite the drink's broad appeal, the consultants opined, many of those who professed to like root beer purchased it infrequently if at all.[78]

In Charles Hires Sr.'s heyday, young people had comprised a major market. But during the 1950s, many had been gravitating to brands that "promise more fun and gaiety," the consultants asserted. To regain the company's mojo in this changed marketplace, they advised Hires to exchange its dated image for a more youthful one.

The consultants summarily dismissed a basic tenet of Hires Sr.'s advertising campaigns: that root beer is good for you. "People don't turn to soft drinks to improve their health," the consultants observed. "They drink for fun." Moreover, focus group members tended to regard root beer drinkers as "conservative—stodgy, conventional and dull." Not surprisingly, panel members described their views of the company in similar terms.

The consultants offered a grab-bag of recommendations calculated to refurbish Hires' image and boost its bottom line—among them: focus advertising at specific markets, make root beer drinking seem fashionable, show more young people drinking Hires, encourage root beer with food (a companion for franks) and as a cocktail mixer, deemphasize health claims, and increase the drink's foamy head. They also recommended a strategy that Hires Sr. had employed but later discarded, substituting "Hires" as a generic term for root beer.

The consultants concluded their analysis on a heady, if unrealistic, note. They reminded the company that "the rewards of a more dynamic sales approach promise to be high. If the aura of old-fashionedness [sic] which now restricts the sale of root beer can be dispelled, Hires may eventually join Coca-Cola and Pepsi-Cola as a member of the Big Three which dominate the lucrative and steadily expanding soft drink market."[79]

The study convinced the company to redouble its appeals to youthful root beer drinkers. Surveys indicated that up to 70 percent of all soft drinks were consumed by the fourteen to twenty-three age group. Peter Hires raised the firm's advertising budget by 10 percent to $1,250,000 in 1956 and pledged to focus its campaign on the youth market.[80] How much more of the consultants' bejargoned advice the company heeded is difficult to determine.

Company sales improved over the next few years, achieving their all-time high in 1959. Peter Hires looked optimistically to the future. He said the company expected the introduction of cans nationwide to become "a major new avenue of business."[81] However, press reports began to indicate a growing interest in Hires as a merger or acquisition candidate.

The conservative company captured national attention in July 1960 when, for the first time in history, it altered the Hires

Root Beer formula. Hires said it was making a slight shift toward acidity as a result in changing public preferences.[82] However, this change may have been dictated by a U.S. Food and Drug Administration (FDA) finding that safrole, a component of sassafras, was carcinogenic. In 1960 the FDA banned the use of sassafras, a key root beer ingredient, in commercially produced foods until a safrole-free substitute could be developed.

THE END OF INDEPENDENCE

A month later the company made an even more dramatic announcement. It had accepted an offer to be purchased by Consolidated Foods for $19 a share.[83] Consolidated was a broadly diversified food conglomerate. Its holdings included Sara Lee Kitchens, Monarch Foods, Eagle Supermarkets, Michigan Fruit Canners, and Shasta Beverages. The value of the deal was reported at $7,267,500. Approximately 222,000, or 58 percent, of Hires' approximately 383,000 shares were owned by family members. The company's assets included eight plants and four hundred franchised bottlers in the United States and abroad. The company was also reported to have estimated holdings of cash and securities worth $3.5 million. In its last fiscal year, Hires had earned $383,747 on sales of $9,214,532.[84]

A joint statement by Hires president Peter Hires and Consolidated chairman Nathan Cummings disclosed that Hires would continue under its present management. Both men spoke optimistically about Hires' future as a brand of Consolidated Foods. Cummings predicted that, backed by strong promotion and the parent company's marketing know-how, Hires could even become "another Sara Lee." Consolidated had almost tripled Sara Lee Kitchens' volume after acquiring that company four years earlier. "Hires will continue operations under present management and the 90 year reputation of the company will be carried on," Cummings announced.[85] (It had been seventy years since the company's incorporation in 1890 and eighty-four years since Charles Hires had introduced his root beer at the nation's Centennial.)

Peter Hires pointed out the advantages of joining a company with Consolidated's "success image." He noted that local bottlers, in particular, would benefit from the parent firm's marketing acumen and aggressive merchandizing plans.[86]

The *Philadelphia Bulletin* reported that Pepsi United Bottlers offered to pay one dollar a share more to purchase the company but had refused to guarantee the retention of Hires' present officers.[87]

President Hires attributed the decision to sell his company to its comparatively small size, which he said had held it back competitively. Sales over the past decade had hovered between $9 million and $10 million a year. Hires told shareholders the company was liquidating because of intense competition, which would have necessitated "large outlays for promotion and advertising." Hires said the company was unwilling on its own to take the risks that such expenditures would involve.[88]

At the time of its acquisition, Hires Root Beer commanded approximately 25 percent of domestic root beer sales. However, root beer comprised but a small fraction of the soft drink market. Cola drinks led with a 64 percent market share followed by lemon-lime and orange-flavored drinks. Root beer and ginger ale were tied for fourth place with 4 percent market shares.[89]

Peter Hires envisioned a bright future for the Charles E. Hires Co. Division of Consolidated Foods. He disclosed plans that included a new headquarters building and plant in Philadelphia, new products, and a more robust advertising budget. He said the division aimed to double its sales in three to four years.[90] Alas, the Hires Division would not remain part of Consolidated Foods long enough to attain its president's ambitious goals. Within two years it was sold to Crush International, a rival soft drink manufacturer.[91] This would not be the last stop for the once-proud root beer pioneer. Its new owner would itself be acquired by Procter and Gamble in 1980 as part of the detergent and household product giant's flirtation with carbonated beverages. Although soap and soda pop share an affinity for bubbles, their union proved less than buoyant.

Nine years later Procter and Gamble sold its Crush International Division to a British conglomerate with impeccable soft drink credentials. The purchase price was reported to be $220 million.[92] Cadbury Schweppes had been formed in 1969 by the merger of British chocolatier Cadbury with Schweppes, an international soft drink maker with eighteenth-century roots. The company appeared intent on becoming a major player in the U.S. market. In addition to Crush and Hires, it had been assembling a stable of American brands—among them Dr. Pepper, 7 Up, and Snapple.

But in 2008 Cadbury Schweppes elected to spin off its U.S. beverage business as a freestanding entity, Dr. Pepper Snapple Group of Plano, Texas.[93] Dr. Pepper Snapple presently maintains the Hires brand among an array of more than fifty beverages, many of which, including Hires, are displayed on its website. However, the company appears to have chosen to promote its other root beer brands—A and W, Stewarts, and IBC—in the national market. The company indicates that producers in Washington, North Carolina, and Arizona are licensed to manufacture and distribute Hires. Dr. Pepper Snapple declines to identify these licensees unless a local zip code is provided.[94]

More recently, twelve-packs of Hires Root Beer in cans could be purchased online through Amazon Marketplace. The product is produced by Dr. Pepper Snapple Group of Ottumwa, Iowa, according to the Dr. Pepper Snapple consumer information telephone line. The cans display the familiar Hires mug and describe their contents as the "Original Root Beer since 1876." However, Charles Hires might be dismayed by the drink's current ingredients, which include high fructose corn syrup, caramel color, and artificial flavors.

CHRONOLOGY

1767   English clergyman and chemist Joseph Priestley invents method for carbonating water artificially.

1806   Benjamin Silliman produces artificial mineral water for sale at a New Haven, CT, pharmacy.

1826   American Temperance Society founded in Boston.

1832   John Matthews begins manufacturing soda water apparatus in New York.

1839   Charles E. Hires' parents, John Dare and Mary Williams, are wed at Roadstown, NJ.

1851   Charles E. Hires born in Elsinboro, NJ.

1851   Maine becomes first state to ban manufacture and sale of alcoholic beverages.

1854   Philadelphia city and county consolidated.

1856   Gail Borden patents process for condensing milk.

1863   Hires apprenticed to his two brothers-in-law who operate a drugstore in Millville, NJ.

1865   American Civil War ends.

1866   Vernors Ginger Ale introduced by Detroit pharmacist James Vernor.

1867   Hires completes four-year apprenticeship and moves to Philadelphia.

1868 Horatio Alger Jr. publishes *Ragged Dick*, tale of a poor boot-black's rise.

1869 N. W. Ayer and Son advertising agency established in Philadelphia by Francis Wayland Ayer.

1869 Panic sparked by gold speculation roils financial markets and adds "Black Friday" to nation's vocabulary.

1870 Hires returns to Millville, NJ, to become partner in Wright, Brooks, and Hires drugstore.

1872 Hires opens his first drugstore at 602 Spruce Street in Philadelphia.

1872 Hires' "first conspicuous success" springs from his discovery of fuller's earth at excavation site.

1872 Hires awarded certificate of efficiency as a pharmacist.

1874 Women's Christian Temperance Union (WCTU) founded in Cleveland, OH.

1875 Hires weds Clara Kate Smith of Philadelphia, daughter of a Quaker merchant family.

1875 Hires sells drugstore and enters wholesale flavorings and botanical drug business.

1875 Charles and Clara Kate Hires are served a tasty herb tea while vacationing at a New Jersey farm.

1876 Hires introduces his recently perfected root beer extract at the Centennial Exposition in Philadelphia.

1877 Hires places first advertisement for root beer extract in Philadelphia's *Public Ledger*.

1878 A total of 876 packages of Hires Root Beer Extract sold.

1880 Hires begins to market a liquid root beer concentrate in addition to his powdered extract.

1884 Moxie Nerve Food, invented by Dr. Augustin Thompson of Maine, is relaunched as a soft drink.

1884 Hires begins advertising root beer in *Harper's Weekly* and other national publications.

1885 Dr. Pepper first served in Waco, TX, pharmacy by Charles Alderton.

1886   Coca-Cola introduced by Atlanta pharmacist John Pemberton.

1888   Jacob Baur founds the Liquid Carbonic Acid Manufacturing Company of Chicago to produce liquefied carbon dioxide in cylinders.

1890   Annual root beer extract sales reach 1.3 million packages.

1890   Charles E. Hires Co. is incorporated in Pennsylvania with capital of $300,000.

1890   Hires opens production facility and headquarters at 117–119 Arch Street in Philadelphia.

1892   Annual sales of Hires Root Beer Extract approach three million units.

1892   William Painter receives patent for crown cork bottle cap.

1892   Hires travels to jungles of eastern Mexico to observe cultivation of the vanilla bean in its native state.

1893   Hires begins distribution of ready-to-drink carbonated root beer bottled by his Crystal Bottling Co.

1893   Financial panic triggers four-year national depression.

1893   Anti-Saloon League (ASL) founded in Oberlin, OH.

1893   Hires awarded highest prize for root beer at Chicago's World's Columbian Exposition.

1894   Hires family moves to Rose Hill, a twenty-acre estate in Merion on Philadelphia's Main Line.

1894   Hires publishes *Recipes for the Manufacture of Flavoring Extracts, Handkerchief Extracts, Toilet Water, Cologne, Bay Rum, etc., etc.*, a do-it-yourself manual for pharmacists.

1895   Michael J. Owens patents a machine to produce uniform glass bottles.

1895   Charles E. Hires Co. moves its executive offices to Philadelphia's Bourse building.

1895   WCTU declares Hires Root Beer is an alcoholic beverage and calls for a national boycott.

1896   Hires relocates root beer manufacturing to factory on Philadelphia waterfront at Delaware and Fairmount Avenues.

1897   Hires elected president of Philadelphia Drug Exchange.

1898   WCTU calls off national boycott of Hires Root Beer after independent tests determine its alcohol content negligible.

1898   Pepsi-Cola introduced by druggist Caleb Bradham in New Bern, NC.

1898   The Spanish-American War occurs. Spain renounces claims to Cuba, cedes Guam and Puerto Rico to the United States, and transfers sovereignty of Philippines to United States.

1899   Hires constructs condensed milk factory on site of former flour mill in Malvern, PA.

1899   Hires begins construction of root beer plant adjacent to Malvern condensed milk factory.

1900   Hires Condensed Milk Co. incorporated in Pennsylvania with capital of $500,000.

1900   Condensed milk production begins at Hires' Malvern condensery. Within six months 20,000 quarts of raw milk a day are being processed.

1900   Hires relocates root beer manufacturing from Philadelphia to Malvern.

1901   Hires files trademarks for production of "Hires Ginger" and "Hires Lemonade."

1901   Rights to bottle and distribute Coca-Cola franchised to independent local bottlers.

1903   Hires' Malvern condensery processes a record 34,000 quarts of raw milk in a single day in March.

1904   Hires relocates root beer manufacturing plant from Malvern to 210 North Broad Street in Philadelphia as a more convenient shipping point.

1904   Hires markets concentrated syrup for production of soda fountain drinks and introduces patented dispenser that mixes syrup and carbonated water in proportion to produce a uniform stein of root beer.

1906   National Pure Food and Drug Act takes effect.

1908   Hires purchases a "fine country mansion" at 842 Buck Lane in Haverford, PA.

1910   Clara Kate, Hires' wife of thirty-five years, dies unexpectedly at age fifty-eight.

1911   Hires marries Emma Waln, a teacher and member of a prominent Quaker family.

1913   Charles E. Hires Jr. joins his brothers John Edgar and Harrison as an employee of the Charles E. Hires Co.

1914   World War I begins in Europe, spurring demand for Hires' condensed milk.

1915   Hires introduces bottled "Champanale," a mock champagne containing the juice of grapes and grapefruit infused with ginger.

1917   Hires publishes *A Short Historical Sketch of the Old Merion Meeting House*, Merion, PA.

1917   Hires consolidates condensed milk operations, which include twenty-two condenseries and thirty receiving stations, with those of the John Wildi Evaporated Milk Co. of Columbus, OH.

1917   Hires relocates Philadelphia plant and company headquarters from North Broad Street to a site on the Schuylkill River at Twenty-Fourth and Locust Streets.

1918   Hires sells its condensed milk business to the Nestlé Co.

1918   Armistice declared on November 11 ends World War I.

1919   Congress ratifies the Eighteenth Amendment to the Constitution prohibiting the manufacture, transportation, and sale of alcohol within the United States, to take effect the following year.

1919   Hires buys 15,000-acre sugar plantation and mill near Cardenas, Cuba, for $2 million.

1920   Hires serves as member of Warren G. Harding's presidential campaign finance committee.

1920   States ratify Nineteenth Amendment to the Constitution giving women nationwide right to vote.

1922   Congress repeals federal excise tax on soft drinks, which had helped to fund the war.

1925   Charles E. Hires, Sr. becomes chairman of the board of the Charles E. Hires Co. He is succeeded as president by his son, Charles E. Hires, Jr.

1925   Charles E. Hires Co. becomes a publicly traded corporation.

1929   Charles E. Hires Co. experiences banner year with sales exceeding $4 million.

1929   Great Depression begins following stock market crash.

1931   Sales of Hires Root Beer decline precipitously.

1933   Pepsi-Cola enjoys sales surge after doubling the size of its bottle to twelve ounces without raising its price.

1933   The Twenty-First Amendment to the Constitution ends Prohibition.

1936   Hires sales begin to recover following its introduction of twelve-ounce root beer bottle.

1936   Hires' second wife, Emma Waln, dies of stroke at age sixty-seven.

1937   Hires Sr. dies of stroke at age eighty-five.

1948   Charles E. Hires Co. earns profits of $457,000 on sales of $8,576,000.

1949   Charles E. Hires Co. sells its Cuban sugar plantation and mill for $1,250,000.

1950   Edward W. David succeeds Charles E. Hires, Jr. as company president.

1955   Peter Hires, thirty-two, son of Charles E. Hires Jr., becomes company president.

1960   Charles E. Hires Co. is purchased by Consolidated Foods, a food industry conglomerate, for $19 per share.

1962   Soft drink manufacturer Crush International purchases Hires Division of Consolidated Foods.

1980   Crush International is acquired by soap maker Procter and Gamble Corporation.

1989   Procter and Gamble sells its Crush International Division to Cadbury Schweppes.

2008   Cadbury Schweppes spins off its U.S. soft drink businesses, including Hires Root Beer, as a freestanding company, Dr. Pepper Snapple Group of Plano, TX.

Notes

Introduction

1. Kate Patton, "Hires Root Beer: The Great Health Drink," Pennsylvania Center for the Book, Fall 2009. Available at: http://pabook2.libraries.psu.edu/palitmap/Hires.html

2. "Letter by Charles E. Hires: Year 1874," *Printers' Ink Monthly*, July 1941, 44–45.

3. Edna Marks, "Hires, Root Beer King, Comes to City to Fish," *The Evening Independent* (St. Petersburg, FL), February 2, 1929, 1.

1. Farm to Pharmacy

1. William L. Hires, *The Hires Family*, privately printed, Philadelphia, 1964.

2. Ibid.

3. Ad in *The Interior* (a Presbyterian journal) Vol. 30, 1899, 339.

4. "Gail Borden," *Encyclopedia of World Biography*. Encyclopedia.com, September 25, 2017, available at: http://www.encyclopedia.com/history/encyclopedias-almanacs-transcripts-and-maps/gail-borden

5. "Union—Troops Furnished and Deaths," The Civil War Home Page, available at: www.civil-war.net (accessed October 15, 2017).

6. Elbert Hubbard, undated recollections, Hires Family Papers, Historical Society of Pennsylvania, 1; hereafter cited as HFP. These papers were recently acquired by the society and were not organized by folder at the time of this research.

7. Ibid.

8. Edna Marks, "Hires, Root Beer King, Comes to City to Fish," *The Evening Independent* (St. Petersburg, FL), February 2, 1929, 1.

9. Hubbard, undated recollections, 1.

10. Ibid., 2.

11. Ibid., 3.

12. Edward Kremers and George Urdang, *The History of Pharmacy*, 2nd ed. (Philadelphia: Lippincott, 1951), 208.

13. Ibid., 276.

14. Ibid., 229.

15. Joseph W. England, ed., *The First Century of the Philadelphia College of Pharmacy, 1821–1921* (Philadelphia: Philadelphia College of Pharmacy and Science, 1922).

16. Passenger service on this Delaware Bay tributary had begun in 1845. See Kimberley R. Sebold, *Southern New Jersey and the Delaware Bay*, National Park Service 1995, available at https://www.nps.gov/parkhistory/online_books/nj2/contents.htm (accessed September 3, 2016).

17. Hubbard, undated recollections, 4.

18. Dorothy Gondos Beers, "The Centennial City, 1868–1876," in Russell F. Weigley, ed., *Philadelphia: A 300-Year History* (New York: W. W. Norton, 1982), 427–428.

19. Ibid., 438.

20. Nathaniel Burt and Wallace E. Davies, "The Iron Age, 1876–1905," in Weigley, *Philadelphia: A 300-Year History*, 506.

21. Beers, "The Centennial City, 1868–1876," 470.

22. "At the World's Fair, Story of a Self-Made Man and How He Won Success," special section, *Public Ledger* (Philadelphia), June 14, 1893.

23. Undated newspaper clipping, HFP.

24. Although never formally enrolled in the Philadelphia College of Pharmacy, Hires would join the college's board of trustees in 1924.

25. Handwritten and undated note, HFP.

26. Copy of Hires' Dyspepsia Mixture ad, HFP.

27. Ibid.

28. John N. Ingham, "Hires, Charles Elmer," *Biographical Dictionary of American Business Leaders* (Westport, CT: Greenwood Press, 1983), 590.

29. "The 'Black Friday' Gold Scandal" available at: History.com/pages/news/blackfridaygoldscandal/www.u-s-history.com (accessed November 15, 2017).

30. Ibid., "Panic of 1873," (accessed November 15, 2017).

31. Charles E. Hires, "Seeing Opportunities," *American Druggist and Pharmaceutical Record*, October 1913, 27.

32. Baldwin H. Ward, ed. *The Fifty Great Pioneers of American Industry* (Chicago: J. G. Ferguson, 1965), 81.

33. Marks, "Hires, Root Beer King," 1.

34. Hires, "Seeing Opportunities," 27.

35. Handbill, February 26, 1872, HFP. A question exists about the year when Hires opened his drugstore in Philadelphia at 602 Spruce Street. Some sources, including an interview with Hires fifty years later ("The Story of Hires," *American Bottler*, May 1921) indicate the year was 1869. However, persuasive evidence supports 1872 as the date of the opening. The

1870 U.S. Census counted Hires as a resident of Millville. A Cumberland County, New Jersey, directory for 1871–1872 lists the Wright, Brooks, and Hires drugstore under Millville businesses. Also, in an 1872 Philadelphia voter registration document (HFP), Hires attested that he had been a resident of the city since November 1, 1871. This appears to be the date when he returned to Philadelphia from Millville. *Gopsill's Philadelphia Business Directory* contains no reference to Charles E. Hires, druggist, at 602 Spruce Street until 1873. Moreover, an editor's note in the Millville *Republican* of March 14, 1872, reads: "We are pleased to learn that our highly esteemed friend, Mr. C. E. Hires, formerly connected with Wright and Brooks in this city has opened a first-class drug store at 602 Spruce St., Philadelphia. He is a worthy young gentleman and we hope he will succeed admirably in the City of Brotherly Love" (newspaper clipping, HFP).

36. Handbill, HFP.

37. Ibid.

38. Ibid.

39. Hires, "Seeing Opportunities," 28.

40. Mark O'Dea, "Charles E. Hires—Pioneer," *Printers' Ink*, August 5, 1937, 53.

41. Hires, "Seeing Opportunities," 28.

42. Ibid.

43. Ibid.

44. Ibid.

45. Joseph J. Fucini and Suzy Fucini, *Entrepreneurs: The Men and Women behind the Famous Brand Names and How They Made It* (Boston: G. K. Hall, 1985), 151. However, the Fucini's estimate, which is undocumented, seems rather high. For example, $6,000 in 1873 would have been equivalent to $118,000 in 2017.

46. "The Story of Hires," 15.

47. Ibid., 27.

48. Hires, "Seeing Opportunities," 27.

49. Ibid., 26.

50. Philadelphia Pharmaceutical Examining Board, report to Mayor William S. Stokley, January 1, 1873, HFP.

51. Transfer certificate, HFP.

52. "Letter by Charles E. Hires: Year 1874," *Printers' Ink Monthly*, July 1941, 44–45.

53. Ibid.

54. Ibid.

55. Ibid.

56. Ibid.

57. Ibid.

58. Hires, *The Hires Family*, 27.

59. Charles E. Hires and Clara Kate Smith Hires, marriage certificate, HFP.

60. William Hires, undated note, HFP.

61. Rebecca Hires, death certificate, HFP.

62. Chares E. Hires ad, *Philadelphia Inquirer*, April 18, 1876, 8.

2. A Rustic Tea Party

1. "The Story of Hires," *The American Bottler*, May 1921, 15.

2. Mark O'Dea, "Charles E. Hires—Pioneer," *Printer's Ink*, August 5, 1937, 53.

3. Stephen Cresswell, *Homemade Root Beer, Soda, and Pop* (Pownal, VT: Storey Books, 1998), 4.

4. "The Story of Hires," 16.

5. Ibid.

6. Charles E. Hires, "Some Advertising Reminiscences, 1869–1913," *Printer's Ink*, July 24, 1913, 17.

7. Charles E. Hires Co., *The Hires Root Beer Manual*, Warren and Reba Lummis Genealogical and Historical Library, Hires Family Folder, Cumberland County Historical Society. (Philadelphia: Charles E. Hires Co., c. 1931), 7. (The HFP contain a similar manual published c. 1923.)

8. Hires, "Some Advertising Reminiscences," 17.

9. Andrew F. Smith, ed., *The Oxford Companion to American Food and Drink* (Oxford: Oxford University Press, 2007), 285.

10. ConAgra Foods, available at: http://www.conagrabrands.com/our -company/company-milestones (accessed June 4, 2016).

11. George S. Fichter, "Products with a Past," *Country Living*, April 1987.

12. Ibid.

13. Ibid.

14. Richard Ohmann, *Selling Culture: Magazines, Markets, and Class at the Turn of the Century* (London: Verso, 1996), 88.

15. Eileen Bennett, "Local Historians Argue Over the Root of the Story of How Hires First Brewed Beer That Made Millions," *Atlantic City Press*, June 28, 1998.

16. David Schmidt, "Hires and the Root of Root Beer," *Main Line Life*, Lower Merion Historical Society, available at: http://www.lowermerion history.org/texts/schmidtd/hires.html (accessed December 3, 2016).

17. Charles E. Hires Co., *Hires Root Beer Manual*, c. 1931, 10.

18. "The Story of Hires," 16. In 1960 the Charles E. Hires Co. reported changing its root beer recipe to produce a more acidic drink. See *New York Times*, July 3, 1960. "Hires Root Beer Gets New Flavor," F9.

19. Charles E. Hires Co., "From Nature's Heart," *Harper's Magazine Advertiser*, August 1893, 26.

20. L. A. Becker, "The Soda Fountain Industry," *Pharmaceutical Era*, May 1913, 243.

21. Tristan Donovan, *Fizz: How Soda Shook Up the World* (Chicago: Chicago Review Press, 2014), 42.

22. Ibid., 43.

23. An American Gentleman and Lady, *Hand Book of Practical Receipts, or, Useful Hints for Every Day Life*, (New York: Barnes and Burr, 1860), 31–32.

24. A. W. Chase, *Dr. Chase's Recipes, or, Information for Everybody: An Invaluable Collection of about 800 Practical Recipes* (Anne Arbor, MI: Scholarly Publishing Office, University of Michigan Library, 2007; originally published by author, 1870), 61.

25. Ed Smith, "Herbal Alteratives, Depuratives and Blood Purifiers: The Balanced Detoxifiers," Herb Farm Chronicles, April 10, 2013, available at: https://www.herb-pharm.com/blog/herbal-alteratives-depuratives -and-blood-purifiers-the-balanced-detoxifiers/ (accessed December 12, 2017).

26. "Recipe and Directions for Making Root Beer," undated company flier, HFP.

27. Ibid.

28. "Russell Conwell Explains Why Diamonds Are a Man's Best Friend," *History Matters*, available at: http://historymatters.gmu.edu/d/5769 (accessed May 30, 2015).

29. Chautauqua was an adult education movement that gained popularity in the late 19th and early 20th centuries. Chautauqua assemblies brought entertainment and culture to rural and small-town America by presenting speakers, teachers, musicians, entertainers and preachers.

30. Russell H. Conwell, "Acres of Diamonds," Temple University, available at: https://www.temple.edu/about/history-and-traditions/acres -diamonds (accessed June 1, 2015).

31. Ibid.

32. Baldwin H. Ward, ed., *The Fifty Great Pioneers of American Industry* (Chicago: J. G. Ferguson, 1965), 82.

33. Joseph C. Carter, *The Acres of Diamonds Man*, vol. 2 (Philadelphia: Temple University; privately printed, 1981), 304; also see Donovan, *Fizz*, 44. Although several secondary accounts attest to Conwell's role in influencing Hires' naming decision, no primary sources were found.

34. James Hilty, *Temple University: 125 Years of Service to Philadelphia, the Nation, and the World* (Philadelphia: Temple University Press, 2010), 18.

35. Letter from Hires to Conwell marking his friend's seventy-fifth birthday, quoted in Carter, *The Acres of Diamonds Man*, 532.

36. "The Story of Hires," 16.

37. Richard R. Nicolai, *Centennial Philadelphia* (Bryn Mawr, PA: Bryn Mawr Press, 1976), 87.

38. Walter Nugent, "The American People and the Centennial of 1876," *Indiana Magazine of History* 75, no. 1 (1979): 58.

39. *The Story of Your Company*, in *The Hires Root Beer Manual*. Philadelphia: Charles E. Hires Co., c. 1923 HFP; "Charles E. Hires," American Council of Learned Societies, *Dictionary of American Biography 1944*, suppl. 10 (New York: Scribner's, 1944), 306.

40. These include James D. McCabe, *The Illustrated History of the Centennial Exhibition* (Philadelphia: National, 1876); *Pennsylvania and the Centennial Exposition: Comprising the Preliminary and Final Reports of the Pennsylvania Board of Centennial Managers to the Legislature*, printed for the Pennsylvania Board of Centennial Managers (Philadelphia: Gillin and Nagle, 1877); *Visitors Guide to the Centennial Exhibition and Philadelphia* (Philadelphia: Lippincott, 1875); and *Frank Leslie's Illustrated Historical Register of the Centennial Exhibition, 1876* (New York: Frank Leslie, 1876).

41. McCabe, *Illustrated History of the Centennial Exhibition*, 848.

42. Elbert Hubbard states that Hires "obtained the agency from a chemical firm in England and during the Centennial Exhibition he made an exhibit" (Hubbard, undated recollections, HFP, 8).

43. William Pierce Randel, *Centennial: American Life in 1876* (Philadelphia: Chilton, 1969), 289. Randel cites soft drink industry historian John J. Riley as a source. Nicolai, in *Centennial Philadelphia*, 74, also states that Hires Root Beer was introduced at the Centennial.

44. John Allen Murphy, "Fairs of the Past," *Nation's Business*, August 1939, 16.

45. John Hope, "Hires to You!" *Pennsylvania*, January/February 1995, 25.

46. John J. Riley, *A History of the American Soft Drink Industry: Bottled Carbonated Beverages, 1807–1957* (Washington, DC: American Bottlers of Carbonated Beverages, 1958), 255.

47. J. S. Ingram, *The Centennial Exposition* (New York: Arno Press, 1976), 287.

48. Donovan, *Fizz*, 33.

49. James W. Tufts, "Soda Fountains," in *One Hundred Years of American Commerce, 1795–1895*, ed. Chauncey M. Depew (New York: D. O. Haynes, 1895), 472.

50. Nugent, "The American People and the Centennial of 1876," 58.

51. Ibid.

52. Murphy, "Fairs of the Past," 16.

53. O'Dea, "Charles E. Hires—Pioneer," 53.

3. Bubbly Water Begets an Industry

1. Joseph L. Morrison, "The Soda Fountain," *American Heritage* 13, no. 5 (August 1962).

2. Mary Gay Humphreys, "The Evolution of the Soda Fountain," *Harper's Weekly*, November 21, 1891, 923.

3. Theodore Weicker, ed., *Merck's Market Report and Pharmaceutical Journal*, vol. 3 (New York: Merck, 1894), 51.

4. Stephen Cresswell, *Homemade Root Beer, Soda, and Pop* (Pownal, VT: Storey Books, 1998), 3.

5. Anne Cooper Funderburg, *Sundae Best: A History of Soda Fountains* (Bowling Green, OH: Bowling Green State University Popular Press, 2002), 5.

6. Ibid., 8.

7. Ibid., 9.

8. "Dr. Physick History," Dr. Physick: America's First Soda, available at: http://www.drphysick.com/drphysickhistory.html (accessed August 9, 2015).

9. Funderburg, *Sundae Best*, 10.

10. Cresswell, *Homemade Root Beer*, 4.

11. Adlard Welby, *A Visit to North America and the English Settlement in Illinois: With a Winter Residence at Philadelphia* (London: J. Drury, 1821; reprint, Carlisle, MA: Applewood Books, 2010), 31.

12. Cresswell, *Homemade Root Beer*, 4.

13. David M. Schwartz, "Life Was Sweeter and More Innocent in Our Soda Days," *Smithsonian*, July 1986, 114–118.

14. Cresswell, *Homemade Root Beer*, 6.

15. "The Soda Fountain," *National Druggist*, March 1906, 79.

16. Morrison, "The Soda Fountain." Article reprinted without pagination on American Heritage website at http://www.americanheritage.com/content/soda-fountain (accessed December12. 2017).

17. Schwartz, "Life Was Sweeter," 114–118.

18. Samuel R. Kaplan, *Beverage World: 100-Year History of the Beverage Market Place, 1882–1982 and Future Probe* (Great Neck, NY: Keller, 1982), 4.

19. Schwartz, "Life Was Sweeter," 114–118.

20. Morrison, "The Soda Fountain."

21. Schwartz, "Life Was Sweeter," 114–118.

22. Humphreys, "Evolution of the Soda Fountain," 924.

23. H. L. Allen, "The Soda Fountain—The New American Bar," *Printers' Ink* 72 (July 1910), 17.

24. Ibid.

25. Schwartz, "Life Was Sweeter," 117.

26. Humphreys, "Evolution of the Soda Fountain," 924.

27. Allen, "The Soda Fountain," 17.

28. Philadelphia Inquirer, advertisement, July 20, 1897, 3.

29. "Vernor's Ginger Ale," Encyclopedia of Detroit, Detroit Historical Society, available at: http://detroithistorical.org (accessed September 9, 2015).

30. John J. Riley, *A History of the American Soft Drink Industry: Bottled Carbonated Beverages, 1807–1957* (Washington, DC: American Bottlers of Carbonated Beverages, 1958) 256.

31. Funderburg, *Sundae Best*, 68.

32. Ibid., 69.

33. Tristan Donovan, *Fizz: How Soda Shook Up the World* (Chicago: Chicago Review Press, 2014), 86.

34. Mark Pendergrast, *For God, Country, and Coca-Cola: The Definitive History of the Great American Soft Drink and the Company That Makes It* (New York: Basic Books, 2013, 3rd ed.), 20–22.

35. Howard Markel, *An Anatomy of Addiction: Sigmund Freud, William Halsted, and the Miracle Drug Cocaine* (New York: Vintage Books, 2012), 56.

36. Pendergrast, *For God, Country, and Coca-Cola*, 23.

37. Donovan, *Fizz*, 55.

38. Pendergrast, *For God, Country and Coca-Cola*, 29.

39. Mark Pendergrast explains these managerial transitions in his company history, *For God, Country, and Coca-Cola*, in a chapter titled "The Tangled Chain of Title."

40. Funderburg, *Sundae Best*, 70.

41. Ibid., 72.

42. Riley, *A History of the American Soft Drink Industry*, 118.

43. *Grocery World and Fruit Trade Bulletin*, September 23, 1893, 1, HFP.

44. Allen's Root Beer Extract trade card, Charles C. Allen Co. (Boston Public Library, American Broadsides and Ephemera).

45. Riley, *A History of the American Soft Drink Industry*, 126.

46. Ben H. Swett, "Dr. Swett's Root Beer," John Swett of Newbury: A Collection of Genealogical Research Papers, May 3, 2012, available at: http://www.swett-genealogy.com/gws/DrGWSwett.html

47. Eric Sortomme, "The History of Root Beer," Eric's Gourmet Root Beer Site, June 29, 2017, available at: www.gourmetrootbeer.com/history.html

48. Riley, *A History of the American Soft Drink Industry,* 256.

49. Mike McCormick, "Historical Perspective: Jacob Baur Still Recognized as 'Father of the Soda Fountain,'" *Tribune-Star*, July 3, 2010, available at: http://www.tribstar.com/news/lifestyles/historical-perspective -jacob-baur-still-recognized-as-father-of-the/article_ba3fb1ac-20ae-54b3 -9949-2acdfc851e17.html

50. Funderburg, *Sundae Best*, 114.

51. Humphreys, "Evolution of the Soda Fountain," 924.

52. Kaplan, *Beverage World*, 41–42.

53. Jasper G. Woodroof and G. Frank Phillips, *Beverages: Carbonated and Noncarbonated* (New York: Avi, 1974), 221.

54. Kaplan, *Beverage World*, 6.

55. Donovan, *Fizz*, 36.

56. Kaplan, *Beverage World*, 6.

57. Ibid.

58. Riley, *A History of the American Soft Drink Industry*, 126.

59. Hires Carbonated ad, *Philadelphia Inquirer*, August 8, 1896, 12.

60. "A Profitable Investment," *Philadelphia Times*, December 15, 1896, 11.

61. Janice Jorgensen, ed., *Consumable Products*, vol. 1, *Encyclopedia of Consumer Brands* (Detroit, MI: St. James Press, 1994), 262.

62. Cecil Munsey, "Hires Root Beer: Its Many Collectible Objects," *Antiques Journal*, January 1977, 46.

63. Advertisement, *Troy (NY) Daily Times*, July 16, 1897.

64. Advertisement, *The Spatula*, vol. 3, October 1896, 281.

65. Charles E. Hires, "Some Advertising Reminiscences, 1869–1913," *Printers' Ink*, July 24, 1913, 19.

66. Donovan, *Fizz*, 76.

67. Ibid.

68. Riley, *A History of the American Soft Drink Industry,* 135.

69. *Printers' Ink,* December 21, 1922, "Curbing the Fraudulent Refilling of Bottles," 81.

70. Riley, *A History of the American Soft Drink Industry,* 243.

71. Kaplan, *Beverage World,* 15.

4. From Sideline to Main Line

1. "10 Dodgy Cough Remedy Ads from the Olden Days," Health 24, available at: http://www.health24.com/Medical/Cough/Cough-medication/10-dodgy-cough-remedy-ads-from-the-olden-days-20150728 (accessed December 5, 2017).

2. Charles E. Hires, "Some Advertising Reminiscences, 1869–1913," *Printers' Ink,* July 24, 1913, 17.

3. Ibid.

4. Public Ledger, Philadelphia, September 1, 1877.

5. "The Story of Hires," *The American Bottler,* May 1921, 16.

6. Ibid.

7. Charles E. Hires Co., "From Nature's Heart," *Harper's Magazine Advertiser,* August 1893, 26.

8. Charles E. Hires Co., *The Hires Root Beer Manual* (Philadelphia: Charles E. Hires Co., c. 1931), 7.

9. *The Red Book: Standard Manual of the Corporations of Pennsylvania, 1893–1894* (Philadelphia: Burk and McFetridge), 106, HFP.

10. "Pepy's Jr. in Philadelphia," *The Illustrated American* 7 (May–August 1891), 625.

11. "As Others See Us," *Philadelphia Daily News,* February 14, 1891.

12. Ibid.

13. Robert B. Zink, letter from former Hires employee to William Hires, June 24, 1955, HFP.

14. "As Others See Us," *Philadelphia Daily News,* February 14, 1891.

15. Ibid.

16. Ibid.

17. Zink, letter from former Hires employee to William Hires, June 24, 1955.

18. *Vanilla planifolia* is a variety of vanilla native to Mexico.

19. Charles E. Hires, "A Talk on Vanilla," *American Journal of Pharmacy,* December 1893, 571.

20. Ibid., 572.

21. Hires' application for insurance to the Mutual Life Insurance Co. of New York, 1909, HFP.

22. Hires, "A Talk on Vanilla," 576.

23. Charles E. Hires Co., *A Talk on Vanilla,* 1897, pamphlet, HFP.

24. "Doings Among the Learned Societies," *Philadelphia Times,* May 28, 1899, 28.

25. "The Panic of 1893," History Central, available at: http://www.historycentral.com/Industrialage/Panic1893.html (accessed December 5, 2017).

26. *Public Ledger* (Philadelphia), June 11, 1893.

27. Anne Cooper Funderburg, *Sundae Best: A History of Soda Fountains* (Bowling Green, OH: Bowling Green State University Popular Press, 2002), 94.

28. "How Is This for Growth?" Company flier, January 1895, box 1 folder 24, Warshaw Collection of Business Americana (Category: Beverages), Archives Center, National Museum of American History, Smithsonian Institution.

29. Richard S. Bond, "Proving Purity Pictorially," *Advertising and Selling*, May 1922, 18.

30. "An Important Decision, Court Decides that Hires Rootbeer Must Not Be Imitated," *Philadelphia Times*, May 5, 1897, 11.

31. "Charles E. Hires Dies of Stroke," *Philadelphia Bulletin*, July 1, 1937.

32. Hires, "Some Advertising Reminiscences," 20.

33. Atlantic Reporter, vol 37, Supreme Court of Pennsylvania, *Hires Co. v. Hires*, cases decided at July and October terms, 1897, 117.

34. "The Hires Cases in Philadelphia," *Bulletin of Pharmacy*, October 1910, 397.

35. Circuit Court, District of South Carolina, July 1, 1910, as reported in The *American Bottler*, vol. 30, 1910.

36. "Substitution Is Dangerous" ad, *The Spatula* (a magazine for pharmacists), vol. 3, 1896–1897, 333.

37. "The Law on Substitution," Introduction, undated Charles E. Hires Co. brochure, HFP.

38. "Hires Gets Heavy Damages for Root Beer Substitution," *The Soda Fountain*, July 1916, 46.

39. "News Department, Philadelphia," *The Pharmaceutical Era,* March 15, 1894, 266.

40. "Philadelphia," *The Pharmaceutical Era*, vol. 17, February 4, 1897, 150.

41. Undated handwritten chronology, HFP.

42. Event program, Cohansey Baptist Church, Roadstown, March 4, 1884, NJ, HFP.

43. "Musical and Literary Entertainment," March 11, 1894, Second Presbyterian Church, Camden, NJ, HFP. The poet was humorist Henry Firth Wood.

44. Event program, HFP.

45. *Philadelphia Inquirer*, December 17, 1883. Unpaginated clipping, HFP.

46. *The Pharmaceutical Era,* vol. 11, May 1, 1894, 429.

47. Unsourced newspaper clipping, HFP.

48. Event program, Haddon Lawn Tennis Club, Haddonfield, NJ, December 16, 1886, HFP.

49. Charles E. Hires, handwritten note, April 7, 1893, HFP.

50. Unattributed newspaper clipping, HFP.

51. Mark O'Dea, "Charles E. Hires—Pioneer," *Printers' Ink*, August 5, 1937, 56.

52. Undated chronology, HFP.

53. Unattributed newspaper ad, 1894, HFP.

54. Nathaniel Burt and Wallace E. Davies, "The Iron Age, 1865–1876," in Russell F. Weigley, ed., *Philadelphia: A 300-Year History* (New York: W. W. Norton, 1982), 477.

55. David Schmidt, "The Mansions," *Main Line Life*, Lower Merion Historical Society, available at: http://www.lowermerionhistory.org/texts/schmidtd/mansions.html (accessed December 4, 2015.

56. John Gunther, *Inside U.S.A.* 50th Anniversary ed. (New York: New Press, 1997), 604.

57. Jeff Groff, "The Hires Root Beer Family Story and Tredyffrin and Easttown Townships," presentation to the Tredyffrin-Easttown Historical Society, September 21, 2014.

58. Ibid.

59. *Main Line Times*, February 7, 2002, 7. The property was located at the corner of Old Lancaster Road and Highland Avenue, presently the site of Temple Adath Israel.

60. Ibid.

61. Charles E. Hires, *Recipes for the Manufacture of Flavoring Extracts, Handkerchief Extracts, Toilet Water, Cologne, Bay Rum, etc., etc.* (Philadelphia: Charles E. Hires Co., 1894).

62. "The Election, Root Beer and Vanilla," *American Druggist*, July–December 1896, 314.

63. "Vanilla Beans—Where to Get Them," *National Druggist*, 1898–1899, 67.

5. Never Wink in the Dark

1. Mark Pendergrast, *For God, Country, and Coca-Cola: The Definitive History of the Great American Soft Drink and the Company That Makes It* (New York: Basic Books, 2013, 3rd ed.), 10.

2. William M. O'Barr, "A Brief History of Advertising in America," *Advertising and Society Review* 11, no. 1 (2010).

3. Stuart Ewen, *Captains of Consciousness* (New York: McGraw-Hill, 1976), 35

4. Roland Marchand, *Advertising the American Dream* (Berkeley: University of California Press, 1985), 10.

5. Charles E. Hires, "Some Advertising Reminiscences, 1869–1913," *Printers' Ink*, July 24, 1913, 18.

6. Frank Presbrey, *The History and Development of Advertising* (New York: Greenwood Press, 1968; first published 1929 by Doubleday), 257.

7. "From Sweet Fern, Sassafras and Teaberries" (New York: Butterick, 1925), 137.

8. Hires, "Some Advertising Reminiscences," 18.

9. Ralph M. Hower, *The History of an Advertising Agency: N. W. Ayer and Son at Work, 1869–1939* (Cambridge, MA: Harvard University Press, 1939), 32.

10. Ibid., 77.

11. "N. W. Ayer and Son," *Advertising Age*, September 15, 2003, available at: http://adage.com/article/adage-encyclopedia/n-w-ayer-son-n-w-ayer-partners/98334/ (accessed December 19, 2017).

12. Bill Double, *Philadelphia's Washington Square* (Charleston, SC: Arcadia, 2009), 96.

13. Jackson Lears, *Fables of Abundance: A Cultural History of Advertising in America* (New York: Basic Books), 1994, 159.

14. Hower, *History of an Advertising Agency*, 114.

15. Hires, "Some Advertising Reminiscences," 20.

16. Hower, *History of an Advertising Agency*, 118.

17. Hires, "Some Advertising Reminiscences," 18.

18. Ibid.

19. Tristan Donovan, *Fizz: How Soda Shook Up the World* (Chicago: Chicago Review Press, 2014), 45.

20. John J. Riley, *A History of the American Soft Drink Industry,* 117.

21. James D. Norris, *Advertising and the Transformation of American Society, 1865–1920* (New York: Greenwood Press, 1990), 118.

22. "Charles Hires Profitable Root Beer Concoction," *Investor's Business Daily*, January 14, 2014, 22.

23. "Charles Hires," The Robinson Library, June 16, 2017, available at: www.robinsonlibrary.com/social/industries/miscellaneous/hires.htm

24. Jennifer Scanlon, "Redefining Thrift: The *Ladies' Home Journal* and the Modern Woman," *Pennsylvania Legacies* 12, no. 2 (November 2012), 12–17.

25. Charles E. Hires Co., "From Nature's Heart," *Harper's Magazine Advertiser*, August 1893, 28.

26. Richard Ohmann, *Selling Culture: Magazines, Markets, and Class at the Turn of the Century* (London: Verso, 1996), 87.

27. Hires, "Some Advertising Reminiscences," 18.

28. Quoted in Pendergrast, *For God, Country, and Coca-Cola*, 11.

29. "From Sweet Fern, Sassafras and Teaberries," 136.

30. "As Others See Us," *Philadelphia Daily News*, February 14, 1891.

31. Margaret Hale, "A New and Wonderful Invention: The Nineteenth-Century American Trade Card," *Harvard Business School Working Knowledge*, September 5, 2000, available at: http://hbswk.hbs.edu/archive/1671.html

32. Ibid.

33. Lears, *Fables of Abundance*, 268–269.

34. Kate Patton, "Hires Root Beer: The Great Health Drink," Pennsylvania Center for the Book, Fall 2009, available at: http://pabook2.libraries.psu.edu/palitmap/Hires.html

35. Cecil Munsey, "Hires Root Beer: Its Many Collectible Objects," *Antiques Journal*, January 1977, 44.

36. William Woys Weaver, *Culinary Ephemera: An Illustrated History* (Berkeley: University of California Press, 2010).

37. "As Others See Us," *Philadelphia Daily News*, February 14, 1891, 4.

38. Hires, "Some Advertising Reminiscences," 18.

39. John McDonough and Karen Egolf, eds., *The Advertising Age: Encyclopedia of Advertising* (New York: Routledge, 2002).

40. Hires, "Some Advertising Reminiscences," 20.

41. Cecil Munsey, "The New Century: Hires Root Beer," *Antiques Journal*, February 1977, 28.

42. "The Advertising of Hires Rootbeer," *Printers' Ink*, September 21, 1898. 3–5.

43. Ibid.

44. Charles E. Hires Co., *The Hires Root Beer Manual* (Philadelphia: Charles E. Hires Co., c. 1923), 73, HFP.

45. "The Advertising of Hires Rootbeer," *Printers' Ink*, September 21, 1898, 4.

46. Hires, "Some Advertising Reminiscences," 17.

47. Charles E. Hires Co., *Hires Root Beer Manual*, c. 1923, HFP, 6.

48. Donovan, *Fizz*, 46.

49. "The Advertising of Hires Rootbeer," *Printers' Ink*, September 21, 1898, 4.

50. Ibid.

51. Norris, *Advertising and the Transformation of American Society*, 118.

52. Hires newspaper ad, 1895, unsourced, Charles E. Hires Co. collection, Dr. Pepper Museum and Free Enterprise Institute. The rough math behind this calculation appears correct. The company calculated that each package of extract would produce 107 six-ounce glasses of root beer. At this rate, 3.1 million packages of extract would yield 332 million glasses, or about five glasses for each of the nation's estimated 69 million residents at the time.

53. Donovan, *Fizz*, 46.

54. Presbrey, *History and Development of Advertising*, 421.

55. Ibid.

56. Donovan, *Fizz*, 57.

57. Ronald Hambleton, *The Branding of America: From Levi Strauss to Chrysler, from Westinghouse to Gillette, the Forgotten Fathers of America's Best-Known Brand Names* (Dublin, NH: Yankee Books, 1987), 59.

58. "The Advertising of Hires' Root Beer," *Printers' Ink*, September 21, 1898, 4.

59. Charles E. Hires Co., *Hires Puzzle Book of Unnatural History* (Malvern, PA: Charles E. Hires Co., 1890). The book can be viewed at National Library of Australia, http://nla.gov.au/nla.aus-vn3945354

60. Donovan, *Fizz*, 45.

61. Although the scene where Ruth pledges her loyalty to her mother-in-law, Naomi, has inspired numerous artists, the portrayal Hires saw in the Louvre appears to be the work of Philip Hermogenes Calderon (1833–1898), a British painter of French and Spanish ancestry.

62. "At the World's Fair, Story of a Self-Made Man and How He Won Success," special section, *Public Ledger* (Philadelphia), June 14, 1893.

63. Hires Root Beer advertorial, *Philadelphia Inquirer*, August 3, 1890, 6.

64. "What Shall We Drink," Hires Root Beer advertorial, *Philadelphia Inquirer*, June 15, 1893, 7.

65. *Philadelphia Inquirer*, June 25, 1892, 6.

66. Unsourced clipping, Charles E. Hires Co. collection, Dr. Pepper Museum and Free Enterprise Institute, Waco, TX.

67. Hires Root Beer ad, *The Cincinnati Lancet-Clinic: A Weekly Journal of Medicine and Surgery*, New Series, Vol. XXXVIII, January–June 1897, 542.

68. Hires' Extract ad, *American Journal of Public Health* 20, no. 2 (February 1930), xi.

69. "Home Guard" Hires' Cough Cure, The Alan and Shirley Brocker Sliker Collection, MSS 314, Special Collections, Michigan State University Libraries, available at: http://www.lib.msu.edu/exhibits/sliker/detail.jsp?id=11763 (accessed December 14, 2017).

70. *Philadelphia Inquirer*, June 25, 1892, 6.

71. *Chicago Tribune*, August 1, 1902, 6.

72. James H. Young, *The Toadstool Millionaires: A Social History of Patent Medicines in America before Federal Regulation* (Princeton, NJ: Princeton University Press, 1961), 61.

73. WebMD, available at: https://www.webmd.com/vitamins-supplements/ingredientmono-783-wintergreen.aspx?activeing (accessed December 9, 2017).

74. Stephen Cresswell, *Homemade Root Beer, Soda, and Pop* (Pownal, VT: Storey Books, 1998), 33.

75. Penn Herb Company, Ltd., available at: http://www.pennherb.com/dog-grass-root-cut-1-144c1 (accessed December 9, 2017).

76. *Philadelphia Inquirer*, June 15, 1989, 6.

77. Munsey, "The New Century: Hires Root Beer," 12.

78. "A Temperance Drink," unsourced newspaper ad, Dr. Pepper Museum and Free Enterprise Institute, Charles E. Hires Co. collection.

79. *Troy (NY) Daily Times*, June 20, 1989, 18.

80. "Hires Improved Root Beer," unsourced clipping, Dr. Pepper Museum and Free Enterprise Institute, Charles E. Hires Co. collection.

81. "Recipe and Directions for Making Root Beer," Michigan State University Library, Special Collections, Digital Collections, Little Cookbooks, The Alan and Shirley Brocker Sliker Culinary Collection, available at: https://lib.msu.edu/exhibits/sliker/jpgview.jsp?id=6095&page=17 (accessed December 11, 2017).

82. "The Election, Root Beer and Vanilla," *American Druggist and Pharmaceutical Record*, July–December 1896, 23.

83. W. W. Williamson, Hires treasurer, letter to editor, *Printers' Ink* 70 (January 5, 1910), 30.

84. Hires, "Some Advertising Reminiscences," 17.

85. "The Advertising World," *Printers' Ink* (November 16, 1892), 638.

86. Quoted in "Charles Hires Profitable Root Beer Concoction."

87. Presbrey, *History and Development of Advertising*, 420–421.

88. Hires, "Some Advertising Reminiscences," 24.

89. Patton, "Hires Root Beer." Although this quotation is frequently attributed to Hires, it was probably not original to him. A November 8, 1870, article in Boston's *Journal* quotes an Illinois editor as saying "Trying to do business without advertising is like winking in the dark; you know that you are keeping up a powerful winking, but nobody else has any idea of it." A similarly worded aphorism appeared as an unattributed filler item on page 166 of the *Pet-Stock, Pidgeon and Poultry Bulletin* 6 (1876). Barry Popik, "Doing Business without Advertising Is Like Winking at a Girl in the Dark . . . ," March 8, 2011, available at: http://www.barrypopik.com /index.php/new_york_city/entry/doing_business_without_advertising _is_like_winking_at_a_girl_in_the_dark (accessed December 5, 2017).

6. Temperance Trauma

1. Daniel Okrent, *Last Call: The Rise and Fall of Prohibition* (New York: Scribner, 2010), 7.

2. David J. Hanson, "National Prohibition of Alcohol in the U.S.," 1, ProhibitionRepeal.com, available at: http://www.prohibitionrepeal.com /history (accessed January 3, 2016).

3. W. J. Rorabaugh, *The Alcoholic Republic: An American Tradition* (Oxford: Oxford University Press, 1979), 20.

4. Andrew F. Smith, *Drinking History: Fifteen Turning Points in the Making of American Beverages* (New York: Columbia University Press, 2013), 170.

5. Okrent, *Last Call*, 8.

6. Ibid.

7. "The Pledge," National Woman's Christian Temperance Union, available at: https://www.wctu.org (accessed December 11, 2017).

8. Okrent, *Last Call*, 35, 36.

9. *Hartford Courant* (Hartford, CN), June 25, 1892, 3.

10. Isaac Barnes May, "Religious Society of Friends (Quakers)," *Encyclopedia of Greater Philadelphia*, available at: http://philadelphiaencyclopedia.org /archive/religious-society-of-friends-quakers/ (accessed June 4, 2016).

11. E. Digby Baltzell, *Puritan Boston and Quaker Philadelphia* (New York: Free Press, 1979), 415.

12. Ibid., 438.

13. May, "Religious Society of Friends (Quakers)."

14. "Our Values," Quakers in Britain, available at: http://www.quaker .org.uk/about-quakers/our-values (accessed Sept. 9, 2015).

15. Philadelphia Yearly Meeting of the Religious Society of Friends. Committee on Alcohol and Other Drugs, Records, 1903–1968, Friends Historical Library, Swarthmore College, Swarthmore, PA.

16. Board of Trustees, Reformers' Gospel Temperance Union, Camden, NJ, to Charles E. Hires, April 9, 1883, letter of appreciation, HFP.

17. *The Voice* article and its author are noted in a Hires company statement published in the *American Druggist and Pharmaceutical Record* as noted below. *The Voice,* a weekly newspaper, was associated with the Prohibition Party. Neither a copy of the article nor its publication date were available.

18. Statement by the Charles E. Hires Co. quoted in "Hires Root Beer a Temperance Beverage," *American Druggist and Pharmaceutical Record*, July–December 1894, 126.

19. Baldwin H. Ward, ed., *The Fifty Great Pioneers of American Industry* (Chicago: J. G. Ferguson, 1965), 82.

20. Undated Hires ad, Charles E. Hires Co. collection, Dr. Pepper Museum and Free Enterprise Institute, Waco, TX.

21. Janice Jorgensen, ed., *Consumable Products*, vol. 1, *Encyclopedia of Consumer Brands* (Detroit, MI: St. James Press, 1994), 262.

22. Charles E. Hires Co. press release, *American Druggist* 25 (1894), 126.

23. Charles E. Hires Co., "From Nature's Heart," *Harper's Magazine Advertiser*, August 1893, 27.

24. Charles E. Hires Co. ad, *Pittsburgh (PA) Dispatch*, July 2, 1892, 12.

25. "Local Union," *The Union Signal*, WCTU, August 29, 1895, 8.

26. Ellen Joiner Thelka, *Sin in the City: Chicago Revivalism, 1880–1920* (Columbia: University of Missouri Press, 2013), 73.

27. "Fermentation," Encyclopedia of Alcohol, available at: http://www.alcohol-encyclopedia.eu/AL_EN/fermentation.shtml (accessed July 24, 2016).

28. Stephen Cresswell, *Homemade Root Beer, Soda, and Pop* (Pownal, VT: Storey Books, 1998), 2.

29. Ibid., v.

30. Stephen Cresswell, e-mail correspondence with the author, May 5, 2015.

31. David B. Fankhauser, University of Cincinnati Clermont College, presents this finding on his website: "Making Root Beer at Home," June 28, 1996, available at: https://fankhauserblog.wordpress.com/tag/root-beer/

32. *Boston Daily Globe*, October 10, 1896.

33. "Against Root Beer, Temperance Women Place the Ban on It," *The Evening Post*, (Denver, CO), June 22, 1895.

34. "Is Root Beer 'Insidious'?" *New York Times* editorial, October 9, 1896, 4.

35. Ibid.

36. Ibid.

37. Tom Masson, "A Limit," *Life* 28 (1896), 317.

38. Jorgensen, *Consumable Products*, 262.

39. Dr. Leffman, undated letter to Charles E. Hires, HFP.

40. Undated Hires ad, Charles E. Hires Co. collection, Dr. Pepper Museum and Free Enterprise Institute, Waco, TX.

41. Hires ad, *The Interior* 30 (1899), 339.

42. Ibid.

43. "Cocaine: A Short History," Foundation for a Drug Free World, available at: http://www.drugfreeworld.org/drugfacts/cocaine/a-short-history .html (accessed September 3. 2016).

44. Jackson Lears, *Fables of Abundance: A Cultural History of Advertising in America* (New York: Basic Books), 1994, 159.

45. Mark Pendergrast, *For God, Country, and Coca-Cola: The Definitive History of the Great American Soft Drink and the Company That Makes It* (New York: Basic Books, 2013, 3rd ed.), 53.

46. Ibid., 84.

47. J. P. Lippincott Co., *Philadelphia and Its Environs: A Guide to the City and Surroundings (1896)* Reprint (Whitefish, MT: Kessinger Publishing, 2010), 155.

48. *The Pharmaceutical Era*, October 28, 1897, news item, 648.

49. "A Profitable Investment," stock prospectus, *Philadelphia Times*, December 15, 1896, 11.

50. Ibid.

51. Ibid.

52. Ibid.

53. Ibid.

54. James W. Tufts, "Soda Fountains," in *One Hundred Years of American Commerce, 1795–1895*, ed. Chauncey M. Depew (New York: D. O. Haynes, 1895), 472.

55. "A Profitable Investment," *Philadelphia Times*.

56. "New River Front, Improvements Fast Nearing Completion," *Philadelphia Times*, October 23, 1898, 15.

57. "There's Alcohol, But Not Much," *Pharmaceutical Era* 22 (1899): 296.

58. Kate Patton, "Hires Root Beer: The Great Health Drink," Pennsylvania Center for the Book, Fall 2009, available at: http://pabook2.libraries .psu.edu/palitmap/Hires.html

59. Champanale ad, *Philadelphia Evening Ledger*, April 2, 1915, 7.

60. *The Pharmaceutical Era*, news item, November 3, 1898, 617.

7. Twenty Years Too Late?

1. Anne Cooper Funderburg, *Sundae Best: A History of Soda Fountains* (Bowling Green, OH: Bowling Green State University Popular Press, 2002), 19.

2. Ibid., 112.

3. Ibid., 92.

4. Roy W. Johnson, "Winning Back the Lost Market," *Printers' Ink*, May 16, 1912, 17.

5. "The Story of Hires," *The American Bottler*, May 1921, 16.

6. Johnson, "Winning Back the Lost Market," 18.

7. "The Story of Hires," 16.

8. Charles E. Hires, "Some Advertising Reminiscences, 1869–1913," *Printer's Ink*, July 24, 1913, 20.

9. Ibid.

10. "The Story of Hires," 16.

11. Ibid.

12. James W. Tufts, "Soda Fountains," in *One Hundred Years of American Commerce, 1795–1895*, ed. Chauncey M. Depew (New York: D. O. Haynes, 1895), 474.

13. U.S. patent numbers US785869 A (Fitzgibbon and Travis) and US1035856 A (Calvert).

14. "Hires Automatic Munimaker," *National Druggist*, November 1908, 375.

15. "Where Root Beer Is Made," *The Soda Fountain*, June 1906, 25

16. Ibid.

17. "Important Apparatus for Dispensing Hires," *The Pharmaceutical Era*, November 5, 1908, 594.

18. Ibid.

19. Johnson, "Winning Back the Lost Market," 19.

20. Charles E. Hires Co., *The Hires Root Beer Manual* (Philadelphia: Charles E. Hires Co., c. 1931), 19.

21. "Hires' Automatic Munimaker," *National Druggist*, November 1908, 375.

22. Ibid., 8.

23. Johnson, "Winning Back the Lost Market," 20.

24. Hires Munimaker ad, *The Confectioners' and Bakers' Gazette* 30 (1908–1909): 38.

25. "Hires at the Soda Fountain," *National Druggist*, January 1907, 33.

26. Funderburg, *Sundae Best*, 114.

27. Hires Munimaker ad, *National Association of Retail Druggists Notes* 9, no. 3 (October 1909): 126.

28. Cecil Munsey, "The New Century: Hires Root Beer," *Antiques Journal*, February 1977, 12.

29. "Patents, Trade Marks, Etc.," *Pharmaceutical Era*, November 5, 1908, 626.

30. *Philadelphia Inquirer*, news item, October 27, 1908.

31. Jeff Groff, "The Hires Root Beer Family Story and Tredyffrin and Easttown Townships," presentation to the Tredyffrin Easttown Historical Society, September 21, 2014.

32. Descriptions of items up for auction in the following paragraphs come from a sale catalog, October 30, 1907, HFP.

33. H. L. Allen, "The Soda Fountain—The New American Bar," *Printers' Ink* 72 (July 1910): 17.

34. "Growth in the Consumption of Hires Root Beer, 1877–1908," HFP.

35. W. W. Williamson, Hires treasurer, letter to editor, *Printers' Ink* 70 (January 5, 1910): 30.

36. "The Soda Fountain—The New American Bar," 18.

37. HFP.

38. Betty C. McManus, "Here's to Hires," *Main Line Times*, March 25, 1995, 9.

39. Unattributed note [Charles Hires to Clara Kate Hires], HFP.

40. Clara Kate Hires to Charles Hires [Christmas eve], HFP.

41. Groff, "The Hires Root Beer Family Story."

42. William Hires, Oral History, interview by Ann Bagley, January 26, 1998, Lower Merion Historical Society.

43. Unattributed handwritten note, May 20, 1915, HFP.

44. Doug Costa, clerk, Merion Friends Meeting, Merion Station, PA, e-mail to author, August 3, 2014.

45. Charles E. Hires, *A Short Historical Sketch of the Old Merion Meeting House* (Merion, PA: self-published, 1917).

46. "The Story of Hires," 16.

47. Charles E. Hires, "Seeing Opportunities," *American Druggist and Pharmaceutical Record*, October 1913, 28.

48. "What Hires Means," item, *Druggists Circular*, July 1921, 50.

49. Charles E. Hires Co., *The Hires Root Beer Manual* (Philadelphia: Charles E. Hires Co., c. 1931), 5.

50. National Soft Drink Association, *Sales Survey of the Soft Drink Industry* (Washington, DC: National Soft Drink Association, 1982).

8. MILK AND SUGAR

1. "Growth in the Consumption of Hires Root Beer," undated company graph, HFP.

2. Mark O'Dea, "Charles E. Hires—Pioneer," *Printers' Ink*, August 5, 1937, 56.

3. Today in Science History, available at: https://todayinsci.com/B/Borden_Gail/BordenGail.htm (accessed December 13, 2017).

4. Joe Bertram Frantz, *Gail Borden: Dairyman to a Nation* (Norman, OK: University of Oklahoma Press, 1951), 223.

5. E. H. Parfitt, "The Development of the Evaporated Milk Industry in the United States," *Journal of Dairy Science*, 50th Anniversary Ed., 1956, 838–842.

6. Frantz, *Gail Borden*, 266. Among Borden's other inventions was the "terraqueous machine," an ingenious amphibious vehicle consisting of a watertight prairie schooner equipped with a sail that could be raised for nautical travel.

7. Mrs. Morris Borden Tucker, "Condensed Milk Popular During the Civil War: Man's Experiments in Preserving Food Leads to Condensed Milk," Capper's Farmer, available at: http://www.cappersfarmer.com/humor-and-nostalgia/condensed-milk-preserving-food-borden-tucker (accessed December 13, 2017).

8. "Condensed Milk," Encyclopedia of Food and Health, available at: http://www.sciencedirect.com/science/article/pii/B978012384947 2001926 (accessed December 13, 2017).

9. Parfitt, "Development of the Evaporated Milk Industry," 839.

10. U.S. Department of Agriculture, *Gross Farm Income and Indices of Farm Production and Prices in the United States, 1869–1937*, Technical Bulletin No. 703 (Washington, DC: U.S. Government Printing Office, 1940), 96.

11. Zink, letter from former Hires employee to William Hires, June 24, 1955, HFP.

12. *Daily Local News* (West Chester PA), March 30, 1899.

13. *Morning Republican* (West Chester, PA), June 20, 1899.

14. Gilbert Cope and Henry Graham Ashmead, *Historic Homes and Institutions and Genealogical and Personal Memoirs of Chester and Delaware Counties, Pennsylvania*, vol. 2 (New York: Lewis, 1904), 415.

15. "Minor News Notes," *American Druggist* 35, 1899, 108.

16. "Root Beer Company's New Move," *Philadelphia Inquirer*, March 31, 1899, 7.

17. *Philadelphia Inquirer*, March 31, 1899, 7.

18. Hires classified ad, *American Druggist*, vol. 42, February 8, 1903.

19. *Daily Local News* (West Chester, PA), January 16, 1900.

20. "Malvern," *Philadelphia Inquirer*, May 14, 1899, 40.

21. *Morning Republican* (West Chester, PA), March 28, 1899.

22. Nancy B. Schmitt, "The Malvern Years with Rootbeer, Condensed Milk and Charles E. Hires," unpublished paper, Malvern Historical Commission, 2012, 5.

23. *Morning Republican* (West Chester, PA), July 17, 1899.

24. Ibid.

25. *Morning Republican* (West Chester, PA), July 11, 1889.

26. *Daily Local News* (West Chester, PA), January 24, 1900.

27. "Receiving 20,000 Quarts of Milk Daily," *Daily Local News* (West Chester, PA.), January 30, 1900.

28. Schmitt, "The Malvern Years," 7.

29. "A Minute in the State," *Philadelphia Inquirer*, February 15, 1900, 4.

30. *Daily Local News* (West Chester, PA), March 22, 1900.

31. "Will They Sign," *Daily Local News* (West Chester, PA), March 28, 1900.

32. Ibid.

33. "The Farmers as Strikers Are Not a Success," *Daily Local News* (West Chester, PA), March 30, 1900.

34. *Daily Local News* (West Chester, PA), April 19, 1900.

35. *Daily Local News* (West Chester, PA), April 30, 1900.

36. Parfitt, "Development of the Evaporated Milk Industry," 840.

37. *Daily Local News* (West Chester, PA), September 3, 1900.

38. *Daily Local News* (West Chester, PA), September 24, 1900.

39. Ibid.

40. *Daily Local News* (West Chester, PA), January 30, 1901.

41. Hires letter to farmers dated January 26, 1901, *Daily Local News* (West Chester, PA), January 30, 1901.

42. *Daily Local News* (West Chester, PA), February 2, 1901.

43. *Daily Local News* (West Chester, PA), February 1, 1901.

44. *Daily Local News* (West Chester, PA), June 12, 1901.

45. *Daily Local News* (West Chester, PA), September 16, 1901.

46. Zink, letter from former Hires employee to William Hires, June 24, 1955, HFP.

47. "521 Prominent Philadelphia Physicians Endorse the Use of Pure Drinking Water Cooled to an Even Temperature through the New Sanitary Cooler," *Philadelphia Inquirer*, November 15, 1927, 27.

48. Charles E. Hires, "Some Advertising Reminiscences, 1869–1913," *Printer's Ink*, July 24, 1913, 24.

49. *Daily Local News* (West Chester, PA), March 11, 1903.

50. *Daily Local News* (West Chester, PA), August 26, 1904.

51. *Daily Local News* (West Chester, PA), November 8, 1935.

52. "Milk Famine" Hires Condensed Milk ad, *Philadelphia Times*, February 16, 1899, 3.

53. Hires Condensed Milk ad, *Philadelphia Inquirer*, February 2, 1899, 13.

54. Hires, "Some Advertising Reminiscences," 24.

55. "Charles E. Hires," American Council of Learned Societies, *Dictionary of American Biography 1944*, suppl. 10 (New York: Scribner's, 1944), 306.

56. John N. Ingham, "Hires, Charles Elmer," in *Biographical Dictionary of American Business Leaders*, vol. 2, (Westport, CT: Greenwood Publishing Group, 1983), 590.

57. James Noce, "Charles Elmer Hires," *Business Leader Profiles for Students*, vol. 1 (Gale Research, 1999), 9.

58. U.S. Bureau of Census, *Census of Manufactures*, part 3 (Washington, DC: Government Printing Office, 1908).

59. Lloyd Abernathy, "Progressivism 1905–1919," in Russell F. Weigley, ed., *Philadelphia: A 300-Year History* (New York: W. W. Norton, 1982), 557–558.

60. Ibid., 560.

61. "Gossip of the Drug Trade," *Meyer Brothers Druggist*, January 1919, 69.

62. "Strang's Soluble Coffee," *Southland Times* (Invercargill, NZ), July 6, 1889, 2.

63. Copy of U.S. War Department citation, 1920, HFP.

64. Mira Wilkins, "The First World War," in *The History of Foreign Investment in the United States, 1914–1945* (Cambridge, MA: Harvard University Press, 2004), 27.

65. "The Society of Friends and the War," *Advocate of Peace* 80, no. 5 (May 1918): 145.

66. "Both Sides of the Quaker Argument," *The Literary Digest*, May 11, 1918, 31.

67. "Some Particular Advices for Friends and a Statement of Loyalty for Others," *Advocate of Peace* 80, no. 5 (May 1918): 146.

68. Hires Condensed Milk Company ad, *Cass City (MI) Chronicle*, December 28, 1917, 7.

69. "Merger of Eastern Condensed Milk Companies," *Western Canner and Packer*, May 1917, 40.

70. Ibid.

71. "Chapter 2, Canned Milk," *Milk and Milk Products 1914–1918*, Federal Trade Commission Report, (Washington, DC: Government Printing Office, 1921), 60.

72. Jean Heer, *Nestlé: 125 Years, 1866–1991*, trans. B. J. Benson (Vevey, Switzerland: Nestlé Co., 1991), 116.

73. Joseph J. Fucini and Suzy Fucini, *Entrepreneurs: The Men and Women behind the Famous Brand Names and How They Made It* (Boston: G. K. Hall, 1985), 151.

74. William Hires, undated letter, HFP. William's letter was written in response to a passage in a 1973 book by Harvey Cox, *The Seduction of the Spirit: The Use and Misuse of People's Religion* (New York: Simon and Schuster, 1973). Cox wrote about growing up in Malvern near the "ruin" of the Hires plant, which remained a local eyesore into the 1930s. In addition to offering a possible explanation for Hires' departure, William pointed out that the company sold the building to the Nestlé Candy Co. soon after World War I.

75. "Production and Uses of Milk in the United States 1919–1921," U.S. Department of Agriculture Yearbook 1921, Table 334, (Washington, DC: Government Printing Office, 1921), 707.

76. U.S. Department of Agriculture, *A History of Sugar Marketing* (Washington, DC: Government Printing Office, 1971), 22.

77. Tristan Donovan, *Fizz: How Soda Shook Up the World* (Chicago: Chicago Review Press, 2014), 85.

78. "Sugar Shortage Charged to Soft Drinks, Political Leaders Display Ignorance Regarding Botting Industry in Suggesting Remedy," *The American Bottler*, June 1920, 48.

79. Donovan, *Fizz*, 86.

80. "Hires Makes Certain of Its Supply of Sugar," *The Scranton (PA) Republican*, June 16, 1920, 4.

81. Charles E. Hires Co., *The Hires Root Beer Manual* (Philadelphia: Charles E. Hires Co., c. 1923), 8, HFP.

82. U.S. Department of Agriculture, *A History of Sugar Marketing*, 22.

83. "Hires Makes Certain of Its Supply of Sugar," *Scranton (PA) Republican*, June 16, 1920, 4.

84. *From Rum Running to Soft Drinks*, undated Charles E. Hires Co. brochure, HFP.

85. Ibid.

86. Thomas R. Winpenny, "Milton S. Hershey Ventures into Cuban Sugar," *Pennsylvania History: A Journal of Mid-Atlantic Studies* 62, no. 4 (Fall 1995): 491–502.

87. Michael Matza, "Ghost Town," *Philadelphia Inquirer*, May 24, 2015, A-1.

88. "Fragrant Instantaneous Coffee," *Harrisburg (PA) Telegraph*, June 5, 1919, 7.

9. LETTING GO

1. Frederick Lewis Allen, *Only Yesterday: An Informal History of the 1920s* (New York: Harper and Row, 1931), 27.

2. "Welcome to Coolidge Starts Campaign Here," *Philadelphia Inquirer*, October 12, 1920, 12.

3. "The Roaring Twenties," History.com, available at: http://www .history.com/topics/roaring-twenties (accessed June 2, 2016).

4. Ibid.

5. Gene Smiley, "The U.S. Economy in the 1920s," EH.Net Encyclopedia, edited by Robert Whaples, June 29, 2004, available at: http://eh.net /encyclopedia/the-u-s-economy-in-the-1920s

6. See Parkway Museums District, Philadelphia, available at: http:// www.parkwaymuseumsdistrictphiladelphia.org (accessed June 9, 2016).

7. It seems that Hires and other prominent applicants, including the manufacturers of Wrigley's chewing gum and Wilbur chocolate, were informed that in addition to their concession fees they would be required to purchase ads costing up to $15,000 in the Sesquicentennial Exhibition magazine. Hires withdrew its application on the grounds that "everything did not appear to be regular." *Philadelphia Inquirer*, October 1, 1925, "Sesqui Grant 'Shakedowns' Now Charged," 1.

8. Martin W. Wilson, "Sesquicentennial International Exposition (1926)," *The Encyclopedia of Greater Philadelphia*, available at: http://philadelphia encyclopedia.org/archive/sesquicentennial-international-exposition/ (accessed October 4, 2016).

9. "The Great Pandemic," U.S. Public Health Service, available at: https://cybercemetery.unt.edu/archive/allcollections/20090305004704 /http://vietnamese.pandemicflu.gov/pandemicflu/envi/24/_1918 _pandemicflu_gov/your_state/pennsylvania.htm (accessed December 20, 2017).

10. Thomas E. Woods Jr., "The Forgotten Depression of 1920," Mises Institute, November 27, 2009, available at: https://mises.org/library /forgotten-depression-1920 (accessed August 3, 2016).

11. "$3,000 Picture," *The American Bottler*, June 1921, 26.

12. Daniel Okrent, *Last Call: The Rise and Fall of Prohibition* (New York: Scribner, 2010), 215.

13. Tristan Donovan, *Fizz: How Soda Shook Up the World* (Chicago: Chicago Review Press, 2014), 91.

14. "Volstead Act Helps Soda Men," *Soda Fountain*, December 1930, 30.

15. Kathleen Drowne and Patrick Huber, eds., *The 1920s* (Santa Barbara, CA: Greenwood, 2004), 140.

16. "American Ginger Ale" ad, *Wilkes-Barre (PA) Times*, May 19, 1903, 3.

17. Stephen A. Brown "Hires, Charles Elmer (1851–1937), Manufacturer and Businessman," in *American National Biography*, vol. 10 (Oxford: Oxford University Press, 1999), 852.

18. "$4500 Jewel Haul Made by Burglar," *Philadelphia Inquirer*, October 27, 1921, 15.

19. Joseph J. Thorndike, "Pop Goes the Soda Tax," Tax History Project, Tax Analysts, available at: http://www.taxhistory.org/thp/readings .nsf/ArtWeb/186B22AE29FA8E15852575CA00439846?OpenDocument (accessed December 10, 2017).

20. Drowne and Huber, *The 1920s*, 139.

21. Samuel R. Kaplan, *Beverage World: 100-Year History of the Beverage Market Place, 1882–1982 and Future Probe* (Great Neck, NY: Keller, 1982), 46.

22. "Factory at 24th and Locust Sold," *Philadelphia Inquirer*, August 7, 1917, 15.

23. "Hires Co's San Francisco Plant," *Retail Grocers' Advocate*, August 27, 1920, 21.

24. "Best Year in History Seen for Soft Drinks," *Santa Ana (CA) Register*, February 6, 1922, 6.

25. Ibid.

26. *Moody's Manual of Investments: Industrial Securities, 1926* (New York: Moody's Investors Service, 1926). Sales and profit statistics herein for Charles E. Hires Co. are derived from *Moody's* unless otherwise noted.

27. "The Coca-Cola Company: 1925–1929," Gurufocus, March 25, 2012, available at: https://www.gurufocus.com/news/169848/the-cocacola -company-19251929 (accessed December 12, 2017).

28. Ernst and Ernst, Accountants and Auditors, report to executors of the Charles E. Hires estate, August 23, 1940, HFP.

29. Chares E. Hires Co. Corporate Profit and Loss Statements, 1921–1925, HFP.

30. *Moody's Manual of Investments, Industrial Securities, 1926*.

31. "Your Career is an Individual Problem, An Interview with the President of the Charles E Hires Co.," *Personal Efficiency* (Chicago: LaSalle Extension University), September 1939, 4, HFP.

32. "Root Beer Pioneer Charles E. Hires Jr. Dies at Age 88," *Santa Cruz (CA) Sentinel*, March 21, 1980, 50.

33. "Football Player is Dying, Gridiron Injury the Cause," *Detroit Free Press*, October 22, 1912, 12.

34. American Council of Learned Societies, *Dictionary of American Biography 1944*, suppl. 10 (New York: Scribner's, 1944), "Hires, Charles Elmer, Jr." 338–339.

35. Obituary, *Philadelphia Inquirer*, January 27, 1951.

36. "Letters to Harrison Hires from Prominent People in Government, Education, Literature, Arts and Science," Haverford Libraries, Quaker and Special Collections, Manuscripts 800, Haverford, PA.

37. Obituary, *Philadelphia Bulletin*, June 7, 1962.

38. See John T. Mickel, review of *Spores. Ferns. Microscopic Illusions Analyzed*, by Clara S. Hires, *Science* 150, no. 3694 (October 15, 1965): 336. Available at: http://science.sciencemag.org/content/150/3694/336.2 (accessed December 14, 2017).

39. "Clara Hires, 87, authority on reproduction of ferns," Clara S. Hires obituary, *Philadelphia Inquirer*, November 9, 1984, F02.

40. William Hires, Oral History, interview by Ann Bagley, January 26, 1998, Lower Merion Historical Society.

41. Letter from Hires dated February 6, 1927, from Shepheard's Hotel, Cairo. HFP.

42. Passport application, 1920, HFP.

43. Haverford Libraries, Quaker and Special Collections, Manuscripts, C. Willis Edgerton Collection, March 23,1919, Haverford, PA.

44. Charles E. Hires, *Bulletin of Friends Historical Association* 13, no. 2 (Autumn 1924): 53.

45. Clayton L. Farraday, *Friends' Central School, 1845–1984* (Wynnewood, PA: Friends' Central School, 1984), 36.

46. Country Day School Headmasters Association pamphlet, quoted in Farraday, *Friends' Central School*, 46–49.

47. Committee minutes, May 4, 1925, Friends' Central School archives, Wynnewood, PA.

48. "Philadelphians' Hobbies," *Philadelphia Bulletin*, August 21, 1926.

49. Jeff Groff family photographs.

50. William Hires, Oral History.

51. Melissa Romero, "20 Grand Hotels of Atlantic City's Past," Curbed Philadelphia, March 25, 2016, https://philly.curbed.com/2016/3/25/11306198/historic-atlantic-city-hotels-photos

52. Unidentified newspaper clipping, "Louis and Hires Get Some Big 'Uns," Key West, FL, HFP.

53. Unidentified newspaper clipping, HFP.

54. Groff, "The Hires Root Beer Family Story."

55. *Philadelphia Inquirer*, February 23, 1919, 42.

56. The Mediterranean Revival–style hotel, designed in 1925 by Henry L. Taylor, rose seven stories above the St. Petersburg gulf front. Its guest list also included Calvin Coolidge, Admiral Byrd, the Pillsburys, and "Babe" Ruth. Anne W. Anderson, *Insiders' Guide to the Greater Tampa Bay Area* (Kearney, NE: Morris, 2010).

57. Edna Marks, "Hires, Root Beer King, Comes to City to Fish," *The Evening Independent* (St. Petersburg, FL), February 2, 1929, 1.

58. Charles E. Hires to Charles Jr. and Harrison Hires, undated letter, HFP.

59. *Moody's Manual of Investments*, 1930.

60. Donovan, *Fizz*, 98.

61. *Moody's Manual of Investments*, 1932, 1936.

62. Donovan, *Fizz*, 106.

63. *The Hires Root Beer Manual*. Philadelphia: Charles E. Hires Co., c. 1923, HFP.

64. John J. Riley, *A History of the American Soft Drink Industry: Bottled Carbonated Beverages, 1807–1957*. (Washington, DC: American Bottlers of Carbonated Beverages, 1958), 143.

65. Charles E. Hires Co., *The Story of Hires* (Philadelphia: Charles E. Hires Co., 1948), 13.

66. "Mrs. C. E. Hires, Sr.," obituary, *Philadelphia Bulletin*, December 16, 1936.

67. Mark O'Dea, "Charles E. Hires—Pioneer," *Printers' Ink*, August 5, 1937, 56.

68. Ibid.

69. Ibid., 61.

70. "Relatives Get Estate of Charles E. Hires," *Philadelphia Bulletin,* August 13, 1937.

71. *Moody's Manual of Investments*, 1949.

72. "Charles E. Hires Co. Sells Cuban Sugar Plantation," *Philadelphia Bulletin*, October 2, 1949.

73. "Soft Drink Business Booms, But Costs Cut Hires' Profits," *Philadelphia Bulletin*, August 23, 1953.

74. "Coca-Cola Co.," *Ad Age Encyclopedia*, September 15, 2003, available at http://adage.com/article/adage-encyclopedia/coca-cola/98398/ (accessed December 10, 2017).

75. *Time*, January 31, 1955, news brief, 82.

76. "Young Hires President Pushes Advertising," *Philadelphia Inquirer*, July 25, 1955, 25.

77. Ibid.

78. Institute for Motivational Research, *A Psychological Research Pilot Study on the Sales and Advertising Problems of Hires Root Beer* (Croton-on-Hudson, NY: Institute for Motivational Research, July 1955), Hagley Museum and Library, Report 627C, Ernest Dichter papers, Accession 2407, Box 23, Wilmington, DE.

79. Ibid.

80. "Along the Financial News Front," *Philadelphia Bulletin*, February 20, 1956.

81. "Hires Pushes Expansion Plan," *Philadelphia Inquirer*, January 4, 1960, 56.

82. "Hires Root Beer Gets New Flavor," *New York Times*, July 3, 1960, F9.

83. "Consol. Foods Buys Control of C. E. Hires Co.," *Philadelphia Bulletin*, August 29, 1960.

84. Ibid.

85. Ibid.

86. Ibid.

87. "Hires Discloses Offer by Bottler," *Philadelphia Bulletin*, August 30, 1960.

88. "Hires Co. Stockholders Unanimously Approve Plan to Liquidate Firm," *Wall Street Journal*, November 2, 1960.

89. Baldwin H. Ward, ed., *The Fifty Great Pioneers of American Industry* (Chicago: J. G. Ferguson, 1965), 83.

90. *Philadelphia Bulletin*, November 15, 1960.

91. "Hires Co. Sold to Crush Firm," *Philadelphia Bulletin*, May 28, 1962.

92. "Cadbury to Acquire P.&G.'s Crush Drinks," *New York Times*, September 1, 1989.

93. "History," Dr. Pepper Snapple Group, available at: http://www.drpeppersnapplegroup.com/company/history (accessed August 9, 2016).

94. Dr. Pepper Snapple Group Director of Consumer Relations, e-mail correspondence with the author, October 28, 2015.

BIBLIOGRAPHY

Allen, Frederick Lewis. *Only Yesterday, An Informal History of the 1920s.* New York: Harper and Row, 1931.

Allen, H. L. "The Soda Fountain—The New American Bar." *Printers' Ink* 72 (July 1910, 17–20).

Anderson, Stuart. *Making Medicines: A Brief History of Pharmacy and Pharmaceuticals.* London: Pharmaceutical Press, 2005.

"As Others See Us." *Philadelphia Daily News*, February 14, 1891.

"At the World's Fair, Story of a Self-Made Man and How He Won Success." *Public Ledger* (Philadelphia), June 14, 1893, advertising insert.

Baltzell, E. Digby. *Puritan Boston and Quaker Philadelphia.* New York: Free Press, 1979.

Beers, Dorothy Gondos. "The Centennial City, 1868–1876." In *Philadelphia: A 300-Year History*, edited by Russell F. Weigley. New York: W. W. Norton, 1982, 417–470.

Bennett, Eileen. "Local Historians Argue Over the Root of the Story of How Hires First Brewed Beer That Made Millions." Cumberland County 250th Anniversary insert, *Atlantic City Press*, June 28, 1998.

Blanding, Michael. *The Coke Machine: The Dirty Truth behind the World's Favorite Soft Drink.* New York: Avery, 2010.

Bond, Richard S. "Proving Purity Pictorially." *Advertising and Selling*, May 1922, 18.

Brown, John Hull. *Early American Beverages.* New York: Bonanza Books, 1966.

Burt, Nathaniel, and Wallace E. Davies, "The Iron Age 1876–1905." In *Philadelphia: A 300-Year History*, edited by Russell F. Weigley. New York: W. W. Norton, 1982, 471–523.

Carter, Joseph C. *The Acres of Diamonds Man.* Vol. 2. Philadelphia: Temple University, privately printed, 1981.

Charles E. Hires Co. "From Nature's Heart." *Harper's Magazine Advertiser*, August 1893, 25–28.

————. *The Hires Root Beer Manual*. Philadelphia: Charles E. Hires Co., c. 1931, Cumberland County Historical Society, Warren and Reba Lummis Genealogical and Historical Library.

————. *The Story of Hires*. Philadelphia: Charles E. Hires Co., 1948.

"Charles Hires Profitable Root Beer Concoction." *Investor's Business Daily*, January 14, 2014, 22.

Chase, A. W. *Dr. Chase's Recipes or Information for Everybody: An Invaluable Collection of about 800 Practical Recipes*. Anne Arbor, MI: Scholarly Publishing Office, University of Michigan Library, 2007 (originally published by author, 1864).

Cope, Gilbert, and Henry Graham Ashmead. *Historic Homes and Institutions and Genealogical and Personal Memoirs of Chester and Delaware Counties, Pennsylvania*. Vol. 2. New York: Lewis, 1904.

Cox, Harvey. *The Seduction of the Spirit: The Use and Misuse of People's Religion*. New York: Simon and Schuster, 1973.

Cresswell, Stephen. *Homemade Root Beer, Soda, and Pop*. Pownal, VT: Storey Books, 1998.

DeLuca, Joe. "The Story of Hires Root Beer." *South Jersey Magazine*, Winter 1999.

Depew, Chauncy, ed. *One Hundred Years of American Commerce, 1795–1895*. New York: D. O. Haynes, 1895.

Dietz, Lawrence. *Soda Pop: The History, Advertising, Art, and Memories of Soft Drinks in America*. New York: Simon and Schuster, 1973.

Donovan, Tristan. *Fizz: How Soda Shook Up the World*. Chicago: Chicago Review Press, 2014.

Double, Bill. *Philadelphia's Washington Square*. Charleston, SC: Arcadia, 2009.

Drowne, Kathleen, and Patrick Huber, eds. *The 1920s*. Santa Barbara, CA: Greenwood, 2004.

England, Joseph W., ed. *The First Century of the Philadelphia College of Pharmacy, 1821–1921*. Philadelphia: Philadelphia College of Pharmacy and Science, 1922.

Ewen, Stuart. *Captains of Consciousness*. New York: Basic Books, 1976.

Farraday, Clayton L. *Friends' Central School, 1845–1984*. Wynnewood, PA: Friends' Central School, 1984.

Frantz, Joe Bertram. *Gail Borden: Dairyman to a Nation*. Norman, OK: University of Oklahoma Press, 1951.

"From Sweet Fern, Sassafras and Teaberries," in *The Story of a Pantry Shelf*, New York: Butterick, 1925, 135–137.

Fucini, Joseph J., and Suzy Fucini. *Entrepreneurs: The Men and Women behind the Famous Brand Names and How They Made It*. Boston: G. K. Hall, 1985.

Funderburg, Anne Cooper. *Sundae Best: A History of Soda Fountains*. Bowling Green, OH: Bowling Green State University Popular Press, 2002.

Furnas, J. C. *The Americans: A Social History of the United States, 1587–1914*. New York: G. P. Putnam's, 1969.

Groff, Jeff. "The Hires Root Beer Family Story and Tredyffrin and East-town Townships." Presentation to the Tredyffrin Easttown Historical Society, September 21, 2014.

Gunther, John. *Inside U.S.A.* 50th Anniversary Ed. New York: New Press, 1997.

Hale, Margaret. "A New and Wonderful Invention: The Nineteenth-Century American Trade Card." *Harvard Business School Working Knowledge*, September 5, 2000. Available at: http://hbswk.hbs.edu/archive/1671 .html

Hambleton, Ronald. *The Branding of America: From Levi Strauss to Chrysler, from Westinghouse to Gillette, the Forgotten Fathers of America's Best-Known Brand Names.* Dublin, NH: Yankee Books, 1987.

Hand Book of Practical Receipts: or, Useful Hints for Every Day Life. By "An American Gentleman and Lady." New York: Barnes and Burr, 1860.

Hanson, David J. "National Prohibition of Alcohol in the U.S." Prohibition-Repeal.com. Available at: http://www.prohibitionrepeal.com/history (accessed June 4, 2015).

Heer, Jean. *Nestlé: 125 Years, 1866–1991.* Translated by B. J. Benson. Vevey, Switzerland: Nestlé Co., 1991.

Hepp, John Henry IV. *The Middle-Class City.* Philadelphia: University of Pennsylvania Press, 2003.

Higby, Gregory, and Elaine Stroud, eds. *American Pharmacy (1852–2002).* Madison, WI: American Institute of the History of Pharmacy, 2005.

Hilty, James. *Temple University: 125 Years of Service to Philadelphia, the Nation, and the World.* Philadelphia: Temple University Press, 2010.

Hires, Charles E. *Recipes for the Manufacture of Flavoring Extracts, Hand-kerchief Extracts, Toilet Water, Cologne, Bay Rum, etc., etc.* Philadelphia: Charles E. Hires Co., 1894.

———. "Seeing Opportunities." *American Druggist and Pharmaceutical Record*, October 1913, 27–28.

———. *A Short Historical Sketch of the Old Merion Meeting House.* Merion, PA: self-published, 1917.

———. "Some Advertising Reminiscences, 1869–1913." *Printers' Ink*, July 24, 1913, 17–24.

———. "A Talk on Vanilla." *American Journal of Pharmacy*, December 1893, 571–584.

Hires, William. *The Hires Family.* Philadelphia: Historical Society of Pennsylvania, self-published, 1964.

———. Oral History. Interview by Ann Bagley, January 26, 1998. Lower Merion Historical Society, News Articles and Ephemera.

Hope, John. "Hires to You." *Pennsylvania* (January/February 1995) 25.

Hower, Ralph M. *The History of an Advertising Agency: N. W. Ayer and Son at Work, 1869–1939.* Cambridge, MA: Harvard University Press, 1939.

Howland, E. A. *American Economical Housekeeper and Family Receipt Book.* Boston: American Antiquarian Cookbook Collection, 1875.

Humphreys, Mary Gay. "The Evolution of the Soda Fountain." *Harper's Weekly*, November 21, 1891, 923–924.

Ingham, John N. "Hires, Charles Elmer." In *Biographical Dictionary of American Business Leaders*. Westport, CT: Greenwood Press, 1983.

Ingram, J. S. *The Centennial Exposition*. New York: Arno Press, 1976.

Institute for Motivational Research. *A Psychological Research Pilot Study on the Sales and Advertising Problems of Hires Root Beer*. Croton-on-Hudson, NY: Institute for Motivational Research, July 1955. Hagley Museum and Library, Report 627C, Ernest Dichter papers, Hagley Museum and Library Accession 2407, Box 23, Wilmington, DE.

J. P. Lippincott Co., *Philadelphia and Its Environs: A Guide to the City and Surroundings (1896)*. Reprint, Whitefish, MT: Kessinger Publishing, 2010.

Jorgensen, Janice, ed. *Consumable Products*. Vol. 1 of *Encyclopedia of Consumer Brands*. Detroit, MI: St. James Press, 1994.

Kaplan, Samuel R. *Beverage World: 100-Year History of the Beverage Market Place, 1882–1982 and Future Probe*. Great Neck, NY: Keller, 1982.

Kremers, Edward, and George Urdang. *The History of Pharmacy*. 2nd ed. Philadelphia: Lippincott, 1951.

Lears, Jackson. *Fables of Abundance: A Cultural History of Advertising in America*. New York: Basic Books, 1994.

Marchand, Roland. *Advertising the American Dream*. Berkeley: University of California Press, 1985.

Markel, Howard. *An Anatomy of Addiction: Sigmund Freud, William Halsted, and the Miracle Drug Cocaine*. New York: Vintage Books, 2012.

Marks, Edna. "Hires, Root Beer King, Comes to City to Fish." *The Evening Independent* (St. Petersburg, FL), February 2, 1929, 1.

McCabe, James D. *The Illustrated History of the Centennial Exhibition*. Philadelphia: National Publishing, 1876.

McDonough, John, and Karen Egolf, eds. *The Advertising Age: Encyclopedia of Advertising*. New York: Routledge, 2002.

McManus, Betty C. "Here's to Hires." *Main Line Times*, March 25, 1995, 9.

Morrison, Joseph L. "The Soda Fountain." *American Heritage* 13, no. 5 (August 1962). Available unpaginated at http://www.americanheritage.com /content/soda-fountain (accessed December 12, 2017)

Munsey, Cecil. "Hires Root Beer: Its Many Collectible Objects." *Antiques Journal*, January 1977, 12–15, 44–46.

———. "The New Century: Hires Root Beer." *Antiques Journal*, February 1977, 26–31, 46.

Murphy, John Allen. "The Business Debt to World Fairs of the Past." *Nation's Business*, August 1939, 14–18.

"N. W. Ayer and Son." *Advertising Age*, September 15, 2003. Available at http://adage.com/article/adage-encyclopedia/n-w-ayer-son-n-w-ayer -partners/98334/ (accessed December 15, 2017).

Nicolai, Richard R. *Centennial Philadelphia*. Bryn Mawr, PA: Bryn Mawr Press, 1976.

Norris, James D. *Advertising and the Transformation of American Society, 1865–1920*. New York: Greenwood Press, 1990.

Nugent, Walter. "The American People and the Centennial of 1876." *Indiana Magazine of History* 75, no. 1 (1979), 53–69.

O'Barr, William M. "A Brief History of Advertising in America.," *Advertising and Society Review* 6, no. 3 (2005). Available at https://muse.jhu .edu/ (accessed December 1, 2017).

O'Dea, Mark. "Charles E. Hires—Pioneer, 1851–1937." *Printers' Ink*, August 5, 1937, 53–61.

Ohmann, Richard. *Selling Culture: Magazines, Markets, and Class at the Turn of the Century*. London: Verso, 1996.

Okrent, Daniel. *Last Call: The Rise and Fall of Prohibition*. New York: Scribner, 2010.

Patton, Kate. "Hires Root Beer: The Great Health Drink." Pennsylvania Center for the Book, Fall 2009. Available at: http://pabook2.libraries .psu.edu/palitmap/Hires.html.

Paul, John Robert, and Paul W. Parmalee. *Soft Drink Bottling: A History with Special Reference to Illinois*. Springfield: Illinois State Museum Society, 1973.

Pendergrast, Mark. *For God, Country, and Coca-Cola: The Definitive History of the Great American Soft Drink and the Company That Makes It*. New York: Basic Books, 2013, 3rd ed.

"Pepy's Jr. in Philadelphia." *The Illustrated American* 7 (May–August 1891): 625.

Presbrey, Frank. *The History and Development of Advertising*. New York: Greenwood Press, 1968. First published 1929 by Doubleday.

Randel, William Pierce. *Centennial: American Life in 1876*. Philadelphia: Chilton, 1969.

Riley, John J. *A History of the American Soft Drink Industry: Bottled Carbonated Beverages, 1807–1957*. Washington, DC: American Bottlers of Carbonated Beverages, 1958.

———. *Organization in the Soft Drink Industry*. Washington, DC: American Bottlers of Carbonated Beverages, 1946.

Rorabaugh, W. J. *The Alcoholic Republic: An American Tradition*. Oxford: Oxford University Press, 1979.

Rush, Benjamin. *Inquiry into the Effects of Ardent Spirits upon the Human Body and Mind*. Boston: James Loring, 1893.

Scanlon, Jennifer. "Redefining Thrift: The *Ladies' Home Journal* and the Modern Woman." *Pennsylvania Legacies* 12, no. 2 (November 2012): 12–17.

Schmidt, David. "Hires and the Root of Root Beer." *Main Line Life*. Lower Merion Historical Society. Available at: http://www.lowermerion history.org/texts/schmidtd/hires.html (accessed June 9, 2016).

———. "History in a Frosty Mug." *Main Line Life*, August 23–29, 2000.

———. "The Mansions." *Main Line Life*. Lower Merion Historical Society. Available at: http://www.lowermerionhistory.org/texts/schmidtd /mansions.html (accessed March 3, 2016).

Schmitt, Nancy B. "The Malvern Years with Rootbeer, Condensed Milk and Charles E. Hires." Unpublished paper. Malvern Historical Commission, 2012.

Schwartz, David M. "Life Was Sweeter and More Innocent in Our Soda Days." *Smithsonian*, July 1986, 114–118.

Smith, Andrew F. *Drinking History: Fifteen Turning Points in the Making of American Beverages*. New York: Columbia University Press, 2013.

———., ed. *The Oxford Companion to American Food and Drink*. Oxford: Oxford University Press, 2007. Root Beer, 508.

"The Soda Fountain." *National Druggist*, March 6, 1906, 79–90.

Sonnedecker, Glenn, David L. Cowen, and Gregory J. Higby. *Drugstore Memories: American Pharmacists Recall Life behind the Counter, 1824–1933*. Madison, WI: American Institute of the History of Pharmacy, 2002.

"The Story of Hires." *The American Bottler*, May 1921, 15-16, 71.

Tchudi, Stephen. *Soda Poppery: The History of Soft Drinks in America*. New York: Scribner's, 1986.

Thelka, Ellen Joiner. *Sin in the City: Chicago Revivalism, 1880–1920*. Columbia: University of Missouri Press, 2013.

Tufts, James W. "Soda Fountains." In *One Hundred Years of American Commerce, 1795–1895*, edited by Chauncey M. Depew. New York: D. O. Haynes, 1895, 470–474.

U.S. Department of Agriculture. *Gross Farm Income and Indices of Farm Production and Prices in the United States, 1869–1937*. Technical Bulletin No. 703. Washington, DC: Government Printing Office, 1940.

———. *A History of Sugar Marketing*. Washington, DC: Government Printing Office, February 1971.

Ward, Baldwin H., ed. *The Fifty Great Pioneers of American Industry*. Chicago: J. G. Ferguson, 1965.

Weaver, William Woys. *Culinary Ephemera: An Illustrated History*. Berkeley: University of California Press, 2010.

Weicker, Theodore, ed., *Merck's Market Report and Pharmaceutical Journal*, Vol. 3. New York: Merck & Co., 1894.

Weigley, Russell F., ed. *Philadelphia: A 300-Year History*. New York: W. W. Norton, 1982.

Welby, Adlard. *A Visit to North America and the English Settlement in Illinois: With a Winter Residence at Philadelphia*. London: J. Drury, 1821; reprint, Carlisle, MA: Applewood Books, 2010.

Wilkins, Mira. *The History of Foreign Investment in the United States, 1914–1945*. Cambridge, MA: Harvard University Press, 2004.

Winpenny, Thomas R. "Milton S. Hershey Ventures into Cuban Sugar." *Pennsylvania History: A Journal of Mid-Atlantic Studies* 62, no. 4 (Fall 1995): 491–502.

Woodroof, Jasper G., and G. Frank Phillips. *Beverages: Carbonated and Non-carbonated*. New York: Avi, 1974.

Yates, Donald, and Elizabeth Yates. *Ginger Beer and Root Beer Heritage: 1790 to 1930*. Homerville, OH: Donald Yates, 2003.

Young, James H. *The Toadstool Millionaires: A Social History of Patent Medicines in America before Federal Regulation*. Princeton, NJ: Princeton University Press, 1961.

INDEX

Note: Page numbers in *italics* refer to pictures or captions.

Bill Double is a Philadelphia-based freelance writer and author of *Philadelphia's Washington Square*.